CAPITALISM IN CRISIS

INFLATION AND THE STATE

ANDREW GAMBLE
and
PAUL WALTON

M

First published 1976 by
THE MACMILLAN PRESS LTD
London and Basingstoke
Associated companies in New York Dublin
Melbourne Johannesburg and Madras

SBN 333 16940 9 (hard cover)
333 19212 5 (paper cover)

Printed in Great Britain by
THE ANCHOR PRESS LTD
Tiptree, Essex

Contents

Preface   v

1. The Appearance of Crisis   1

    The Depth of the Crisis   4
    Income and Inflation: The Long Debate   12
    Types of Inflation   21
    The State   26

2. Economics and the Experts   34

    The State of the Discipline   34
    The Heyday of Marginalism   37
    The Keynesian Revolution   42
    The Keynesian Paradigm   48
    The Phillips Curve   50
    Paish's 'Lash'   52
    Cost or Profits Push   53
    Monetarists: Paper-Thin Excuses   58
    The Debate on Policy   63
    'Morton's Fork'   74

3. Monopoly Capitalism   77

    Underconsumption and the 'Economic Surplus'   88
    'Economic Surplus'   92
    Monopoly Capital   94
    The 'Surplus Eaters'   101
    Boom and Bust   105

4. Value, Price and Profits   111

    Money and Value   112
    Capital   119
    Accumulation   122
    Crises of Accumulation   125
    The Real Crisis   131
    Value and Profit: The Present Controversy   137
    The Falling Rate of Profit: The Long Debate   140

CONTENTS

5. The End of the Boom   145

   The Great Depression   145
   The Long Boom   147
   The International Monetary System   148
   Profitability   158
   The State   162
   Inflation   170

6. Political Prospects   175

   The Approach to Doomsday   175
   Slump and Hyperinflation   180
   The End of Consensus   189
   The Conservative Predicament   194
   Left Turn   197
   Conclusion   200

Notes and References   207

Index   217

Preface

This book has grown out of the 1973 Isaac Deutscher Memorial Lecture, entitled 'Late Capitalism in Crisis', which we were privileged to deliver at the London School of Economics in February 1973. Versions of the lecture later appeared in the *Bulletin of the Conference for Socialist Economists* (Autumn 1973) and in *Neues Forum* (July–Aug 1974). This present work – with the exception of Chapter 4 – attempts to handle the analysis of crisis in a non-technical fashion.

This book, originally conceived by us as a short extension of the argument in the lecture, has taken us over two years to complete. Such are the difficulties of political economy. We wish to thank the following for their active encouragement, criticism and support at various stages along the way: Robin Blackburn, Keith Burgess, Ben Fine (see also his *Marx's 'Capital'* published by Macmillan in 1975), Karl Kruhm, Mike Morrissey, Charles Posner, Keith Povey, Henrietta Resler, Chris Rodway, Ian Roxborough, Bob Sutcliffe, John Westergaard; everybody involved with the Glasgow Media Project, particularly Brian Winston; and friends, students and colleagues at the Universities of Glasgow and Sheffield. Our debt to Shaie Selzer as Editor and Friend remains.

The contradictions inherent in the movement of capitalist society impress themselves upon the practical bourgeois most strikingly in the changes of the periodic cycle, through which modern industry runs, and whose crowning point is the universal crisis. That crisis is once again approaching, although as yet but in its preliminary stage; and by the universality of its theatre and the intensity of its action it will drum dialectics even into the heads of the mushroom upstarts of the new, holy Prusso-German Empire.

Karl Marx, *Capital*, Afterword to the Second German Edition (Moscow: Foreign Languages Publishing House, 1961) p. 20.

By the same authors

Andrew Gamble
THE CONSERVATIVE NATION
(Routledge & Kegan Paul)

Andrew Gamble and Paul Walton
FROM ALIENATION TO SURPLUS VALUE
(Sheed & Ward)

L. Taylor, P. Walton and J. Young
THE NEW CRIMINOLOGY
(Routledge & Kegan Paul)

L. Taylor, P. Walton and J. Young (*editors*),
CRITICAL CRIMINOLOGY
(Routledge & Kegan Paul)

I

The Appearance of Crisis

The quadrilateral of full employment, free collective bargaining, free elections and reasonably stable prices, has become a figure of unstable forces.

The Times (18 Oct 1974).[1]

It is merely another indication of the depth and breadth of the present economic and political crisis that the leading establishment newspaper is found to share the occupational pessimism of the economic pundits. During the post-war boom which has recently been so rudely terminated, *The Times* together with leading politicians regularly assured us that class struggles and crises were things of the past, that a new society was emerging, that, with properly run government, prosperity and expansion were assured. Academics discussed the post-industrial and affluent societies, television programmes began to cover the so-called 'leisure problem'. Economists were cheery, optimistic men, and the trade-union shop steward was something of a media joke.

All of that jocular bulldog confidence now seems to have evaporated. It has been replaced by accusations of social irresponsibility and greed, by renewed appeals to Dunkirk and other spirits, and by a mood of growing pessimism and despair. Capitalism's face is no longer very acceptable even to its admirers. In the search for quick solutions and easy scapegoats inflation has been singled out and blamed for the end of the boom. If inflation is not brought under control, dire consequences are threatened. By October 1974 *The Times* was arguing in its editorials (as in the opening quotation to this chapter) that 'unfortunately the probability is that we shall not be able to maintain our present system in its present form, because it does

not appear to have any good answer to inflation'. In the midst
of the apparent alarm which has gripped wide sections of our
rulers there is an unspoken agreement. The problem and the crisis
have been labelled. The mass media, the politicians, the experts
and the other paid pundits all agree. Solve inflation and somehow the crisis will disappear. But inflation is not the real crisis.
It is only its expression. The real crisis is the threat of slump
which haunts the capitalist economy. This threat grows out of the
impasse of the post-war 'mixed economy'. Inflation postpones this
real crisis by warding off slump.

Crisis is a complex phenomenon, and the term itself has many
meanings. It was first used to denote the point in the progress of
a disease at which an important development or change takes
place which is decisive for recovery or death. It has since been
used metaphorically to refer to similar turning points in the
development of society. Marx used the term in the main to refer
to economic and commercial crises which were interruptions to
production and the process of capital accumulation, and took the
form of (i) goods piling up because they could not be sold profitably, (ii) widespread bankruptcies, (iii) financial panics, (iv) cut-
backs in production, and (v) mounting unemployment. But he
also spoke of the periodic economic crisis that crowned the trade
cycle, through which the capitalist economy developed, as the
universal crisis – distinguished by the 'universality of its theatre'
and the 'intensity of its action'. Such crises are not merely
economic but political and social as well. The barriers that appear
to additional expansion of capital are rooted in the political
economy and so cannot be overcome by technical means. Political and economic solutions are necessary.

A proper explanation of the nature and causes of the present
crisis must look at the reasons for the existence and termination
of the long post-war boom. It must examine the growing and
central importance of the state in determining the outcome of
economic affairs. Superficial arguments which suggest that the
irresponsibility of the trade unions is the chief cause of the crisis
must be rejected. Those who support the right to strike and the
right to work are justified in seeing no good economic reason why
either should be sacrificed. The post-war mixed economy is now
reaching a decisive turning point. The options both politically and
economically are increasingly between a socially planned

economy, which can safeguard living standards and employment, and the unplanned market economy, which cannot. The mass of working people, given proper understanding of the alternatives, would surely choose work rather than unemployment, consensus against conflict, people before profits. The book is about the causes, outcomes and choices presented by the crisis.

A few years ago inflation was the preoccupation of economists and government advisers, but in 1975 it had become such a household term that it constantly featured in news broadcasts. Inflation is associated with a range of other economic ills, the repeated balance-of-payments crises, a floating and falling pound, bankruptcy and unemployment. The experience of economic hardship is all the more harsh following as it does upon the long and unequalled period of post-war expansion and prosperity. During this period the United Kingdom's relative decline as a major power has been masked. The recession and present crisis has not arrived with the shock that has hit Japan or West Germany, whose economies and future had never looked better. Yet for the United Kingdom too, once again, with fears for prosperity, the threat of world slump, falling living standards and mass unemployment, the whole bundle of economic ills have returned to darken prospects for the future.

The chief response of the Labour and Conservative leadership to the present crisis has been to threaten unemployment as if suddenly it was beyond their power to prevent it. That power exists, but rather than control investment and prices, they try to ensure that wages rise more slowly than prices. In effect this means that we buy less in quantity and less in quality, so consumption falls and unemployment mounts. Governments hope that extra unemployment will cure inflation by reducing wage demands. Inflation and unemployment, however, have been rising together. The annual rate of inflation in the United Kingdom reached 19·1 per cent in 1974, a year in which unemployment grew to 653,000 (figures from the Department of Employment).

The combination has encouraged some political pundits to start thinking the unthinkable again. A prize for the most dangerous thought of that year would probably go to Charles Douglas-Home who, in an important and widely read article in *The Times,* argued that 'an annual rate of inflation of 20% would soon bring us to the point where either there had to be a stabilization plan involving great hardship to most of the country, or – even without a stabilization plan – the effects of rising prices and shortages had caused such chaos that conventional economic and social life was being overthrown'. He goes on to suggest that, 'in either case the civilian government – the Cabinet – would probably have to call on the armed forces either to provide essential services to the public in areas where these had broken down through economic paralysis or industrial action, or to protect the community from the more violent consequences of a state of hyper-inflation – food riots, looting, major demonstrations'.[2] The article reassures us, however, that all this would be constitutional and indeed democratic because approximately only one-third of all army officers come from upper-class public schools. The degree of panic and gloom displayed in the establishment paper is a sign that this crisis is already the most profound since the 1930s, and perhaps destined to be even more far-reaching. In the West there is a mounting tide of bankruptcies. Fringe banks fold, the pyramid of credit totters, and prices soar to unthinkable levels as unemployment slowly climbs.

For most Britons, indeed for most people, such occurrences are outside personal experience. The collapse in the 1920s and 1930s is merely a folk memory handed down by their parents. Like many other folk memories it is treated with suspicion. Another capitalist collapse on a large scale has generally been thought impossible. For nearly thirty years capitalism in the 'advanced' countries has been seen by its supporters and even by many of its opponents as impregnable, as the most sound and sensible society which could be achieved. Today the economic and social policies which supposedly made it permanently stable are breaking down; where there was stability, now there is flux. The essential nature of capitalism is being revealed. Its driving force is on display for all to see. The present crisis in the U.K. economy is larger than that of mere inflation. To reduce it to 'inflation' therefore is to ignore its real dimensions.

THE DEPTH OF THE CRISIS

It is not difficult to find signs of the crisis. They crowd in on every side. The problem is distinguishing between what is fundamental and what is not. By all conventional indicators, the capitalist economy has suffered a remarkable *volte-face* in its fortunes and prospects in the last few years. The United Kingdom's own crisis is at once a reflection and a contribution to the crisis of the larger system to which she belongs. Because the U.K. economy has been steadily declining, compared with its main competitors in Europe, economic 'crisis' has seemed to be part of the U.K. experience ever since the Second World War. She has suffered austerity and rationing, balance-of-payments and sterling crises, 'stop–go' policies, wage freezes, flagging investment and niggardly growth. Her present troubles may seem to many only a few degrees worse. In the 1930s, a peak unemployment total of three million in the United Kingdom made less impact than did unemployment in many other countries, because right through the 1920s, when the the rest of the capitalist states were enjoying a rapid boom, the United Kingdom never had less than one million unemployed.

Yet the scale and seriousness of the present crisis cannot be doubted. Since 1945 governments have generally set themselves four basic economic objectives – full employment, economic growth, a balance or surplus on foreign-trade payments and price stability. It was common to fail to achieve one out of the four in any one year, but it is now common to achieve none.

Unemployment, despite temporary lulls, has been gradually rising in the United Kingdom. Since 1968 it has on average been much higher than the very low levels (around 1 per cent) common since 1945. In 1972 it rose above one million. After falling in 1973 it has risen again. By April 1975, 939,767 were officially out of work – 3·5 per cent of the work force. The male unemployment rate reached 5·2 per cent, and over 100,000 workers were on short-time working. In the United States unemployment reached 7·5 million (8·2 per cent), and in Japan over one million. In the E.E.C., over four million were unemployed in early 1975 – over one million in West Germany and Italy. West Germany had a further 830,000 workers on short time, while France and Italy both had more than 300,000. In Denmark the unemployment rate had reached 14 per cent. (The data comes from the Labour Research Department's *Fact Service*, vol. 37, issue 18 (3 May 1975).)

Economic growth in the United Kingdom since 1945 was higher when compared to growth rates in the past, but it has been much slower than her main industrial rivals. Table 1 gives an indication of this phenomenon.

TABLE 1

Underlying rates of growth 1955–68[3]

Annual percentage rates	G.D.P.	G.D.P. per employed person
Belgium	3·9	3·5
France (1959–68)	5·5	4·9
West Germany	5·0	4·3
Italy	5·3	5·8
Japan	9·7	8·3
United Kingdom	2·8	2·3
United States	3·9	2·4

More recently, economic growth has been faltering. It became increasingly erratic after 1968. Booms have grown sharper and shorter, as was the case in 1973; the underlying drift to recession has grown. In 1974 and 1975 growth rates in the O.E.C.D. area have been stagnant and in a few cases negative. The classic definition of an economic crisis under capitalism is an interruption to production and to the process of growth. This happened in 1974 – the first time since 1945 that economic activity declined in all parts of the capitalist economy simultaneously. A period of generalised recession began then, which was expected to last until the end of 1975.

A trading surplus – the symbol in the 1950s and 1960s of a buoyant and thriving economy – is no longer in the grasp of most capitalist countries. Indeed some like the United Kingdom and Italy face deficits which make those of the past look puny. The 'astronomical' deficit of 1964 for the United Kingdom was £800 million. In 1974 the figure was £3828 million (see, for example, *Economic Trends* of March 1975). The cause is partly, but not solely, the higher prices that now have to be paid for oil and other primary commodities. It is a gap that can only be bridged by borrowing.

But of all the main objectives it is price stability that has been most completely missed. In drawing up their policies in the past, U.K. governments assumed a trade-off between growth and a trading surplus, and between inflation and unemployment. Having more of one meant having less of the other and vice versa. Now growth declines and the balance-of-payments deficit soars, unemployment rises and so do prices. Inflation has reached record levels for a peace-time economy. A creeping annual inflation of 2–3 per cent in the 1950s rose to 3–4 per cent in the 1960s, above 5 per cent after 1968 and accelerated to 10 per cent and beyond in the early 1970s. In the United Kingdom inflation reached 19 per cent in 1974 and had passed 27 per cent in 1975. Record inflation has been a global phenomenon not confined to the United Kingdom.

While economic policy goals are no longer being met, there are many other ways of observing the depth of the present crisis. One is strikes. In the United Kingdom after the strike wave following the First World War which continued into the 1920s, strikes dwindled away to negligible proportions. In the 1950s it even became fashionable among some industrial sociologists to talk about the 'withering away' of strikes. But in the 1960s a new wave of official and unofficial trade-union militancy swept many countries. The United Kingdom was no exception.

Between 1960 and 1967 the annual averages for number of strikes, workers involved, and days lost were : 2371 strikes; 1,200,000 workers involved; 3,001,000 days lost.

Between 1968 and 1972 the comparable figures were : 2820 strikes; 1,717,000 worker involved; 11,994,000 days lost.

TABLE 2[4]

Average duration (days)		Average number of workers involved per strike
1960–7	2·5	506
1968–72	7·0	609

Most of these strikes were merely defensive. While the target today for some of the higher-paid workers who are striking is the share of profits, the real goad to larger and larger wage demands is the combination of accelerating prices and the growing burden of taxation.

The Ford workers, for instance, prepared a claim in 1973

that showed their company to be making in 1972 pre-tax profits
of £60 million or approaching £1000 per Ford worker. Their
demand for an extra £10 a week appeared moderate in this
context. For a majority of workers, however, with no access to
the high productivity increases in other industries, the late 1960s
saw declining or stagnating real wages and growing unemployment. As one study put it : 'In face of the stagnation of wage
earners' real income which begins to be evident from 1965, the
number of wage increase strikes rises sharply from 1966 to the end
of the decade, despite the almost equally sharp rise in unemployment, so that the previous inverse relation between wage disputes
and unemployment is completely disrupted.'[5] Indeed it is noticeable that the number of strikes about wages as a percentage of all
strikes increased from around 32 per cent (1960–4) to over 55
per cent (1969–70).[6] Faced with declining real income, workers
take defensive action. A recent study by John Shorey discovered
that during the post-war period the number of strikes was related
to price changes not to wage changes.[7] The result has been industrial disruption and growing dislocation. People have learnt to
expect and adjust to growing breakdown of services, especially in
the cities. Shortages and queues for essential foods and other goods
are increasingly common. The economy is gradually becoming
unable to provide the same level of goods and services that were
once taken for granted.

In the meantime, the Stock Exchange has collapsed. The falls
in the principal stock exchanges in 1973 and 1974 were the
greatest ever, greater even than the famous Wall Street crash of
1929–32. Rallies have occurred and will occur, but further slumps
are expected. Such a steep fall cannot be blamed on evil finan-
ciers and speculators selling U.K. industry short. The fact that the
shares of one of the United Kingdom's leading manufacturers
had fallen so low by 1975 that the assets of the company,
British Leyland, were valued at only a few weeks' wage bill, reflected something deeper. In general the Stock Exchange is a baro-
meter for the future prospects for profitability and growth in
industry. Despite its recovery in early 1975 it is no longer set to
'fair'.

One of the causes of the collapse on the exchanges has been
the behaviour of profits. In the United Kingdom, as in West
Germany and the United States, there has been a long-term

decline in the profitability of industrial and commercial companies. On Andrew Glyn and Bob Sutcliffe's figures, the pre-tax rate of profit declined from 16·5 per cent in 1950–4 to 9·7 per cent in 1970. The post-tax rate of profit fell from 7·1 per cent to 4·1 per cent between 1964 and 1970. The pre-tax share of profits in company net output has fallen from 25·2 per cent in 1950–4 to 21·2 per cent in 1964 and 12·1 per cent in 1970.[8]

At the same time there has been a steady worsening of the United Kingdom's performance in the world market, which has affected the goals of both economic growth and a favourable balance of payments. As Robin Blackburn has put it : 'A comparison of the percentage share of world exports of manufactures by the major capitalist powers gives a sharp picture of the consequent decline of British Imperialism, despite the high level of its continuing export of capital.'[9] The United Kingdom's share of manufactures from the twelve main exporting nations declined from 21·9 per cent in 1951 to 14·2 per cent in 1964 and 10·6 per cent in 1970.[10] There have been repeated and ever deeper balance-of-payments crises, which culminated in the pound, formerly both the symbol and the instrument of U.K. capital's international strength, being thrown overboard after 1967 and allowed to float. Despite the long battles in the past of the City and finance capital to maintain a fixed parity for the pound, sterling now floats, or rather sinks.

Since 1968 the international monetary system has been crumbling. A succession of sterling and then dollar crises in the 1960s have undermined the use of both as international currencies, and forced the suspension of the convertibility of the dollar into gold. The regime of floating exchange rates that followed has been one of the main causes of a rapid expansion in the world money supply and of the acceleration in world inflation. No agreement on how to restore monetary stability to the world economy is in sight. Yet such agreement has never been more necessary. Faced by the drift towards recession and the new burdens imposed by high oil prices and the trebling of primary-commodity prices between 1970 and 1974, the maintenance of world trade and the avoidance of tariff wars and isolationist policies has become essential in order to keep employment and output high.

The steady deterioration of the western economy since 1968

has been matched by the increasingly gloom- and doom-laden
thoughts of the pundits. Books like *The Second Great Crash*,[11]
written jointly by the Financial Editor and the Economics Cor-
respondent of the *Guardian* are now multiplying, unrelieved in
their forebodings of disaster. They see an inevitable collapse : 'It
may be that, this time round, we escape a return to something
like the dark years of the 1930s. But if we escape this time, then
we have only gained a breathing space. Either uncontrollable
inflation and/or unfathomable slump will catch up with us later
in the 1970s' (p. 9). The merchants of economic doom proclaim
an inescapable destiny for the world economy. Their gloom is
shared and amplified by the believers in ecological disaster, who
see the three evils of population growth, the exhaustion of irreplaceable raw materials, and industrial pollution of the planet as
bringing, at the very least, an end to economic progress, and at
worst the destruction of mankind. The middle classes were once
famed for their optimism. But there is little faith in the future
to be found anywhere any more, except in the recesses of the
Hudson Institute. Social tensions are rising. The middle classes,
fired by resentment and fear at the threats to their savings and
their jobs, are turning to organisations like the Middle Class
Association and General Walter Walker's private army for pro-
tection and consolation.

Indeed the most alarming features of the present crisis are not
the economic aspects, which are powerful and depressing enough,
but the present ragbag of political solutions. These solutions are
often nationalist, that is they see the crisis in the United Kingdom
as special, as peculiar to this country. Inflation is home-grown, we
are told. Increasingly, and without serious evidence, the politicians and the media blame the idleness and the greed of the
trade-union movement for our present situation. These ideological myths are perpetuated and maintained by those who are
especially keen on demanding authoritarian solutions to the
present crisis. These same people, a few years ago, dismissed as
sterile dialectics any suggestion that capitalism was an inherently
unstable system. These same people now stock larger larders and
order bigger deep-freezes as their contribution to stability and
prosperity whilst confidently recommending wage freezes or
unemployment for the rest of us. Such double standards make
the remedies they suggest indigestible.

Mass unemployment is already a reality in the West, yet most politicians suggest that if wage demands are not moderated, then more unemployment will be generated. If wage demands were merely the problem, why is it that inflation rates and unemployment have risen sharply in all of these countries despite huge differences in wage increases? If, as it is now argued, unemployment is uncontrollable when high wages are demanded, how is it that full employment and increasing real incomes seemed only yesterday a permanent feature of the post-war boom? If there is a drift towards world recession, can it really be that the only escape from such depression is the restoration of high profits at the expense of the mass of real incomes? If the problem is obtaining funds for investment and expansion, why should the state not provide them and assume a commanding position in the economy, instead of using its resources to prop up ailing private companies?

At one time, full employment seemed an unshakeable commitment accepted by both major political parties in the United Kingdom. Such guarantees are now being broken – not because full employment is impossible, but because it is not profitable. Profits and the concerns of property still dominate government policy. They inspire the false set of options at present being paraded. The fall in the *rate* of profit, and rising unemployment, cannot be blamed on one or two years' wage increases. The increasing rate of inflation does not follow any direct relationship to wage increases. The present crisis is a world-wide crisis of capital accumulation, not the results of a temporary burst of wage militancy. The factual evidence is difficult and often contradictory. Some of the most popular arguments are plausible, but false. One of these is that the state alone is solely responsible for inflation, by printing too much money and by raising taxes and spending too much. The other favourite is that the trade unions are causing inflation with excessive wage demands. More recently, another scapegoat, alongside inflation and the trade unions, has been found. This is the Arab sheik with his oil supplies. That is the supposed cause of the crisis. When North Sea Oil arrives, it is suggested, all the United Kingdom's present economic difficulties will vanish. But it is untrue. As Wilfred Beckerman argues, the effects of the rise in the price of oil are often exaggerated. He estimates it has only increased

the G.N.P. price level by 2 per cent.[12] Cairncross and McRae
put the case against oil still more firmly :

> even if oil, unlike almost every other commodity had gone on
> being cheap . . . the international economy would still have
> been in a fragile state in 1974. There would still have been
> raging inflation, there would still have been some uncomfort-
> ably large balance-of-payments deficits to be financed, the
> industrial economies would still have plunged into a dangerous,
> simultaneous recession, as governments clamped down on their
> spending and raised taxation in an effort to slow inflation
> down.[13]

The problems of the world economy go deeper than oil. The
most favoured scapegoat of all, however, remains the trade
unions.

INCOME AND INFLATION : THE LONG DEBATE

> The onrush of inflation is due in great part to mounting pay
> claims.
>
> E. M. Phelps Brown[14]

The initial problem with inflation is to decide what it is that is
under examination. That late master of capitalist economics, Lord
Keynes, once observed of inflation : 'Lenin was right. . . . There
is no subtler, no surer means of overthrowing the existing basis of
society than to debauch the currency. The process engages all the
hidden forces of economic law on the side of destruction and does
it in a manner which not one man in a million is able to diagnose.'[15]
Keynes, as was so often the case, isolated the real problem that
occurs with rapid inflation. The currency becomes debauched
and unpredictable as a measure of value; in a hyperinflation it
becomes worthless. In Germany in 1923, as soon as workers were
paid they rushed to the nearest shops and bought whatever goods
were still on the shelves. A man who left a basket full of banknotes outside a shop for a few moments found the money still
there when he returned. The basket, however had gone. In cafés
it was quite possible to eat a meal and be unable to pay for it
at the end, because during the course of it the price level had
risen so much.

Whenever inflation appears, this is the real fear which hits at millions of people, that suddenly the money in their pocket and their bank will no longer guarantee them comfort and security. The concern of economists and governments becomes an everyday concern when it is seen that the currency can change enormously in value. There is a growing flight from paper currency into other assets that may hold their value, like land, diamonds and works of art. New inflation hedges are sought eagerly. During rapid inflation, people become concerned less with what they earn, more with what they can buy. In periods of economic stability everybody more or less knows what their weekly or monthly wage will buy. In a period of rapid inflation in which prices continually soar, the value of one's income cannot be taken for granted. What is a manageable income in January may prove to be unmanageable by July or December.

But one major myth can be laid to rest immediately, namely that rising prices, whether for labour or goods, are necessarily bad for the capitalist economy. In most periods and under most conditions rising prices accompany prosperity and boom. It makes any easy generalisations about inflation difficult to sustain. If we take the United Kingdom as an example, the post-war situation has been one of expansion and relative prosperity, yet consumer prices have not fallen in any year since 1933. There was always a 2 or 3 per cent increase in prices per annum in the early post-war years, which rose to 4 per cent and then 6 per cent per annum in the late 1960s, and which has now reached double figures. The problem of rising prices only becomes an economic strain when an inflationary spiral occurs – a situation when the rate of inflation is accelerating so fast that large numbers of people can no longer make predictable calculations. If the inflation rate is rising by a relatively constant factor each year then economic problems need not necessarily emerge. It is accelerating inflation that makes market forces run amok and brings the whole economy lurching towards destruction.

The politicians and the media are presenting the crisis as if price inflation was primarily determined by wage inflation. The greatest possible use is being made of the Department of Employment's figures published early in 1975 which reveal that, during 1974, basic wages rose around 28·6 per cent in money value whilst prices as measured by the retail price index rose only 19·1 per cent. The argument that wage increases cause inflation seems irresistible. But this simple equation is implausible for a number of reasons.

In discussing the relationship between rises in pay and rises in prices several other factors must be considered. First, in an expanding economy either wages should rise faster than prices or prices should fall because productivity is increasing. Otherwise real wages will be stagnant and all the increased income that comes from the higher productivity will accrue to owners and controllers of capital. Increases in productivity, however are often hard to measure and vary greatly between industries. That makes any comparison between total increases in pay fairly meaningless. Yet it is often made.

Secondly, the figures for wages or average earnings are normally given before tax. The figure that should be used is take-home pay. A large percentage of any money increase is immediately removed by government taxation, so that the real increases in money terms will be around one-third less than that figure. In the example above, that means the wage increase is around 18 per cent, significantly less than the rise in the retail price index. As *Labour Research* has shown :

> a single man earning £40 a week gross receives no more than £28·37 take-home pay. An increase of 19·1 per cent in take-home pay would add £5·42 to this figure making £33·78 altogether. To get such an increase he requires an extra £8·80 in gross pay, making this up to £48·80. This means that he needs an increase in gross pay not of 19·1 per cent but 22 per cent. Again a married man with two children earning £40 gross has take-home pay of £31·87. An increase of 19·1 per cent would add £6·08 to this figure. To get this he requires an extra £9·90, bringing his gross pay up to £49·90, an increase fo 24 per cent. The wage earner needs such an increase just to stand still in real terms.[16]

A *Financial Times* editorial suggested, when the figures were published, that 'A progressive system of taxation helps to ensure that net wages and disposable income rise less rapidly than gross wages.'[17] The same editorial actually termed 'disruptive' the argument of some unions that the net wages of their members, that is take-home pay, should rise in line with retail prices. As presently constructed, the retail price index itself systematically understates the rise in retail prices, because it takes the pattern of expenditure over the average of the three previous years. In a period of inflation this greatly underestimates the price increases in food and housing costs for the average buyer. Thus, even on the assumption that it underestimated by only 5 per cent over all, for most people this means that incomes only increased by 18 per cent in a period of a 24·1 per cent rise in prices. The truth is that even during 1974–5, a period in which the voluntary 'Social Contract' replaced statutory wage controls, wage increases were still less than price increases. The notion that wage increases help sustain inflation is plausible, the notion that they are the cause is not.

Thirdly, the figures are always presented in a very biased form. Income from employment in the form of average earnings is compared with the rise in prices, and inferences are drawn. Profits and other property income are never treated in this way. If profits are mentioned at all it is the profits of a particular company or industry. Total profits and their rate of increase are never given by the media in the way in which wages are. The period given for comparison is also very important. A single year's results are often meaningless. Studies show that wages tend to increase faster after a period in which they have fallen behind prices. So a 'wage explosion' may be nothing more than a process of catching up. A study of possible contributions to the rise in prices between 1967 and 1970, the period in which inflation began to accelerate in the United Kingdom, revealed that rises in the price of unit labour costs accounted for much less of the rise in the consumers' price index than did rises in indirect taxes and import prices, until the end of 1969.[18] Finally, the chucking around of gross percentages ignores the obvious point that 40 per cent of very little can never add up to very much, whereas 20 per cent of very much is seldom very little.

Even if one accepted that increases in incomes not merely sustain but actually push up the rate of inflation, and it is by no means proved, there still remains the question of whose or what kind of income. Much of the narrow ideological debate which is being conducted by both the media and many politicians refuses to recognise that inflation has deeper causes and cannot simply be blamed on the aspirations and militancy of the working classes. But the complexities are ignored.

In any case, do the aggregate figures actually support the idea that money increases in wages and salaries are the prime cause of inflation? The figures show that if we take 1970 as a base year then total industrial production had risen 15·1 per cent by the end of 1973, whilst output per man-hour worked in the crucial manufacturing sector of the economy had risen by 17·5 per cent. Yet in the same period, the period during which the annual rate of inflation first rose to above two figures, average real weekly earnings only rose by 12·3 per cent.[19] Despite this, from 1970 to the end of 1973, retail prices rose by 33·2 per cent but real weekly wages only 12·3 per cent. How could average wage rises of a little over 12 per cent cause inflation of nearly 35 per cent? This in a period when the real increase in weekly earnings was less than the productivity increase of over 15 per cent. Once this is grasped, two arguments immediately fall. First, that money-wage increases automatically cause inflation, and, secondly, that if real wages are kept lower than increases in productivity, then somehow inflation will magically disappear. On the contrary, in the period 1970 to 1973 average real wages were kept lower than productivity increases, yet prices shot up nearly 35 per cent. To take another more homely example, again with 1970 as a base year, whilst the money, as against the real, earnings of employees rose on average 49·9 per cent, by the end of 1973 the average prices of new houses mortgaged rose 110 per cent.[20]

The relationship of price increases to real-wage increases is not straightforward and causally determined in the manner that many would wish trade unionists to believe. Rapidly rising money wages do of course contribute to an inflationary spiral of costs and final prices, but they are only part of the transmission mechanism – they do not cause the inflationary pressure in the first place. There are many other factors involved. Another major factor that sustains inflation is the price increases which arise from the demand for higher profits or the need for more and more money for re-investment as the amortisation rate of capital drops. For some years now there has been a growing liquidity and profit crisis in U.K. manufacturing industry, though its precise dimensions are uncertain. It has been largely due to the failure of industrialists, for a variety of reasons, to maintain

and raise investment and productivity fast enough since 1945.
Full employment and consumption have been supported by
government expenditure and the expansion of credit. Capital
has attempted to maintain its relative position by increasing prices.
To justify investment and attract capital, firms must show a rate
of return higher than the market rate of interest. When this is
over 10 per cent it is not easy, especially when costs are rising
fast.

The crisis of profit realisation is frequently blamed either on
government, or on the working class, or on both. Wage freezes
or short-time working become necessary to pay the price of
industry's inability to produce profits. Industry demands tax cuts,
subsidies and government support in controlling wages to restore
its profitability. The cost has to be paid in taxation by the mass
of taxpayers. Cuts in welfare, social services and education are
often demanded by the same industrialists who are to be aided
from public funds. The real crisis arises from the barriers to
further private capital accumulation. These go much deeper than
inflation and wage rises on which all the problems are so often
blamed. Besides, increases in workers' money wages have to be
viewed alongside the huge increases in other incomes.

One often ignored aspect of the inflation has been the large
increase in income from property – rent, dividends and interest.
Rates of profit in manufacturing industry may have declined, but
the mass of property income has not. New ways of protecting
and increasing personal wealth are always being developed.

Furthermore, not all of the income from employment goes
to trade unionists; a large and unknown percentage goes to the
upper-income groups in salaries and fees. Not only does a dis-
proportionate amount of income from employment go directly to
these groups, but they also get special treatment through the
various perks, fringe benefits and tax dodges arranged with the
help of a veritable army of accountants and financial lawyers.[21]
59,000 individuals received over £10,000 per annum in 1970–1[22]
and their earnings have to be taken into account in considering
figures for aggregate increases in real income from employment.
Indeed, in general, the incomes of industrialists and rentiers have
benefited more from inflation than have the incomes of wage
earners. Those who argue that incomes from employment are a
larger absolute figure and that therefore any increase in income

from employment, however small, is more inflationary than that in dividends or rents, conveniently forget that trade-union incomes as a percentage of all personal incomes are much less than 50 per cent.

What also needs to be understood, however, is that real disposable incomes depend increasingly on changes in taxation, and different categories of income are treated differently in the tax system. Progressive income taxes continually increase the percentage of wages and salaries removed by tax during a period of inflation, unless the government takes action to prevent it. At the same time, however, that its revenue from taxes on incomes is rising, the government can vary the rate of tax on companies to reduce their tax burden. Company taxation fell dramatically in the United Kingdom in the 1950s and 1960s, and offset increases in costs caused in increased money wages. As Tony Cliff has shown in his useful socialist anlaysis of the present crisis, something like one-third of any wage rise is taken in tax and national insurance. To compensate for a 1 per cent price rise, there needs to be a 1·5 per cent wage rise. He points out that, although gross real wages rose by over one-third between 1959 and 1970, about one-half of the gain was taken back in tax and social insurance deductions.[23] So the tax system is used to redistribute income between employment incomes and corporate incomes.

A cursory examination of the figures on inflation and income cannot by itself settle the debate, for the debate is old and long, and like the chicken and the egg, no one can agree which came first. The index of retail prices rose to 124·3 in March 1975, an increase of 2 per cent over the previous month. If this figure was representative of the rest of 1975, it would give us a record annual figure of close to 30 per cent. With such a rate expected, and with 40p being deducted in tax from each pound of a pay rise, 30 per cent wage-demand increases are hardly surprising. They are needed just to maintain the *status quo*.

Speculation over what causes inflation is at least as old as the history of economics. Economists still occasionally investigate real questions and, since the late 1950s and 1960s, there have appeared an avalanche of academic papers on inflation. These displayed every hue of every view, yet they have produced no final proof of what causes inflation. In part, no such proof is possible, for society is the outcome of interacting forces, and to try to isolate and measure one cause and its outcome is as impossible an undertaking as alchemy. Some still tried, however, and a quick survey of a few findings helps to clarify the problems as seen by the professionals. Not one has so far been able to demonstrate that wages are the main cause of inflation. That has not prevented many other economists and economic correspondents from continuing to assert it.

One important contribution to the debate was that of Mr Dicks-Mireaux who, in 1961, using complex statistical regression analysis, examined changes in the general level of both wages and prices in the United Kingdom from 1946 and 1959 and concluded that 'the least certain results concern the estimates measuring the mutual influence of wages on prices and of prices on wages'.[24] This study showed that both wages and prices tended to rise irrespective of rises in each other. It also revealed that even the short-term effect which it could demonstrate between wage increases and price changes was only in the order of one-third of the wage change. What wage effects on prices could be shown are the least certain and, in any case, only show weak effects. The case for cost-push inflation, as economists termed it, meaning wage-push, looks pretty poor on such evidence. This finding received still more dramatic confirmation recently. A report of the Price Commission, established by a Conservative Government, has shown that from late 1974 to early 1975 less than one-third of price increases could be attributed to direct increases in labour costs.

A further aspect of Dicks-Mireaux's study was his examination of the share of national income going to wages and salaries. The study demonstrates that since 1938 the figures issued by the various governments themselves show that there has been no large shift. Indeed, many argue that labour's share has not shifted at all since 1870. The cake has got larger, but the share has not varied significantly. His conclusion from this evidence is very clear : 'Thus, *in the long run* the changes in real wages/salaries has been equal to the change in productivity.'[25] Any decline in productivity has not been due to the workers pushing and getting a larger share of the national cake. Table 3 also shows that, despite belief to the contrary, no significant shifts have occurred lately.

The cake is not being eaten away by worker militancy, for, if

TABLE 3[26]

Percentage of National Income going to the three main divisions.

Year	Dividends, rents etc.	Self-employment	Wages and salaries
1966	12·66	8·82	75·29
1967	12·68	8·89	74·40
1968	12·57	9·05	74·55
1969	12·93	9·20	75·84
1970	12·18	9·39	77·54
1971	11·54	9·71	76·48
1972	10·86	10·26	76·56
1973	11·27	11·10	76·24

it was, labour's share would be rising rapidly. This is *not* the case. Another study conducted by Klein and Ball in 1959 looked at the determinants for absolute prices and wages between 1948 and 1957 and showed that 'wage-rate adjustment to price changes has in effect roughly compensated for the effects of price increases between the times at which increases in wage rates have been obtained'.[27] Such relationships still hold. Most wage increases tend merely to compensate for price increases. In fact, many fail to do even that, and any proposal for take-home pay to be linked automatically to increases in the retail price index is resisted. At the same time a great campaign has been waged, joined even by the General Secretary of the Trades Union Congress (T.U.C.), Len Murray, insisting that unions must not enter claims which anticipate price rises. Yet if they do not, wages will not rise as fast as prices, and taxes due on the increase will make real income fall even faster.

The problem with many studies is that they were carried out during the period of creeping, not rapid, inflation. The present inflationary spiral has magnified the problems. It has not, however made the wage-push thesis any more plausible. Relationships which once held now collapse. A good example of this is the work of Professor A. W. Phillips who studied the relationship between unemployment and wage rates and came up with a rather unpleasant curve which demonstrated, on evidence from 1861 to 1957, that there would be 'a lower average rate of increase of wage rates if unemployment is held constant at a given level'.[28] This relationship has been largely discredited by the events of the past few years which have brought increased unemployment and accelerating inflation. It is all to the good, for one of Professor Phillips's dismal policy conclusions was that, if we want stable money-wage rates, 'the associated level of unemployment would be about $5\frac{1}{2}\%$'. 5·5 per cent unemployed of today's work force would mean around 1·25 to 1·5 million people out of work on a permanent basis.

If creeping inflation cannot be blamed on wage-push by workers neither can other kinds of inflation. From an analysis of seven hyperinflations occurring in six countries in the 1920s and 1940s, P. Cagan concluded that, 'By implication, the rise in wages and the depreciation of the foreign exchange rate in hyperinflations are effects of the rise in prices.'[29] The author blames hyperinflation on the monetary policies of successive governments.

Finally in the United Kingdom, Michael Parkin of the Manchester Inflation Workshop recently reviewed the evidence for five major explanations of inflation put forward by economists : excess demand, inflation expectations, frustrated real-income growth, structural excess demand, and wage-push. On the media favourite – wage-push – he concluded that the U.K. evidence gave no support to it. Wage demands were only part of the mechanism that sustained inflation, not its cause. Indeed Parkin stated that 'in an environment of full employment . . . only a complete abolition of trade unions and any other forms of monopoly would have the effect of guaranteeing a slowing down of the inflation rate'.[30]

TYPES OF INFLATION

Perhaps the most important study of all, and certainly one of the most technically competent is the recent study by a group of Cambridge University economists entitled *Do Trade Unions Cause Inflation?*[31] This is really two studies, one on the relationship between various forms of inflation and social conflict, the other on the relationship between wages, taxes, and labour militancy. The authors distinguish between four types of inflation : the first is 'suppressed inflation' a condition existing in most eastern bloc countries where state intervention and control corrects any upward pressure on costs and incomes. These policies have been very successful and have meant, with the exception of Yugoslavia, which is a mixed economy and often experiences around 25 per cent inflation, the eastern bloc price levels are immensely stable, an achievement much envied in the 'advanced' capitalist countries. Professor Alec Nove of the Soviet Studies Department at the University of Glasgow, although critical of the Soviet Union, summed up his recent examination of the Soviet statistics in *The Times* by stating : 'There is evidence of hidden or disguised inflationary pressures, but it is undoubtedly the case that prices show greater stability than in the West.'[32]

Comparative analysis of economic systems shows that the problems of permanent inflation reflect problems inherent in the modern capitalist economy. Free from inflation, these eastern bloc countries are also free of the real problem in capitalist economies, of which inflation is an expression – the threat of slump. Ernest Mandel in an important article entitled 'The Generalised Recession of the International Capitalist Economy' points out that 'while the recession is hitting all the capitalist countries . . . the countries with non-capitalist economies are escaping the overall effects of the recession. In 1974 and 1975 they will experience their usual growth rate, which will appear all the more pronounced when counterposed to the stagnation or decline in production in all the imperialist countries.'[33]

The second type of inflation discussed in the Cambridge study is normal or 'equilibrium inflation' – a steady annual upward creeping of prices, which was the experience until recently of most of the advanced capitalist countries. This permanent inflation averages around 3 per cent per annum and contrasts with previous experience in capitalist economies, when big fluctuations in prices were common, prices rising and falling with the trade cycle. For many years equilibrium inflation was thought manageable and even beneficial because it provided a constant stimulus to expansion.

The third type of inflation is 'strato-inflation' – a condition seen most clearly in Latin America, but not confined to those countries. In this situation, there is a kind of panic ceiling level of around 50 per cent inflation and a floor rate of about 10 per cent whilst prices on average rise around 30 per cent per annum. The effects of this are great social unrest, especially as there are repeated and arbitrary redistributions of income between various groups. As the authors comment: 'The condition is generally marked by severe socio-industrial conflict, high political instability, and repeated external devaluations.'[34] Finally there is hyperinflation of more than 50 per cent per annum in some cases just running away to the unbelievable figure of 1000 per cent per annum. Invariably there is collapse of countries' currencies and often of the political system as well. Naturally hyperinflations can last only for a very short time.

The dangers of the present situation are obvious, for there are now inflation rates in many of the capitalist countries which have shifted them from the 'normal' or 'equilibrium' band to the strato-inflation type. Intensified social conflict and social unrest will follow. The authors of the Cambridge study argue that inflation is endemic to the modern capitalist economy and that the exent to which inflation is controlled or controllable depends on 'the political capacity and wisdom of governments'. They also stress the fact that 'a failure or inability to control or hold inflation will itself invoke a parallel degree of social conflict that will limit the government's power to keep back inflationary pressures'.[35] Their study demonstrates the central importance of government activity in controlling the modern economy, a fact still not assimilated by much economic analysis. They reject the simple causal approaches, which suggest that wage-push or expansion of money supply cause inflation, in favour of an approach which places political conflict and the role of the state very much at the centre.

The politics of the issue become crucial as the move from an equilibrium to a strato-inflationary economy occurs. In the former, conflict is usually concerned with marginal additions to the national product (who gets what of the additions to the size of the national cake); whilst in strato-inflation, social and industrial conflict comes to centre on the basic distribution or share of the cake which each class or group gets. For, under strato-inflation each major social group can experience a real and perceptible fall in its real standard of living, and this can occur even if overall standards of living are rising. For example, if prices are rising 15 per cent a year, even if a wage claim and settlement of 20 per cent is granted, loss of real income can be experienced for most of the year. Prices in a strato-inflationary situation are rising month by month whilst wages are usually increased only once a year. It is therefore likely that in the present situation most people experience a real fall in their standard of living for part of the year. This is true even if over the year as a whole their real income increases slightly.

The Cambridge study also claims that an annual inflation rate of above 10 per cent may well prove to be irreversible.[36] The O.E.C.D. figures from the *Economic Outlook* for December 1974 reveals that this 10 per cent figure has been exceeded by most of the member countries for the last 2 years.

So that technically, with the exception of West Germany, all of the major seven nations are now approaching strato-inflation. The most recent figures however show the rate of increase to be slowing for all the O.E.C.D. countries except the United Kingdom. Significantly enough, the United Kingdom often has the lowest number of unemployed in this group of countries and the fastest rate of inflation. This tends to support our view that inflation is only the indicator of the real crisis. For the rate of inflation can always be slowed or 'repressed' by either an interventionist state policy or by controlling the money supply and increasing unemployment. The most likely immediate outcome in most capitalist countries will be a turn to 'monetary correction' and so unemployment. This tends to lower the level of total effective demand for goods, reduce credit and private debt and, when very high, to reduce wage demands.

Despite this, the situation remains unstable. It was reported in early 1975 that Italy had, temporarily at least, improved its economic situation, despite the severest financial problems of all of the major O.E.C.D. countries, by short-time working and a rise in unemployment. This was coupled, however, with an acceptance by the Governor of the Central Bank that the measures taken would bear hardest on private business and would mean a further expansion of state participation in the economy.[37] This is a price that most economists, politicians and industrialists in the Unted Kindgom are refusing to countenance. Inflation can be vastly reduced, if not eliminated, by real controls over private companies' ability to increase prices. But this would involve an unacceptable extension of the state. So monetary correction, and hence unemployment, is favoured. Yet already the pressures, especially in West Germany and the United States, for reflating the world economy are building up again.

TABLE 4

Consumer prices in seven major countries

Percentage changes seasonally adjusted at annual rates (estimates and forecasts)

	Average 1959–60 to 1971–2	1972 to 1973	1973 to 1974	1974 to 1975	1973 I to 1973 II	1973 II to 1974 I	1974 I to 1974 II	1974 II to 1975 I	1975 I to 1975 II	1973 Q4 to 1974 Q4	1974 Q4 to 1975 Q4
Canada	2·3	6·1	10	11·5	8·6	9·6	12	12	10·5	11·25	11
United States	2·4	5·5	11·5	11	8·8	12·5	12	11·25	9·5	12·5	10
Japan	5·5	11·7	25	16	18·6	29·3	22·5	15	12·25	26·75	11·5
France	4·3	7·1	13·75	13	10·1	14·9	15·25	13·25	10·5	15·5	11·5
West Germany	3·0	7	7·5	7	7·9	7·5	7	7	6·75	7·5	6·75
Italy	4·1	10·8	19·25	20·25	11·0	20·0	26	21·75	12·5	25·5	14·5
United Kingdom	3·8	8·6	14·75	18	8·3	17·1	16·25	19	17·75	17·75	18
Total of above countries	3·3	7·3	13·75	12·25	10·4	15·2	14·25	12·5	10·5	15·5	10·75

Source: O.E.C.D., *Economic Outlook* (Dec 1974).

The evidence then does little to support the view that the causes of the crisis lie in a rise in expectations, or an expansion of militancy. Such a view commands widespread support partly because of the complexity of the issues involved and partly because of the deliberate attempt, through the media, to blame inflation upon the rest of society. It is characteristic of the modern media, particularly television, that they are used to direct attention not to the causes but to the manifestations of crises. If attention were directed to causes, then the legitimacy of the system itself would be questioned. By focusing only on the manifestations and reactions to the crisis such as wage demands, the system itself is made to appear legitimate, and these reactions illegitimate and subversive. The causes of the crisis lie not in wage demands but in the way capital is accumulated and production organised. Whenever accumulation falters and profits fall, a crisis allows capital to be restructured and profit expectations to recover. Attempts are made to lower or hold down wages and salaries. The mass of society has to pay for the uncontrollable outcomes of a production system orientated to private profit – if the present private market can be graced with the term 'system'.

In the present 'crisis', however, no major interruption to production has yet occurred, inflation is still rampant, profits continue to be squeezed. In this situation, the government has been blamed by a section of political opinion – the so-called 'monetarists' – for printing too much money and for allowing such massive rises in prices. The size of the state sector itself and the government handling of the economy come under attack.

THE STATE

> The proximate cause of the crisis and imminent decline of Britain is the expansion of public spending and money supply that began under Mr Reginald Maudling in 1963–4, and which continued with only a short pause in 1969 for ten years.
>
> Alan Walters[38]

This increasingly influential position, thoroughly right wing in its implications for policy, which has re-emerged during this present crisis, argues that the government causes most of the inflation,

and therefore the crisis, by allowing the money supply to expand
too fast. It tends to evade the thorny problem of how the government should control the money supply. There are severe restrictions on governments' ability to achieve this. It would create a
vast credit crisis if it refused to print sufficient money to meet
existing claims and demands for more cash transmitted through
the clearing banks. Much of this credit is in personal debt, over-
drafts, hire-purchase of cars and other goods – any real cut here
would send unemployment spiralling. One alternative is to cut
back government expenditure itself and create a budget surplus.
Much of the public spending, however, is in highly profitable areas,
such as arms manufacture or contract building. Such a cut would
only reduce profits further and add to unemployment. The cuts
would have to fall on welfare services, pensions and education;
but such a rolling back of public expenditure may not be sufficient to keep the money supply in check. Besides, a cut in such
areas would lead to an increase in political conflict and a cut in
effective demand for goods, which would again extend the
unemployment rate.

Despite the fact that restricting money supply means a liquidity
crisis, a credit crisis and perhaps as much as four million unemployed, it is still advocated by many people. The desire to cut
back on government spending is at once both politically and
economically reactionary. Inflation is not purely a monetary
phenomenon, nor is it the cause of the crisis. Yet the monetrist
and other free-market crusaders against state intervention seem
prepared to pay any price in unemployment and social conflict
in their desire to dismantle the state. It is true that the state sector
is large. Indeed, by some measures, the private sector is now
the smaller part of the so-called mixed economy. Public expenditure in the United Kingdom, as a proportion of G.N.P. rose
from 13 per cent before 1914 to 27 per cent after 1918; by 1948
it had risen to 42·4 per cent and by 1974 it was 50 per cent.
The government now employs around one-quarter of all those in
employment. Taxation as a percentage of G.N.P. has risen from
23·2 per cent in 1936 to 48 per cent in 1970.[39] All other states
in the O.E.C.D. showed a similar trend.

The enlarged state sector can be viewed as the bin for dump-
ing increasingly vast amounts of surplus for which industry can
find no profitable outlets. On this view the capitalist system has

B

an inherent tendency, if left to itself, to stagnation and under-consumption. We find this view in the work of Paul Baran and Paul Sweezy, as well as in that of Keynesians of all kinds. The crucial point of reference and departure for all these theorists is the Great Depression of the 1930s. The post-war boom is interpreted in the light of the apparently hopeless stagnation of that time.

Of the major industrialised countries only two got to grips with the crisis of the 1930s, Germany and the United States. But it is clear now that neither were really successful. The New Deal did not prevent a new recession starting in 1938, and the only way out for Germany was the attempt to enlarge its markets and investments by force of the arms it had been producing single-mindedly since 1933. Since 1945 a very different picture appears; steady, sometimes bounding, growth for all the major capitalist states; general amazement at the productive forces locked away in a mode of production widely believed to have reached its limit.

Monetarists argue that the state does encroach upon private capitalism, but they forget that it stabilises it as well. It is this contradictory nature of state activity that throws doubt upon the monetarist thesis. If, to avoid depressions and inflation, the government has merely to balance money supply and output and balance its own expenditure against revenue, why does public expenditure rise so much in the first place? No equilibrium balance between money supply and output that eliminates the causes of inflation is in fact possible through the market but this is not to deny that there is a relationship between the size of the state sector and inflation.

Since 1945 the nature of government expenditure and private credit has helped to create continual inflationary pressure. For a long while inflation was moderate, so long as expansion was both rapid and profitable throughout the world economy. For a number of reasons to be examined later in the book, barriers to further expansion have been growing in recent years. This has hit U.K. industry, already less competitive than its rivals, particularly hard. The direct consequence has been a declining rate of profit. In response, successive governments have adopted policies including increased taxation, devaluation, and incomes policies which have strengthened trade-union resistance and militancy. At the same time they have attempted to maintain demand and employment by increasing the money supply through greater spending and more private credit. An accelerating rate of inflation has been the result.

The government has been forced to step in to restore rates of profit through the tax system, by investment incentives, reducing company taxes and direct aid to private industry. This has to be paid for if the state sector is to be maintained at its present level and, under recent governments, this has meant an increase of taxation on wages. It is a policy which cannot be extended indefinitely. Its immediate effect indeed is to increase claims for wage increases, by reducing real wages, and to make accumulation still more difficult by encroaching further on the productive sector.

The debate on how to control inflation within the framework of a mixed economy centres on the state sector. If inflation is primarily a monetary phenomenon monetarists argue that it can only be contained by a drastic reduction of state activities, the elimination of the budget deficit, the exercise of monetary restraint, and the deliberate creation of unemployment. This view in most of its variants regards the unions as only a marginal cause of inflation. Wage demands are but the expression of an inflationary situation, the mechanism by which excess demand is translated into higher prices. The monetarist secret for controlling it is to restore the responsibility for resisting wages to individual employers. They will be forced to resist because, once there is no longer excess demand in the economy, which would allow price rises, and no more government handouts to industry through the tax system, by granting wage increases which the company could not afford, the result would be bankruptcy. The old economic law of capitalism would be restored – discipline would once again be imposed by the market and no longer by the state.

This strategy is that of Enoch Powell, Sir Keith Joseph and leading sections of the Conservative Party. The alternative strategy still clings to the wage-push theory, which accepts, for practical purposes, the level of public expenditure and hence the size of the state sector as it exists at the moment, and therefore generally denies that this has anything to do with inflation. On the contrary, this theory assumes that, were the level of public expenditure cut, private investment would not expand, and slump and depression would ensue. It therefore regards the level of public expenditure as necessary for prosperity and accumulation to continue. Inflation is blamed on the monopoly power of firms and unions which enable them to cause a wage–price spiral. Amongst other things such a spiral is resisted because it makes exports uncompetitive. The remedy is the control of wages, through the 'Social Contract' or some other kind of incomes policy. In order to align wages with productivity, such a policy is expected to work by educating the unions and employers into a true understanding of the 'facts' about the economy and helping them perceive the sacred truth that inflation is caused when wages rise faster than productivity.

So on the one hand one side urges a return to the discipline of the market, a discipline it knows can only be re-established by cutting back on public expenditure, whilst the other has moved steadily to advocating the conquest of inflation by the control of wages at source, and thus the restriction of free collective bargaining. Conservative Governments are elected with pledges to cut back public expenditure drastically and in office are soon muttering about economies and cost effectiveness. Yet the level of government spending goes on rising. The wage-push theory is a convenient ideological tool for the ruling class for it turns attention away from the level of government spending towards the control of wages. But since wage demands are not, in fact, the root of inflation but only the scapegoat, the government becomes steadily committed to greater and greater intervention in the economy in order to make labour and not profits suffer from the effects of the inflation its own spending generates in the attempt to render capitalism profitable.

Today the state and recipients of public expenditure are voracious and unproductive consumers as far as capital is concerned. What is consumed cannot be accumulated, and so there is a contradiction between the size of the state sector and productive capital. On the one hand, government spending cuts short the business cycle, and government intervention helps to restructure capital and socialise many industrial costs. On the other hand, the cost of the state sector encroaches on accumulation. State action is intended to overcome the problems of realising profits, but finally it intensifies the crisis of accumulation. The more the state ensures the first through its own spending the more it endangers the second. The accelerating inflation suffered by all developed capitalist countries since 1945 is, in conventional terms, a sign of excess demand in the economy, that is 'too much money chasing too few goods'. The reason for this excess demand, however, is partly the size of the state sector. Inflation is produced by the manner in which the modern state intervenes in the economy attempting to ensure conditions for profitable accumulation and to avoid recessions. The capitalist state helps create the conditions for inflation, although the forces that actually initiate, transmit and sustain it are varied.

Increases in both public expenditure and the money supply, which have occurred in all the advanced capitalist economies in this century, is by no means all at the expense of accumulation. Much of it directly aids accumulation. In looking at the modern state, we must distinguish a number of aspects of its role in the economy. First, it manages demand in order to achieve full employment and other economic objectives. Secondly, it is the most visible expression of the unproductive sector within the capitalist mode of production; most obviously this is the case in the area of defence. Thirdly, it has the task of restructuring capital and ensuring the most favourable conditions possible for profitable accumulation. Fourthly, it is there to legitimate class rule. It is clear that these different roles can be contradictory.

Faced by the acceleration of inflation, governments have an unpalatable choice. Short of an attempt to restore free competitive capitalism and drastically restrict its own activities, the government has two basic remedies to the wage offensive – direct control of wages and conditions, and the redistribution of national income to profits through taxes. Both are aimed at restoring and raising profits, and both have appeared together in the policies of recent governments. Control of wages at source, however, cannot ultimately be successful unless either the trade-union movement is completely shackled or real control of prices is introduced. In the latter case, government must gradually take over from private capital the responsibility for maintaining investment and employment.

The economic and political options that are presented by those who wish to maintain class rule boil down to a choice between wage restraint and unemployment. From a monetarist position Samuel Brittan has written in the *Financial Times*: 'A liberal democracy is subject to unbearable tensions if the public sector and thus the area of political decision is stretched too far.'[40] But the alternative – dismantling the state sector – would mean, in present circumstances, mass unemployment and a prolonged slump.

Our argument so far may be briefly summarised. Since 1968 the performance of the western economy has been deteriorating. The most obvious sign of this deterioration is accelerating inflation. The creeping inflation of the 1950s and 1960s has been replaced by rates of inflation much closer to Latin American experience. Inflation is blamed for many of the other ills of the economy – declining growth, rising unemployment, international monetary chaos, and so on. In fact, inflation is only a symptom of the real crisis. The real crisis is caused by the obstacles that now stand in the way of further growth and expansion in the framework of a capitalist economy. Inflation has accelerated in the last few years as governments have sought to overcome these barriers and maintain prosperity and full employment. In this situation governments put the blame for inflation on trade-union militancy. But the trade unions are not responsible for inflation. Most of their actions are defensive. The real cause of inflation lies in governments' expansion of the money supply and credit to finance their own expenditure and maintain prosperity by ensuring that the goods produced by industry can be sold at a profit. The realisation of this fact has produced an alternative strategy to control inflation – the path of monetary correction and cutting back on public expenditure. But this also means breaking up the mixed economy that has established and underpinned the prosperity and the long boom since 1945. It requires a major shift in the balance of political power between labour and capital, and some alternative means of providing the conditions that will make the accumulation of capital possible.

This impasse of the mixed economy reflects the size and importance of the state sector in modern capitalism. The barriers to further expansion are rooted deep in the political and economic features of the mixed economy as it exists in the capitalist world. The problems facing the United Kingdom are only one expression of a crisis that is international. In the chapters that follow, we shall examine explanations of the post-war boom and of the various aspects of the present crisis, particularly inflation. One

theme will guide our discussion. It is impossible to understand
what is happening without grasping the role and nature of the
modern state and its contradictory relationship to the process of
capital accumulation.

Since 1945 all the parties that have administered the mixed
economy have chosen to use public expenditure and credit to
ensure prosperity and, consequently, inflation. But sustained
inflation, encourages militancy over pay at the same time that an
enlarged state sector and a falling rate of profit makes accumulation more difficult. In 1975 even 3, 4, 5 per cent unemployment does not discipline the labour force and reduce their wage
demands. The state is obliged to step in directly to confront the
working class on behalf of capital. The political struggle is beginning in earnest. The calm of the long boom is over.

2

Economics and the Experts

Creeping inflation is the malaria of the modern mixed
economy. Like malaria it is uncomfortable to live with and
just will not go away. But unlike the case of malaria, there
seems to be no known cure for creeping inflation that is better
than the disease.

Paul Samuelson, *Newsweek* (1971).

THE STATE OF THE DISCIPLINE

The professional experts on inflation, the economists, have long
preened themselves on the scientific nature of their enquiries. For
two hundred years, ever since Adam Smith published *The
Wealth of Nations*, economists have been busy refining concepts,
gathering facts, constructing models, and laying claim to be practitioners of the most rigorous and scientific of all the social
sciences. From being a despised and vulgar utilitarian branch of
knowledge economics has risen, side by side with industry, to
become one of the most acceptable academic disciplines.

Economic knowledge has never accumulated in a straight and
steady path, nor in direct proportion to the efforts or numbers
of its high priests. Like the capitalist economy that it studies,
economics has suffered crises, periods of stagnation and periods
of boom. The immediate character of these crises is intellectual,
and at times they have temporarily threatened the coherence of
the discipline and its scientific pretensions. Such crises arise
because economics reaches the point where it explains either too
much or too little about the real world. The logic of intellectual
enquiry and the logic of real economic events are different yet
related. Despite the devoted efforts of many of its practitioners
to keep economics forever pure, the dirty fingers of reality occa-

sionally mark the ivory walls. At such times economists are rudely awakened to the inability of their theories to continue to render the capitalist economy intelligible.

In philosophers' models of ideal scientific research, such discrepancies between theory and observation lead to gains in understanding, through a change in the theory. The economics profession is a curious scientific community. Many of its members are attached to the building of theoretical models that aim to explain but can rarely, if ever, be falsified by events. The present marked disjunction between the assumptions of its theoretical models and what is actually happening in the real world is not new for economics. It is a characteristic mode of procedure. Intellectual crisis only erupts when part of the profession is forced to recognise that the predictions based on the theoretical models have become so at variance with what is going on in the economy as to cast doubt on the assumptions on which these models are based. Such a reappraisal can occur with such an explosive force that changes in the boundaries and landmarks of the subject are brought about. In the history of economic thought there have been many minor crises in various corners of the discipline but only two revolutions – the marginalist revolution in the second half of the nineteenth century, and the Keynesian revolution in the 1930s. In 1975 a new crisis had gripped economics, but there are as yet no signs of any theoretical advances that can help overcome it.

The marginalist revolution is the best example of an intellectual crisis which arose because economics was plainly beginning to examine and explain too much. It was overcome by shifting the whole focus of economic enquiry on to a narrower plane. The political economy of the early classical economists took the subject-matter of economics to mean an examination of how wealth was created and distributed. This meant they were obliged to develop some historical notion of the society and economy they were studying, some idea of different forms of economic organisation, and some judgement as to the relationship between politics and economics. Their starting-point was the labour theory of value – the idea that only human work could give exchange-value to commodities. Value was, therefore, a social relation and the only objective and independent measure of wealth. It represented the labour-time spent producing commodities. This con-

cept marked out the boundaries of the new subject and provided the basis for a historical theory of different forms of
economic society. A theory which argued that labour rather than
land or gold was the direct source of wealth devoted attention
to those forces that increased the productivity of labour and permitted it to develop most rapidly. It supplied a tool which could
be used to criticise existing economic reality and conditions,
especially where these hindered the development of the productive
power of labour and the extension of competition and the free
market. The political economists used it to attack restrictive
government policies and laws which favoured the interests of
landed property, and to support the interests of the rising class
of industrial capitalists, whose ownership of capital (which represented past, stored-up labour in the classical theory) gave them
the power and opportunity to direct the labour process.

In the United Kingdom after the 1840s, when the political
power of the industrial capitalists was relatively secure following
the repeal of the Corn Laws, the labour theory of value began to
appear more dangerous than useful. Dominant liberal opinion
preferred a theory that could justify the existing economic order
rather than criticise it. The labour theory of value in the hands
of Ricardian and other socialists was used to call both rent *and*
the profits of capital, exploitation, and to support the claims of
the working class for a more just distribution of wealth.

A special talent of the professional academic mind has always
been to suppress dangerous thoughts. So a great volume of
academic criticism began to rain upon the labour theory of value.
All kinds of unsuspected logical flaws were discovered lurking
within it, and it was soon gratefully abandoned as a tissue of
contradictions and confusions. The economics profession gradually adopted a new theory of value no longer dependent on
labour and labour-time, the marginal utility theory, which,
as it unfolded in all its grisly circularity, successfully removed from
economics any subversive taint. It also stripped from it the
limited historical dimension it had possessed and allowed
economists to assume henceforward as a matter of course that
the existing order of things, as far as economics was concerned,
was unchanged and unchanging.

THE HEYDAY OF MARGINALISM

The marginal utility theory of value was evolved over a long
period by a number of economists, among whom Jevons, Menger
and Walras were the most prominent. But it was only really con-
solidated and formalised in the works of the followers – Alfred
Marshall (despite his dislike for Jevons's work), the 'Austrian
School', and Pareto, although all developed different interpreta-
tions and emphases. Some of the reasons for the revolution were
straightforwardly intellectual – the clearing up of what were seen
as the theoretical shortcomings of the labour theory of value.
But many of the main figures in marginalist economists, particularly on the continent – such as Böhm-Bawerk, Ludwig von
Mises and Pareto, also saw the new theory as a powerful
weapon against socialism and as an intellectual defence of the
liberal order of capitalism.[1]

This new theory of value stated simply that value only had one
dimension. Commodities no longer had both a value in use and
a value in exchange. Their value was only the subjective valu-
ation which individuals placed upon them – the degree of utility
they possessed for each individual. Markets were composed of
economic agents acting independently, pursuing the greatest
possible 'utility' by maximising their returns and minimising their
costs. No essential difference existed between buyers and sellers,
producers and consumers. All were 'economic men' subject to the
external discipline of the market, the invisible hand of competition. Rational behaviour meant maximising benefits.

The subjective preferences of all individuals together added up
to consumer demand. Competition among producers would
bring forth a supply of goods at the lowest possible cost to meet
that demand. The point at which the curve of total demand
intersected the curve of total supply would be the price of the
product. This price would be the value of the commodity in
question – its market value. It turned out that for the marginalists the only measure of consumers' preferences in practice were
the preferences that were revealed in the market, that is what was
bought and sold. Whatever price a good sold at must therefore
be its value, its utility to consumers. Price equalled value and
value equalled price. The cobwebs of metaphysics were blown
away by the airy breeze of tautology.

The consequence was that the focus of economic enquiry altered. It was still centred on the market, but no longer on the political and economic conditions and consequences of a free market; only with the interplay of demand and supply, and therefore with the structure of relative prices within the market. The problem of what created value had been defined away. Other problems – income distribution, economic growth, trade cycles, concentration of production, export of capital, economic crises – all received little attention. Since value now equalled price, whatever could command a price had value and was 'productive'; capital for instance.

Extreme versions of marginalism went still further and argued that not only did the market define what was productive and what was not, but also ensured that each factor of production received as income the value of what it contributed to production. So it was a closed circle. The market was the only reality, and the only function of economics was to understand how it worked. Economics became, in Lord Robbins's famous definition, 'the science which studies human behaviour as a relationship between ends and scarce means which have alternative uses'.[2]

The marginalist revolution as it unfolded served both to re-affirm the economist's concentration on the market as the central feature of the capitalist economy, and at the same time to narrow the scope of economic enquiry to processes of price formation and determination within the market. This encouraged the construction, by one school, of formal general equilibrium models of the economy. These showed with enormous mathematical sophistication and elegance that there was one and only one point for the whole economy where all sectors would be in balance and all factors of production would be employed. This point was the point of general economic equilibrium. It was also the point which ensured the highest possible level of individual satisfactions and the most efficient allocation of resources. The 'equilibrium' was the 'optimum', where no one could be made better off without making someone else worse off. The road to this earthly paradise lay through perfect competition, free markets, free trade, no state interference, and every economic man maximising to his heart's content. As Professor Shackle has written :

The forty years from 1870 saw the creation of a Great Theory or Grand System of Economics, in one sense complete and self-sufficient, able on its own terms to answer all questions which those terms allowed. . . . This Great Theory was . . . the theory of general, perfectly competitive, full-employment stationary (or better, timeless) equilibrium. . . . In its arresting beauty and completeness this theory seemed to need no corroborative evidence from observation. It seemed to derive from these aesthetic qualities its own stamp of authentication and an independent ascendancy over men's minds.[3]

Marginalist economics accepted without question many tenets of classical political economy, particularly the 'law' laid down by Jean-Baptiste Say – that 'supply creates its own demand'. Say's Law ruled out the possibility of an economic crisis arising from the malfunctioning of the market. Whatever was produced could be sold, because paying the factors of production would produce sufficient incomes to buy all the goods that had been produced. Such a proposition could be happily incorporated into the general equilibrium and partial equilibrium models of the marginalists. Only price movements had any meaning for them, and the movements of prices were determined by the demand and supply of commodities in all markets. Since value was the same as price, it offered no alternative insight. The idea, insisted upon by Marx, that supply and demand only determined relative prices on the market, and that over-all fluctuations in prices had to be understood as fluctuations around labour-time values determined not in the market but in the production process, was ignored or rejected. For the marginalists, basking in the warm sun of the Pareto optimum, the market was the only reality. They loyally accepted the structure of ownership that gave one small class control of the economic process, and merely analysed the character of price formation and resource allocation in such an economy. Though there were important differences between the different schools, all were in general concerned only with how the political conditions for such an economy could be established and maintained.

The marginal revolution was, however, too successful. The security of economics was purchased at the expense of its relevance, and though economists showed themselves very good at donning blinkers, they could not forever remain indifferent to what was happening in the economy they were supposed to be studying. Perfect competition, free trade and *laissez-faire* capitalism had already received some hard knocks before 1914, in a world of cartels and trusts, trade unions and rival imperialisms. By the 1930s, however, a major depression had settled on the economics profession, following the destruction of the world of free trade and the gold standard, and the arrival of prolonged unemployment, stagnation, tariff barriers, and mounting restrictions on competition.

The great slump appeared to most economists like some vast natural phenomenon over which man could exercise no control. As John Strachey observed in his classic book on the 1930s:

> Capitalist crises are in truth to the [*sic*] inhabitants of our highly developed industrial communities, to modern Europeans and Americans, what the tempest and earthquake are to the savage. . . . The savage, it is true, has his experts, his medicine men who by chant or howl, by sacrifice or incantation attempt to cajole the destroying force. The capitalist world also has its experts, its economists. The phenomena of crisis lie, however, outside the scope of their science.[4]

Strachey's socialist judgement was shared by the liberal Keynes. Economics had nothing fundamental to say about the slump because, according to its own model of how the economy worked, the slump could not happen. There were automatic forces at work in the economy that always brought the economy back to full-employment equilibrium and Pareto's optimum. Even Pareto, however, seemed to lose faith in the power of capitalism to restore his optimum and maintain public order. He preferred to back Mussolini's fascists. For other economists, since the slump was hardly a figment in the imaginations of the unemployed, it had to be blamed on the intrusion of political and external factors into the workings of the market. Its basic causes were held not to be economic. Incredibly, the greatest convulsion the world economy had ever experienced was ruled to be outside the scope of the science intended to explain economic events. The relevance and appeal of general equilibrium and the optimum level of income and use of resources established through the market were not very apparent during the 1930s.

This still did not trouble many economists. Those amongst them with more advanced views had come to the conclusion that it was impossible to compare the relative satisfactions which different individuals derived from their money incomes. Pursuing the individualist premises of marginal utility theory to their logical conclusion, it was decided that each individual's judgement of utility was unique and could not be compared with anyone else's. Hence there was no way of knowing whether a millionaire derived more satisfaction from his millions than the unemployed worker from his dole. It was not an economic question, but a matter for ethics, to decide which of two real incomes was the larger. This was the dictum of Robbins, Hayek, and Haberler. As John Strachey commented sardonically :

> The mind's eye detects the doctor (Haberler) contemplating in turn the incomes of Herr Thyssen (a leading German industrialist) and of a man in a Nazi labour camp drawing three marks a week. After prolonged reflection Dr Haberler turns sadly and modestly away with the report that he is quite unable to decide which of these two is the richer. What scientific scruples, and, above all, what tact! We cannot help feeling how extraordinarily convenient these scruples must be for the good doctor. In a world which rocks and reels because of an unparalleled inequality in the distribution of wealth, how soothing to have come to the conclusion that the magnitudes of wealth enjoyed by different individuals cannot be compared at all.[5]

Strachey argued correctly that economics had reached this absurd position because it had no objective theory of value, no measure of value that was independent of price, hence no theory of the social relationships of the economic process which were expressed through the market, but were not identical with it. An economics that was based on a subjective theory of value, the impenetrable preferences of 'sovereign' individuals, was logically forced to exclude from the scope of economics all the most fundamental and important events and characteristics of actual economies.

Such a position could be maintained only at the cost of denying that economics had any relevance to the understanding of the economy, in particular to the overriding problem of that economy in the 1930s; the fact of prolonged depression. From its

beginnings, economics had always focused on the capitalist
market and how government policy could help to make it work
better, despite the efforts of purists to separate analysis from prescription. In the work of the classical political economists,
economics had been strongly associated with rising capitalism, that
is with liberalism and the economic programme of liberalism –
free trade, open markets, wider division of labour, minimum
state interference, and this aspect of classical political economy
was retained by the marginalists. The implicit belief governing
the study of economics has always been a formally rationalist one
– that a correct understanding of the principles of economic
order and economic progress could assist politicians to pursue
economic policies in conformity with them. The appearance of
prolonged economic disorder and stagnation, which could not be
understood within the framework of economics and ran counter
to all the expectations of general equilibrium, threatened both
the theoretical and the ideological basis of capitalist economics.

THE KEYNESIAN REVOLUTION

The intellectual crisis was largely overcome by Keynes,[6] but the
economic crisis proved more stubborn. Keynes waving his intellectual wand was not sufficient to dispel it, though such is the
romantic faith in the magic of great men and the alchemy of
ideas that the Keynesian revolution is often claimed as the reason
why the depression ended. What Keynes did was to restore the
relevance of economics to government policy by dispensing with
many parts of the orthodox economic model and integrating into
a new analysis many of the 'political' and 'institutional' factors
which economists had carefully winnowed from their theories.
Keynes devised a new theory for handling the facts and causes
of depression in a modern capitalist economy with its imperfect
markets and its growing public sector. Perhaps the most important feature of Keynes's ideas for the later development of
economics was his new and positive conception of the state.
Keynes was the first capitalist economist to analyse the importance
and potential of the growing state sector within capitalism. He
broke away from the notion, assumed by all the orthodox models,
that the only function of the state within a market economy was
to be the nightwatchman – enforcing contracts, balancing the

budget, and maintaining the stability of money. The new size of the state sector and the new institutional organisation of the private sector – particularly the concentration of production and the growth of trade unions – meant that the state could no longer afford a passive stance. Keynes realised that the size of the state sector gave governments the power to create and manage prosperity by manipulating its spending and tax policies and thus the income and expenditure of other sectors in the economy.

Much of Keynes's work may therefore be interpreted as an attempt to recognise the existence of the state as an economic agent within the economy, to justify its new role, and thereby recommend that it should assume responsibility for conditions in the economy as a whole. The consequences for economics are not hard to see. Keynes's ideas taken up by a generation of young economists only too anxious to overthrow the tutelage of orthodoxy produced a revolution in economic thought, and a new kind of economics – one interested in intervention.

The Keynesian revolution made state intervention respectable for professional economists. What made it respectable for governments was something else – urgent practical necessity, first in Nazi Germany and New Deal America in the 1930s, then in the United Kingdom during the Second World War. The economy in the United Kingdom revealed that state planning and state intervention, in particular Keynesian budgetary policy, were practicable and could be successful. The social and political upheaval the war caused committed all parties to a new consensus when the conflict was over – an expanded state sector, greater spending on social services, nationalisation of basic industries, and government commitment to full employment. Keynesianism supplied an economics of the real world and a useful set of beliefs and maxims for the administration of the economy. A whole branch of the 'new' economics after the war became concerned with practical questions – how to achieve higher growth, how to manage demand, how to raise productivity, how to stabilise prices, and so forth.

For a time the 'new' economics triumphed.[7] The remarkable and dramatic transformation of the fortunes of capitalism carried all before it. The system which had seemed incapable of further expansion and had been sunk in world-wide depression advanced once more. In the 1930s the symptoms of crisis and decay had been evident everywhere – the inequalities of wealth, the triumph of fascism, bitter social conflict, the unemployment of men and machines in the face of hunger and want. But after 1945 the reconstructed system found new life – a great boom began during which living standards rose, full employment was maintained, the fluctuations of the trade cycles were mild, and productivity increased faster than ever. Keynesians and Marxists alike were confused. Both had predicted a return to the chronic unemployment of the 1930s once the war and the expected post-war boom was over. The best Keynes had thought could be achieved was an economy which guaranteed full employment but which did not grow. Yet it was the application of Keynes's ideas that was widely held responsible for a large part of capitalism's new success. Keynes died at the start of this new era for economics and for capitalism, yet his figure bestrode it. The famous Bloomsbury dilettante was admitted posthumously to the company of the great economists, the Valhalla of the dismal science.

The extraordinary recovery of capitalism bred a facile optimism. Some believed that Keynesianism had solved the capitalists' 'economic problem' for all time. If the trade cycle could be moderated by government intervention and full employment secured, if markets could be kept expanding both domestically and world wide, then there were no further obstacles to uninterrupted economic growth, so long as ever larger doses of technology were fed into the productive process to raise the productivity of labour.

Yet there was one economic problem of the post-war world which Keynesianism could not master and had not really been expected to – permanent inflation. A modest secular inflation of prices became the normal experience of all the advanced capitalist states. At first, rising prices were regarded as a minor irritation. It was frequently dismissed as 'one of the most inconsequential economic problems'. A moderate inflation of 2 to 3 per cent per annum was thought to be a reasonable exchange for full employment and a growing national income. Besides, many economists thought it would only be a matter of time before the techniques of demand management were perfected, so that governments could run the economy at full employment, yet simultaneously maintain both stable prices and growth.

As techniques and experience of the problem increased, however, so did inflation. During the 1960s more and more people became convinced that policies for curbing inflation based on a Keynesian analysis would not work. The result was to discredit Keynesianism gravely. By the end of the 1960s, with inflation nearing double figures in many capitalist countries, with major currency crises, with rising industrial militancy, with sudden fears about the possible exhaustion of irreplaceable raw materials, the confident Keynesian worldview was ripe for overthrow. Dulled knives gleamed again in the common rooms of the economics profession. Economics began exploding in all directions – a strong monetarist anti-Keynesian counter-revolution erupted, alongside a big revival of radical and Marxist economics.

Inflation has opened huge cracks within the economics profession. The Keynesian paradigm ceases to command general assent. A babel of conflicting analyses and proposals for policy have arisen in its place. The prestige of Keynesianism, like the best of earlier branches of economics, was based on its ability to explain and overcome economic problems. It was therefore highly vulnerable when a real economic problem arose which it seemed unable to explain and overcome. Its period of ascendancy has been much shorter than the reign of marginalism. Today neo-Keynesians, vulgar Keynesians, Left Keynesians, Cambridge Keynesians, even Marxist Keynesians consort and dispute both with each other and with a growing ragbag of anti-Keynesians – among them monetarists, neoclassicals, gold fetishists, institutionalists, 'Austrians' and marginalists.[8]

The collapse of Keynesian certainty has revealed how diverse the views of economists have become on almost all questions of analysis and policy, and how poorly many economists have digested the central insights of Keynes and his followers. On every major policy, whether it be the European Economic Community, economic growth, inflation, devaluation, floating exchange rates, or monetary policy and taxation, economists provide for the benefit of the public a parade not only of different recommendations, but different facts and evidence, different methods of analysis, and different predictions.

Post-war economics was divided into two halves, macroeconomics and microeconomics. Macroeconomics, concerned with questions of output, employment, and the determination of national income, was marked out for the Keynesians. Microeconomics, dealing with the economics of the firm, welfare economics, price determination and the like, remained the preserve of the marginalists, or neoclassicals as they became known. Within this framework Keynesians never dug up the roots of orthodoxy. It merely felled the marginalist theory of employment, and erected its own in its place. But in time, marginalism sprouted again and threatened to choke the 'new' economics. Neoclassical theories of growth and distribution began once more, spurred by the new energy and resilience of capitalism and the market. Not that all the Keynesians were standing idle. One school, based in Cambridge, were pursuing their own onslaught on orthodoxy, developing the critique of marginalism into new areas, particularly capital theory, distribution theory, and finally marginal utility theory itself.[9]

On the practical level, surveying the economic scene in 1976 an observer might be forgiven for thinking that the argument had come round in a circle, back to the 1930s once again. Indeed, in retrospect, the Keynesian revolution of the 1930s may not appear so much as a major breakthrough in economic thought, but rather as the beginning of a long period of confusion and decomposition within economics, which was masked for a time by the success of Keynesianism as a practical technique. In the first decade after 1945 Keynesianism seemed supreme and unchallengeable; yet in some respects it had not routed, still less converted its adversaries. It had merely silenced them for a time. Even during this period, critics of Keynes were busy undermining the Keynesian edifice. A fashion developed among some orthodox economists, and Marxists too, though for different reasons, to belittle the theoretical importance of Keynes's achievement and to reassert the validity of the older economic models. The defenders of marginalism said that Keynes's whole analysis was only a special case of the general marginalist analysis, and therefore not a truly general theory of employment at all. Instead of replacing orthodox theory it only added special assumptions reflecting 'institutional factors', in particular the notion that wage rates were generally inflexible downwards.[10]

These anti-Keynesians strongly believed that if money-wage rates fell low enough during a slump, investment and production would be made profitable once more, and employment would recover. A falling price level was the market mechanism that counteracted the downturn of the trade cycle and speeded recovery and a return to full employment. Many made the further assumption that there was a point of general equilibrium in all markets towards which the economy was forever tending. Such a tendency depended on all prices being flexible, able to move up and down as the occasion demanded in order to restore balance between all economic variables. The Keynesian answer was that most prices were no longer very flexible, and many were highly inflexible. They argued that prices in modern capitalist markets were more often determined by costs than by demand, and that even if wages were to fall sharply in a slump, that would not necessarily stimulate investment since prices might fall as fast. So real wages would be unchanged. In the absence of a change in expectations there was no reason to suppose that a fall in money-wage rates by itself would have any appreciable impact on investment, saving and interest rates. But the anti-Keynesians were unmoved. They believed they had vindicated orthodoxy by showing that the Keynesian theory, far from being revolutionary, was only an application of the orthodox theory to the special case where wage rates would not fall.

This sly attempt to assimilate Keynes to marginalist orthodoxy obscured the central contribution Keynes made to economic analysis. Keynes denied that there was any automatic tendency to equilibrium or balance in the economic system at full employment, and made it possible for economists to study once more the economy as a whole using economic aggregates, like total consumption and total investment, and how political and economic factors interacted. To do this he was compelled to shift the focus of economics back to the kind of questions that interested the classical political economists. Moreover, he had re-adopted a modified version of the labour theory of value. Marginalist economics had removed aggregates that covered the whole economy from the scope of their enquiries. To analyse aggregates once more Keynes needed some independent measure of them. Monetary quantities only measured economic variables in money prices. He chose wage units – the amount of money paid for one hour of work, thereby making a version of labour-time once again the measure of value created in the process of production. Keynes's aggregates – consumption, investment, national income – were all made up of these wage units. This enabled the national accounts to be expressed in terms of both income and expenditure.

Keynes showed that if economists wished to study the real development of the economy they had to dispense with the polite fiction that the economy could be treated as though it were simply a technical process and that private ownership of capital made no difference; or that capital was a factor of production just like labour, was productive like labour, had a price like labour, and received a reward like labour. Such assumptions gave answers to certain microscopic questions, but ruled out proper understanding of how the accumulation of capital, and the determination of shares in the national income, depended on the way in which production was socially organised. The social and political relations were, in fact, inseparable from it. In Michael Kalecki's summary of this important aspect of Keynesian theory, capitalists get what they spend, and workers spend what they get. Such an insight into the workings of an actual as opposed to a mythical capitalist economy was not available to the marginalists, stuck as they were with 'economic men'. Though innocent of many of the implications of his theories himself, Keynes, through his work on the factors that determined employment in the economy, opened the path which some at least of his followers have pursued.[11]

THE KEYNESIAN PARADIGM

In the days when the Keynesian paradigm ruled and inflation was merely a problem of fine-tuning the economy, two basic approaches to inflation developed. They were labelled 'demand pull' and 'cost push'. As their names suggest, one approached inflation from the side of demand, the other from the side of costs. To suggest prices were pulled up by demand meant that a general imbalance between demand and supply had arisen.[12] In the simple Keynesian breakdown of national income and expenditure this indicated that the spending of consumers, capitalists and the government amounted to more than the quantity of goods being produced. The gap could only be bridged by rising prices.

The mechanism by which excess demand could cause continual inflation was analysed by Keynes in a pamphlet entitled, *How To Pay for the War* (London: Macmillan, 1940). His analysis here was simplified because he was discussing a war economy –

an unusual situation in that one overriding goal was imposed upon economic production : the winning of the war. This meant that he could assume that the share of government in G.N.P. should be as large as possible, and could therefore concentrate on how this expenditure should be financed and how the incomes of other groups should be controlled. In a war economy the demands on the productive resources of a country naturally tend to become unlimited. Consumption by all other groups has to be restrained to a bare minimum. The traditional means by which the government commandeers production for its war machine and consumes the vast bulk of everything that is produced is a mixture of direct controls and inflation. The former channels production, labour and raw materials into desired areas, the latter reduces the effective purchasing power of the incomes of the rest of the population. Governments stay ahead of the inflationary upsurge because they control the presses. They print the money. In his pamphlet, however, Keynes argued that inflation was not the only means to enforce a balance between planned spending and production. Instead of financing the war through inflation, and as a consequence enriching the owners of the country's industries at the expense of the rest of the community, the government could choose to finance it through a mixture of voluntary and forced saving. By persuading individuals to lend to it and by taxing all incomes to leave only the minimum required for subsistence, the government could balance spending and production without inflation. Instead of a free-for-all scramble in which governments and employers stayed ahead because they had the power to print money and raise prices, some rough equality of sacrifice could be imposed on the community.

These ideas were taken up by Keynesians after the war in grappling with the problem of rising prices in a fully employed economy. If consumers, capitalists and government together planned to spend more than the economy currently produced, the excess demand would cause prices to be forced up. In an economy where production resources, both men and machines, were idle, then an increase in demand might mean only a rise in output, with prices remaining stable. But once full employment was reached a situation of potential excess demand was threatened, unless by strange coincidence the plans of consumers, capitalists and government happened to balance. As in the war economy the potential full-employment output of an economy in the short run could be calculated, and so, it was thought, could the amount of aggregate demand that would be necessary to keep that economy at full employment with stable prices. One important difference from the war economy, however, was that war production was geared overwhelmingly to producing use-values for immediate consumption, not to maximising profits and enlarging productive capacity. Increases in productivity were important but secondary. In times of peace, however, the normal accumulation of capital would be resumed. A portion of national income would be devoted each year by capitalists to investment in plant and machinery to increase labour productivity, so enlarging their capital. This increase in productivity could partly offset the increase in prices caused by excess demand. Specifically, if money costs rose no faster than the rate of increase of productivity, then in principle these rises in costs could be absorbed without any rise in prices.

This became a central focus of the Keynesian analysis of inflation – the relationship between the rate of increase of productivity and the rate of increase of money costs at full-employment levels. The most important part of costs was supposedly labour, so analysis was focused on the money wage. If there was general excess demand in the economy, this would be reflected in the prices of consumer goods through employers bidding up wage rates, as they would be anxious to secure as much labour as they could. Money wages would rise and, after an interval, so would all costs, and capitalists would then protect their profit margins by raising the prices of their final products. This simple analysis was refined by studies which suggested that excess demand in particular industries and for particular types of labour could exist without there being general excess demand in the economy as a whole. Variation by region and sector were thus introduced into the argument.

THE PHILLIPS CURVE

Perhaps the most striking example of the demand-pull analysis lay in the attempts to devise measures of the amount of excess demand existing in the economy at any one time, with the aim of controlling it and reducing inflation. The great spur to such speculation came from Professor Phillips who in 1958 unveiled the memorable Phillips Curve.[13] Phillips claimed that over the past hundred years there was a definite relationship between the amount of unemployment in the economy and the rate of increase in money-wage rates. The greater of the one the less of the other, and vice versa. He backed this up by a detailed statistical analysis going back to 1861. Through all his scatter diagrams the curve ran like a golden thread.

The Phillips Curve delighted economists. It is not often that a firm relationship of any sort between economic variables can be discovered, still less of a relationship that appears to be of major importance. Yet it was not easy to say how the Phillips Curve should be explained. It was one thing to deduce a relationship between excess demand and inflation from a simple general model of the economy; it was harder to see how unemployment could be treated as a reliable measure of excess demand and how the apparent relationship could reflect the concrete processes of decision-taking, price-fixing and wage negotiation in particular industries. However, theoretical explanations were in time thought up and, meanwhile, economists could marvel at the progress of their science and accept as axiomatic that there existed a trade-off between inflation and unemployment. Many drew a simple lesson for policy – if governments wanted to control inflation they would have to permit higher unemployment.

Phillips himself estimated that given the shape of the curve, a level of unemployment just below 2·5 per cent would keep final prices stable, and a level of 5·5 per cent would keep money wages stable. He showed how for each of three periods, 1861–1913, 1913–48, and 1948–57, knowing what the unemployment rate was, allowed a fairly accurate prediction to be made of the rate of increase of money wages in that year. In the five years 1953–7, the accuracy was particularly strong. Phillips presented his results as a tentative conclusion, and advanced no explanation of why the relationship should hold, but they were quickly seized on by others. Attempts were made to show that if governments persisted with policies to maintain full employment (or over-full employment, as it was quickly christened, which made it sound disreputable), then they would have to put up with creeping inflation.

paish's 'lash'

Such a straightforward guide to policy was formalised in the writings of Professor Paish,[14] who claimed relentlessly during the 1960s that if governments would only permit unemployment to rise to 2·25 per cent then inflation would abate, and the country could have rapid growth with stable prices. Paish defined inflation as a condition in which the national money income is rising faster than the national real income. He dismissed wage-push explanations, arguing that there was no tendency for profits to fall, because average earnings were increasing much faster than basic rates. Unions were only able to push up basic rates. The real cause of inflation, according to Paish, was excess demand, the tendency for the economy to produce too close to the ceiling of its productive capacity. This led to a competitive scramble amongst employers for scarce labour, thus forcing up average earnings. In a situation of excess demand, there was thus constant pressure for the gap between union-negotiated basic rates and average earnings – which included overtime, incentives, bonuses and fringe benefits of all kinds – to widen. This gap was called 'wage drift' by the economists.

It followed that controlling inflation meant controlling excess demand. Rises in profit margins, wages and salaries were not the cause of inflation, but only its symptoms, the means by which excess demand was transmitted into higher prices in the shops. Long-run price stability depended on finding that 'margin of unused capacity at which money incomes will rise at an annual rate equal to that of the growth of productive capacity'.[15] Paish calculated that for the United Kingdom this meant a margin of unused capacity of between 5 and 7 per cent, which represented 2 to 2·5 per cent unemployment, or around 500,000 working people without jobs. If the government maintained this margin permanently then competition for labour would fall, money wages would not be bid up, costs would not increase, and final prices would be stable.

Like so many economic prescriptions, this one seemed too tidy, too logical to be a real solution. Naturally, none of the economists supporting Paish offered to join the ranks of the unemployed in the cause of national policy, neither did they have much to say about how the government would secure greater unemployment only in those sectors and regions of the economy where there was already excess demand for labour and avoid increasing it in those where unemployment was above 10 per cent.

More seriously, the theory supposed that there was some automatic regulator ensuring a perpetual trade-off between inflation and unemployment. But it ignored changes in the rate of growth of productive capacity, and above all the role of expectations in inflation, which could cause the trade-off between inflation and unemployment to shift violently, as indeed happened after 1968. Then both inflation and unemployment rose together, and even Paish was forced to concede that his theory no longer applied.

COST OR PROFITS PUSH

The alternative Keynesian explanation of creeping inflation centres on costs.[16] These Keynesians accept many of the conclusions of the demand-pull school, in particular the central importance of the relationship between money wages and productivity. This meant that they too could accept the Phillips Curve, though they interpreted it differently. The relationship between unemployment and money-wage rates revealed by the curve was in principle compatible with either theory. Where cost-push theorists differ from the demand-pull approach is where they thought inflationary pressures started. Both sides can agree on the mechanics of the inflationary spiral, the endless chase of costs after prices and prices after costs. But they cannot agree on what started the spiral in the first place and what maintains the momentum.

The cost-push theorists argue that the initial impetus comes not from excess demand, but from an autonomous increase in prices which reflects either higher costs or a desire for higher profits. Such an autonomous increase is possible because of the new institutional realities of the modern economy – the replacement of free competition in many markets by varying degrees of monopoly. Modern companies have become price-makers rather than price-takers and are therefore able within fairly wide limits to vary output and prices independently of the state of demand. In the labour market unions have secured a virtual monopoly in many branches through the establishment of the closed shop and have therefore gained the right to negotiate the sale of the labour-power of their members. Furthermore, their bargaining strength has been increased by new government policies, specifically the commitment to full employment.

Cost-push explanations became exceedingly popular in the 1950s and 1960s, and not merely among Keynesians. Some anti-Keynesian economists like Haberler and Hayek were equally fond of them.[17] But whereas the Keynesians accepted the dwindling validity of models of free competition for analysing how prices were established in many markets, the anti-Keynesians thought the institutional structure a fundamental perversion of how the economy could and should work. The Keynesians point to the dominant feature of modern markets – the existence of imperfect competition and oligopoly and the concentration of production and employment in the hands of a few firms. This means that firms can set their own prices within certain limits and vary output to maximise sales, profits and growth. Prices in such markets are a mark-up on costs and price competition tends to disappear. In many industries one firm comes to act as the price-leader; if it alters its prices the other firms in the industry follow suit. Competition revolves around market shares and is conducted through advertising and marketing strategies of all kinds. The aim is to make each firm's product unique for the consumer, however essentially similar in reality most of them remained. Detergents and petrol are typical examples.

The result is an industrial structure in which production in most branches is concentrated in the hands of a few giants; the process of production is organised in ever larger plants to reap economies of scale, and in which financial control is increasingly centralised in the hands of holding companies, multinationals and conglomerates of all kinds. It has produced a growing division between those sectors of the economy where businesses are still small and numerous and usually run by the owners and their families, and the corporate sector, run by professional managers, and accounting for an ever-greater proportion of total production, employment, research, investment and growth in the private sector.[18]

Labour markets have been similarly transformed. The rise of trade unions had ended individual competition among workers for jobs in many sectors. Using weapons such as the closed shop, restrictive practices, strikes and go-slows, unions have gradually developed collective bargaining over wages and conditions, and built up their bargaining strength. They are essentially defensive organisations, and their economic power is clearly of a different order compared to that of the great corporations.[19] However, such is the influence of marginalist economics that the same abstract analysis of 'monopoly' – meaning control over either demand or supply in a market, and therefore control over price – is applied equally to such dissimilar 'economic men' as General Motors and the National Union of Railwaymen.

As far as the anti-Keynesians are concerned, most of the developments in the modern markets of capitalism are deplorable. The marginalist vision of perfect competition is of markets made up of a myriad of small buyers and sellers, whose actions and decisions all taken together set prices and determine output. No one individual firm or consumer can alter the price of a product by varying output or consumption because no one firm produces enough of total output to make any difference to total supply. Such firms are price-takers, ruled by the market, unable to mould the economic environment to suit themselves. For *perfect* competition it is also essential that there should be no barriers to new firms entering the industry, no significant differences in the product manufactured within an industry (hence on marketing, packaging or advertising), and full information available to buyers and sellers about any variations in price.

It is readily understandable how such an ideal makes contemplation of the modern economy a waking nightmare for marginalist economists. The gross interference with the workings of free markets, which they see on every side, makes the attainment of equilibrium almost impossible. As a result they differ strongly with the Keynesians on questions of policy, such as the control of inflation. The Keynesians seek to restrain inflation by taking account of institutional realities – notably the degree of monopoly exercised by firms and unions. The anti-Keynesians recommend the overthrow of the realities.

The very choice of the label 'cost push' shows the direction in which the theory was weighted. An alternative label would have been 'profits push'. But, in fact, economists have concentrated overwhelmingly only on how the unions could exert their 'monopoly' power to force employers to raise wages. Few have considered the plausible alternative – that firms might use their monopoly control over markets to raise prices to increase their profits. Whenever it is raised, it is instantly dismissed.[20] The monopolistic organisation of industry only enters the cost-push explanation because it means that firms can accede to demands for higher wages in the knowledge that they can raise prices to protect their profit margins. In a competitive market, any one firm that agrees to a wage increase and then raises its prices would be priced out of the market. Making use of the 'full information' at their disposal, buyers would merely switch their orders to one of the firm's rivals. Since both would be producing an identical product, only a difference in price could affect the choice of the consumer. But in an oligopolistic market, firms are subject to no such constraint. Costs can be passed directly on to the consumer. Firms set their prices at a level that maximises their cash flow. They can mould their own economic environment to a significant degree. For a small firm in a competitive market, profits are the mark of efficiency, the ability to hold costs down below the ruling market price. For the modern corporation, profits are also the chief goal because they make possible all other goals of the corporation. But profit maximisation becomes more calculating and rational, for the corporation must consider not merely what price will maximise revenue in the short run, but how best to secure the maximum profitability for the company in the long run, when so many of the factors that can affect profitability are both unpredictable, yet at the same time open to possible influence by the company's own actions. This means attending to growth, research and development, labour policy, investment, marketing strategy and much else. What achieving all these goals requires, however, is a constant and rising flow of profits.[21]

The cost-push explanation gained many adherents because of its apparent ability to explain many facts which the demand-pull theory in its aggregate wisdom passed over. In particular, cost-push theorists pointed out that prices continued to rise even when there was considerable unemployment, and demand (by all available indicators) was falling. In formal terms, they defined inflation as money wages outstripping productivity. Whilst most of them acknowledged that earnings could be bid up in high productivity industries by competition between employers for labour, they pointed out that in a growing number of industries in the modern economy, for instance the services sector and much of the public sector, the scope for increasing productivity was low. This is because such sectors of the economy were labour-intensive. The great bulk of their running costs are wages and salaries. Productivity increases fastest in those industries where new machines can be introduced that simultaneously cuts the work force and raises output. In industries which require a large labour force, such as the railways and the mines, increases in productivity may come from getting the workers to work harder, longer or more efficiently, but they will not be substantial. New capital investment to raise productivity dramatically would have to be labour-saving. The scope for such investment is small in many industries. In other sectors, such as education or hairdressing the very meaning of productivity is doubtful, because the output is a service, difficult to measure, hence difficult to increase meaningfully. Yet workers in these industries can demand and receive wage increases that keep their wage rates 'comparable' to the wages of workers boosted by wage drift in the high-productivity sector. The wage edifice, the procedures of collective bargaining and government policy all conspire to produce an irresistible wage-push which is reflected in rising costs at every stage of the production process and which employers happily pass on to the consumer by raising prices.

The principle on which cost-push explanations are firmly grounded is that money wages are almost completely rigid downwards, but highly flexible upwards. This unites Keynesians and anti-Keynesians. In the 1930s when prices were falling, it meant that profits and capital values could only be protected by closing down factories and sacking workers. In the 1950s it meant that, if unions exerted their monopoly power to demand higher wages, profit margins in general could only be protected by increasing prices. Inflation thus appears to Keynesians and anti-Keynesians alike as a symptom of the struggle over how the national income and the annual increase of productivity are to be distributed. The Keynesians, however, mostly hold that, in the absence of government regulation, prices and relative shares in national income will be determined by the balance of power between the major producer groups – the degree of monopoly each can exercise over the market.[22] They accept that monopolistic control of markets is irreversible. Prices in each industry are a mark-up on costs, the size of which depends on the degree of monopoly. For the anti-Keynesians, the fact of monopoly introduces cruel distortions into the workings of the capitalist economy and creates a struggle over the distribution of income which is strictly unnecessary. Both camps came to accept that the price level is now determined by a labour standard – the level of money wages that is established by collective bargaining. If wages rise the price level has to rise too. The external monetary constraints of the gold standard have been swept away. Governments can expand the money supply to accommodate whatever level of prices emerges from the process of collective bargaining.[23]

MONETARISTS : PAPER-THIN EXCUSES

The debate over the relative importance of cost-push and demand-pull factors was largely a Keynesian one, conducted in terms of the Keynesian model of the economy. The anti-Keynesians, who continued the debate of the 1930s, claimed the Keynesian system did not replace the earlier orthodox model, merely that it based its analysis on certain assumptions, particularly that wage rates were inflexible downwards. By this means, Keynes's 'General Theory' could be shown to be not general at all, but only a particular application of the general equilibrium analysis of a competitive economy. If wage rates could be made to fall as well as rise then the orthodox analysis would apply as before. Economists had no responsibility for the shortcomings of the real world, so it was argued they should not feel obliged to modify their theories about it. They advised their fellow economists – 'do not adjust your theories, there is a fault in reality'.

This attempted deflation of the importance of Keynes's 'revolution' in economic theory, however, though often repeated, did not for a long time constitute an all-out attack on the Keynesian system. That was launched during the 1960s by another group of anti-Keynesians who called themselves 'monetarists'. By the 1970s the economic journals were speaking of a 'monetarist counter-revolution in economics'.[24] This particular counter-revolutionary orchestra was conducted from Chicago by Milton Friedman, where it had been tuning up, in fact, since the 1950s. Accelerating inflation and the disarray of the Keynesians allowed the monetarists their chance.

The most striking contribution of the monetarists to the speculation over the causes of inflation is the apparently banal assertion that inflation is always a monetary phenomenon. Since inflation is usually defined as rising prices, and prices are a monetary phenomenon, it could hardly exist in an economy that did not use some form of money to conduct exchange. That might be thought common ground between all disputants. But the monetarists' interpretation of their own statement is novel in the extreme and carries important implications for the analysis and control of inflation. For they argue that monetary phenomena do not simply reflect real phenomena, but have an independent form and influence of their own. In other words, according to the monetarists, the Keynesians in practice investigate economic phenomena as a set of use-values. Consumption and investment are related to the actual spending plans of individuals reflecting their desire for material objects to satisfy their material needs. They disregard the most important feature of the market economy – the fact that all goods must appear in it in the form of commodities, that is in the form of money. They have an exchange-value as well as a use-value and these are very different. Money for the Keynesians is only a veil behind which the real forces affecting production and distribution operate. In their analysis they neglect it and concentrate on the real spending plans of consumers, capitalists and governments that determine the actual level of effective demand, hence of national income and employment. Money does not matter – it is a mere token, a unit of account.

This was what the monetarists claimed the Keynesians said. It was certainly never what Keynes said. But it sounded plausible. It followed that if money were to be reinstated as one of the prime movers of the modern capitalist economy, then the Keynesian analysis and prescriptions could be declared invalid. Governments could control the rest of the economy by controlling the money supply, not by intervening directly. The implications of monetarism were, from the start, highly conservative. *Ultra* monetarists began rewriting economic history, gaily demonstrating that all fluctuations in the history of capitalism, all slumps

C

and booms, crises and recessions were due primarily to changes
in the money supply, and that therefore government and central
banks were responsible for them. If governments only learnt
how to manage the monetary supply properly and ceased inter-
fering with the delicate workings of a free-enterprise economy,
cycles would be eliminated, and steady growth without inflation
would be achieved.

The idea around which this shiny edifice was built was the
quantity theory of money – which had attracted such scorn from
Keynes and his followers. The quantity theory simply declared
that the level of prices was determined by the quantity of money,
$MV = PT$. Prices (P) multiplied by the number of transactions
(T) had to equal the quantity of money in circulation (M),
multiplied by the velocity of circulation (V), the speed at which
money changed hands. In itself the formula might seem innocuous
because it is true by definition. But it was always interpreted to
mean that money was the prime mover and any change in
prices (P) would depend on a prior change in money (M) (V
was assumed to be constant).

The monetarists revived and updated the quantity theory of
money. Keynes had argued that the velocity of circulation of
money was not a constant and that the money supply and therefore the price level rose or fell in response to the behaviour of
real forces, the interaction of the plans of government, capitalists
and consumers. The price level was determined by these real
factors not by the money supply. The monetarists believed the
opposite. To understand how prices were determined, the changes
in the money supply had to be studied, changes which were
independent of changes elsewhere in the economy.

Monetarists do not argue that the rate of inflation is directly
proportional to the rate of increase of the money supply, at least
not immediately. In the short run, changes in the money supply
affect primarily the level of output. According to this view, it was
the precipitate fall in the money supply of one-third at the beginning of the Great Depression in the United States, brought about
by the ineptitude of the federal authorities, that led to the sharp
fall in output.[25] In the long run, however, changes in the money
supply *do* affect prices. It is a central monetarist proposition that
a sustained inflation can only result from the quantity of money
increasing more rapidly than output. If the flow of money and

the flow of real goods and services are not balanced, the gap has to be bridged either by rising or by falling prices.

The simple Keynesian retort is that this will only be so if the velocity of circulation – the speed at which money changes hands – remains constant. If it should rise, then prices could rise without there being any change in the amount of money circulating. Keynes indeed argued that the velocity of circulation would be highly variable, and the monetarists have therefore devoted much attention to showing that normally it is highly stable. They argue that the demand for money is determined by each individual's level of income. Individuals choose to hold a certain proportion of cash in relation to their income, independently of whatever the current rate of interest is. This sets definite limits to the possible variations in the velocity of circulation of money supply. Milton Friedman argues further that only where money as a standard of value has completely collapsed, as in hyperinflations, when the price level may double every month, does the velocity of circulation rise very fast. But in that case, the supply of money is being increased very fast at the same time, and the whole monetary system must soon collapse. The only example of a rapid increase in velocity since the war in the United States is the Korean War inflation of 1952. Then inflation was extremely rapid, but without any increase in money supply to sustain it, it only lasted about six months; then it petered out. Clearly there do exist definite limits to the amount that velocity can rise.

The basic Keynesian objections to the monetarists is rather different. It is that the money supply and the demand for money are not directly connected to the forces that determine national income – primarily consumption, investment and government spending. Keynes argues that part at least of the demand for money is determined by the desire of individuals to hold cash ('liquidity preference'), but that this in turn depends on the rate of interest. In the orthodox theory, the rate of interest was the link between savings and investment, and brought them into balance, so that a decision to save always meant a corresponding decision to invest. Keynes argued, however, that the rate of interest had very little impact on either savings or investment – it only determined how much cash individuals wished to hold. Saving was a stable proportion of income, the amount left over

after consumption. To each level of income corresponded a level
of consumption ('propensity to consume'), and therefore a level
of savings. Investment was quite separate. It was determined
not by the rate of interest, but by businessmen's expectations of
the profitability of new investment (the 'marginal efficiency of
capital' as Keynes called it). National income was determined by
the level of effective demand, the amount that consumers, capitalists and government planned to spend, not by changes in the
supply of money and in interest rates.

Keynes argued that national income, the level of prices and
the money supply were all inevitably linked in the long run, by
definition, but that, in the short run, it was changes in spending
that determined the level and the distribution of national income.
Once such changes had occurred, no purely *monetary* changes,
whether in the price of goods, wage rates, or rates of interest,
could counteract them. Changes in money flows could not
reverse changes in real flows. The functioning of the modern
capitalist market economy, Keynes insisted, is not the smoothly
adjusting system pictured in the models of general equilibrium.
On the contrary, rigidities and discontinuities within and
between all its different sectors and markets are its distinguishing characteristic, but even if they were not, there would still
be no automatic tendency for the system to move towards full
employment.

So the argument between Keynesians and monetarists is really
an argument about how the market works. Monetarists put stress
on the money supply, because they believe the price mechanism
is still the major factor that can create balance and adjustment
throughout the economy if it is allowed to work. Since by
definition inflation must mean that somehow the money supply
is expanding faster than output, the monetarists argue that health
can be restored to the market economy by rigorously controlling
the money supply. Naturally that is formally correct, and there
can be no doubt that if such a policy was enforced, *eventually*
inflation would be stifled.

The Keynesians argue that the monetarists see everything from
back to front. They start with accounting identities, propound
simple cures, and end by disregarding the real nature of the
modern market economy. In a very revealing metaphor, Milton
Friedman, like David Hume before him, describes the effect of

an increase in the quantity of money brought about by discharg-
ing a heap of new banknotes from a helicopter. (Hume described
what would happen if everyone woke up to find a gold sovereign
in their pocket; or if overnight the currency of the economy
increased five times.) In either case, of course, with output
unchanged, the extra money if it is to be spent, can only be
accommodated in the economy through prices rising.

In the real market economy, however, increases in the supply
of money do not come about in this way – the analogy is misleading. According to the Keynesians, the money supply only
rises because consumers and capitalists raise their expenditure and
therefore their demand for cash. Initially this is financed from
exisiting cash balances, from an expansion of credit, from running down bank deposits, and the like. This reduces the amount
of liquidity in the system, thus raising or threatening to raise
interest rates. Rising interest rates would mean falling prices for
government securities. The government's ability to borrow in the
future is thus weakened, the burden of present repayment on the
National Debt and on short-term lending is increased. To prevent
this from happening the Central Bank increases the money supply.
For the Keynesians, therefore, the expansion of the money supply
is an effect and not a cause of inflation. The reason why governments are so ready to expand the money supply on request is the
size of the public sector and the volume of government expenditure (over 25 per cent of G.N.P. in every major capitalist
economy), and the commitment to full-employment policies. So
the policy of monetary restraint preached by the monetarists
could only work if governments were at the same time prepared
to cut back drastically on their own expenditure.

THE DEBATE ON POLICY

The monetarist counter-revolution has helped to clarify the
alternatives for inflation both in analysis and in policy. It has
made the outlines of the Keynesian system far sharper and has
shown that what is at stake is not just another technical argument in economics but different conceptions of the political
economy. What Keynesians and monetarists offer are rival political–economic strategies for managing the most important contemporary economic problem – inflation. It is impossible to make

sense of the debate without taking this dimension into account, however abstruse, technical and unreachable so much of it may appear. The cost-push/demand-pull division which pre-dated the split between monetarists and Keynesians was also a debate over policy and had important practical implications, but the disagreements between the two sides were much narrower. Both in general shared the central assumptions of the Keynesian model, so both were primarily concerned with fine-tuning. Cost-push economists naturally advocated some form of incomes policy to enable governments to intervene directly to control costs, whilst demand-pull economists recommended refinement of government policies to eliminate excess demand and, specifically, in the case of Paish and others, to raise unemployment to 2·25 per cent.

The split between Keynesians and monetarists, however, has become a disagreement over the nature and role of the state sector and threatens the maintenance of the consensus on running the 'mixed economy'. By placing such emphasis on control of the money supply in defeating inflation the monetarists break with one of the central tenets of this consensus – that the government's primary responsibility is to maintain full employment. All consistent monetarists among economists and politicians are prepared to see unemployment rise if this is necessary to control inflation. What the monetarists demand is that money should resume its proper function in a capitalist economy – a universal standard to facilitate exchange and one that keeps its value. They therefore seek to take away from governments the power to vary the money supply at will. If the money supply is made predictable like the seasons, it ceases to inject uncertainty into economic affairs. Economic man must adjust his behaviour to money and stop expecting money to adjust to him.

At this point it becomes clear how the monetarist argument joins pre-Keynesian and anti-Keynesian economic thinking. If the government is to lose its power to vary the money supply, then it also loses its power to reflate the economy through deficit financing. It must balance its books and only spend what it can raise through taxes or borrowing. It can no longer print more money to finance new expenditure. It follows that the government is no longer responsible for maintaining full employment. That is to be made once again the responsibility of the unions. According to this reasoning unemployment was only prolonged in the 1920s and 1930s in the United Kingdom and elsewhere because trade unions refused to accept sufficiently large cuts in their wage rates. Thus the implication of the monetarist position is that trade unions are never responsible for inflation, but do cause unemployment.

Underlying all varieties of the anti-Keynesian position is the central belief that left to itself a competitive market economy always moves towards some kind of equilibrium at full employment of resources. Hence all cycles, troughs, slumps, inflations and dislocations are caused by some interference with the competitive mechanism. This is very clearly expressed by Hayek,[26] who has argued consistently against Keynes and the Keynesians that the real cause of unemployment is not lack of demand, but the fact that the distribution of labour does not coincide with the distribution of demand. This makes production unprofitable. Unemployment and cuts in wage rates to force labour mobility between industries and raise profit margins are the solutions he has always advocated. Monetary expansion to overcome unemployment, Hayek believes, will only solve the problem temporarily. It creates an artificial prosperity that does not solve the underlying problems. It prevents competitive forces from operating and, before long, further doses of 'inflation' are required to maintain employment. Thus full-employment policies lead to accelerating inflation because they create the need for repeated and ever larger monetary expansion, and give trade unions the power and the opportunity to push up wage rates. Since inflation cannot continue for ever at an accelerating rate, sooner or later capitalist states will face a new collapse of output and employment. The basic need, therefore, is to restore the stability of money by making the trade unions once again responsible for unemployment – 'the long-run problem remains the restoration of a labour market which will produce wages which are compatible with stable money'[27] – and to re-create an 'unhampered' market in which full employment again becomes compatible with real not 'artificial' growth, by redistributing labour so that it 'corresponds' with the distribution of demand.

Hayek's faith that such an underlying harmony exists is remarkable, but it runs through all the anti-Keynesian thinking, including the monetarists. As one critic of the monetarists has pointed out – despite their name the real belief of the monetarists about money is that money does not matter, so long as governments do not interfere with its supply. In the long run, money is a passive factor in the economy provided its growth does not run on ahead of the growth of the G.N.P. It is merely the medium through which the market mechanism works. The task of policy is therefore to neutralise it.

The differences in the anti-Keynesian camp are largely differences of political approach. All wish to take away the power of governments to interfere with the money supply, and demand that money be reconsecrated as a stable standard of exchange. Some wish this to be done on a national, others on an international basis. Some advocate a return to the gold standard, the restoration of gold to its historic role as world money; others back freely floating exchange rates.[28]

Monetarists in particular are not blind to the global aspects of the present inflation. They stress that, ever since the gold standard was finally abandoned in 1931, the international money supply has lacked a secure and stable base in some precious metal or other commodity. A metal can, of course, be debased, but never so easily nor so fast as a paper currency. No one government controls the international money supply, which consists in the main of gold reserves, international credit of various kinds, and those national currencies that are acceptable as international currencies. The stability which world-wide acceptance of the dollar and its junior partner, sterling, provided after the war has been steadily eroded during the 1960s. The cause has been the mounting U.S. deficits to finance their overseas military spending and foreign investment, and the increasing financial power of countries in surplus, for example West Germany and Japan.

The succession of sterling and dollar crises in the 1960s led to the inauguration of freely floating exchange rates in 1971 – the formal abandonment of dollar hegemony over the international monetary system. Floating exchange rates naturally appeal to many economists who see in the market the infallible instrument for creating general equilibrium and harmony, and maximising efficiency. It is a natural feature of world free trade. However, it ignores the fact that the capitalist economy is still divided up into nation states. Freely floating exchange rates in such a situation spell monetary chaos, for there is no one country to take responsibility for regulating the world money supply for the whole system. A world central bank is needed, a world currency, and therefore a world government. Realms of fantasy indeed. Without an international monetary authority, freely floating exchange rates mean a potentially dangerous acceleration of world inflation. On the one hand, there is the growth of new 'stateless' forms of money such as Eurodollars (dollars deposited in European banks) which have been used as the security on which to make loans and erect a gigantic pyramid of international credit, for which no national government is responsible, and for which there is no lender of last resort. The Eurodollar market had risen from $3 billion in 1960 to $56 billion in 1969.[29] On the other hand, there is no external reason for individual countries to restrain their domestic rate of inflation. If they inflate faster than their neighbours their exchange rate will merely decline. There are thus no sanctions. World money supply increases as fast as the domestic money supply of the different states. Monetarists freely describe the present situation as explosive.

This has encouraged calls for a return to gold, or to some kind of commodity standard. The great joy of a gold standard to its beholders is that the rate of expansion of the money supply, both internationally and domestically, is fixed. Only so much gold can be mined every year. It therefore provides stability. Paper currency can only be issued in amounts that are backed by gold reserves. Countries in deficit on the balance of payments have to export gold to pay their debts. Since their gold reserves will not be unlimited and they cannot augment them, they have to take stringent domestic measures to get rid of the deficit – cutting imports by deflating demand and increasing unemployment. World inflation is halted in its tracks because the money supply cannot be increased in excess of gold reserves. The problem of providing sufficient liquidity can be solved by fixing a sufficiently high price for gold at the outset.

The main alternative to a gold standard is the gold exchange standard, under which the capitalist economy prospered in the 1950s and 1960s. Here all currencies were pegged to the dominant international currency, the dollar, which was itself pegged to gold. Deficits had again to be dealt with by deflating home demand and occasionally by devaluation. The problem with both kinds of standard, however admirable though the goal of a stable monetary standard for international trade may seem, is that both require either political agreement or political domination. In the circumstances of the post-war world, it was relatively easy for the United States to reconstruct the international monetary system under the supremack of the dollar. But its power was significantly eroded as other nations recovered. Moreover, the United States refused to abide by the rules of its own monetary system. It used the special international status of the dollar to force other countries to finance growing U.S. deficits. Since these deficits were used to help the United States retain its global supremacy through military adventures and foreign investment, particularly in Europe, resistance and speculative pressure grew until the dollar was toppled from its eminence.[30] To restore fixed exchange rates pegged either to gold, a commodity standard, or to one national currency, requires a type of political agreement that is nowhere in evidence in the mid-1970s. No country any longer has the power to impose it.

Despite the obvious difficulties, the re-establishment of the stability of money remains the priority. It would prevent inflation and restore the preconditions for a market economy to function once more. Though it does not eliminate all further problems, it does make clear where responsibility lies. If unemployment is prolonged for more than a temporary period, the cause must be the monopolistic procedures of collective bargaining. As Hayek puts it : 'What is needed is that the responsibility for a wage level which is compatible with a high and stable level of employment should again be squarely placed where it belongs : with the trade unions.'[31]

All the anti-Keynesians would agree on this. Where they would disagree is over the means to re-establish the kind of economy which could once more suffer from permanent depression due to trade-union intransigence. Here the veterans of the 1930s are far more realistic than the starry-eyed monetarists. The monetarists prefer to believe that merely a change in government policy is needed – a firm commitment to hold the growth in the money supply steady, a return to gold, and a readiness to countenance rising unemployment. They say nothing about the unions, who are not in their view in any way to blame for inflation. But more seasoned warriors like Hayek, Haberler and Robbins recognise that the political strength of the trade unions has been the major factor in promoting the adoption of Keynesian full-employment policies, so that to change government policy requires first that the political strength of trade unions be weakened. Here a real dilemma arises, and one reason for the monetarists' caution becomes plain. For how can the power of the unions be curtailed? For an extreme liberal like Hayek unions perform no useful economic function and should be abolished whenever possible. 'Economic men' have no business to be acting collectively. As Hayek himself sadly confesses : 'It is probably equally impossible in our time for a student to be a true friend of labour and to have the reputation of being one.'[32] To some extent his view on unions is shared by all the anti-Keynesians, although many are more ready, if only grudgingly, to admit the fact of the unions' existence and concentrate on ways in which the unions' power can be slimmed down and their existence made more palatable. There is, therefore, great support for legal curbs on union power. The Industrial Relations Act was much admired. Economists like Haberler supported such legislation because it was directed at increasing competitive forces in the labour market, and thereby at increasing the bargaining strength of the employers in opposition to the trade unions.[33]

Any impact of such legislation, however, could only be long term. Much more serious for the monetarists is another less discussed aspect of union power – power exercised through the ballot box. Whereas it has proved possible in certain periods in a number of countries to impose legal curbs on the trade unions by mobilising 'public opinion' against them, that is very different from the wholesale change in government policy urged by the monetarists. Governments have come to assume general responsibility for economic conditions and are so identified by national electorates. All governments have learnt that economics may be manipulated to foster booms before elections. For any government to countenance rapidly rising unemployment and refuse to take the measures within its power to reflate the economy would be electoral suicide. No one knows how many years of severe monetary restraint would be necessary to control inflation. But it has become clear that it will be too many for any government seeking re-election.

The monetarists themselves do not suggest it will be easy or short. Depending on how severe the inflation is, it will take anything up to ten years of 'monetary correction' to restore stability. A leading monetarist, Professor Friedman, in one of his pamphlets,[34] argues that the path can be smoothed by indexing all incomes and taxes to the cost of living through escalator clauses in contracts in the Brazilian style. That, of course, would not prevent unemployment, nor would it cause the political problems to vanish. Two years of monetary correction seems too great for most present countries, let alone ten. In the United States the Nixon administration committed itself to a monetarist strategy for two years. In 1971, it capitulated to political pressures and the Keynesians, reflated the economy, and introduced extensive wage and price controls.

Friedman states that the techniques for controlling inflation are available. It is only a matter of political will. But political will means willing higher unemployment, blighting the mighty tree of private credit, and willing a large reduction in government expenditure. A sustained policy of monetary correction will steadily reduce expectations, says Friedman. Expectations are greatly stressed by monetarists and non-monetarists alike But they are viewed much too narrowly. Workers, too, form expectations about the future rate of inflation, which, it is hoped, they will moderate given a policy of tight monetary restraint. They have also acquired expectations about what government can and should do in maintaining and improving living standards. These are much harder to moderate. In a society where the only effective consensus is the consensus between the party leaderships on priorities for administering the existing state, falling living standards focus attention directly on the highly unequal distribution of income and wealth. To be acceptable, sacrifice has to be universal.

The decisive weakness of the monetarist strategy is therefore that no government adopting it in its full sense could be expected to survive at the polls. The power of the unions is not merely their bargaining strength in their particular industries but the voting strength of the great mass of wage earners and their families. As capitalism has sucked in ever greater proportions of the population into the industrial economy, so the industrial working class has come to dominate numerically the political markets of all the western 'democracies'. Not surprisingly no means has yet been found for persuading their electorates to vote for mass unemployment. It thus appears that in order to implement a monetarist strategy the political market must be closed down in some way – either completely by the substitution of an authoritarian regime for free elections, or by the existing parties ceasing to compete with one another and forming a national coalition. Such implications of their theories are rarely discussed by mere economists who prefer to remain technical experts, and even politicians like Enoch Powell and Sir Keith Joseph who have embraced the monetarist analysis are understandably shy about stating the social and political cost.

The dilemma for the monetarists is acute. It is the same as that faced by Hayek and other followers of the 'Austrian School' in the 1930s who advocated immediate wage cuts and an increase in profit margins as the only way to stimulate recovery. As Martin Bronfenbrenner has pointed out, however, 'Austrian' economics is no longer practicable even if true. The consequences, he reckoned, of attempting such a solution given strong trade unions and resentment against the existing distribution of income, would precipitate either socialist or fascist revolution. Furthermore :

> The incompatibility of political democracy with the 'Austrian' remedy for the business cycle is not limited to this single pre-scription of deflation and liquidation. It extends . . . to the entire nineteenth century mechanism of combating labour's demand for a higher share of the national income through the constant threat and occasional fact of mass unemployment.[35]

Bronfenbrenner poses the problem in terms of distribution. What is certainly true is that inflation is the modern mechanism that prevents redistribution through the market. To dispense with it would mean that future crises could only be overcome by the 'Austrian' means of deflation and direct wage cuts, and hence a massive confrontation with organised labour. But then the monetarists conveniently believe, even as the city blazes around them, that once money is under control again, there will be no more booms and slumps, only uninterrupted progress.

The Keynesian strategy is quite different. The Keynesians have, in general, much greater realism than the monetarists about the institutional realities that perpetuate and sustain infla-tion, but neglect its monetary aspects and its roots in the money supply. Keynesians do not accept that underlying the rubble and confusion of the modern capitalist economy is slumbering an

economic order of perfect harmony and balance only waiting
to re-emerge into the light. On the contrary, they recognise that
markets are inherently imperfect, inherently unstable and that to
understand how any capitalist economy works it is necessary to
study its social and political institutions, and how economic forces
are inescapably expressed through them. The best Keynesian
writing is less rigorous in the strict sense than that of the anti-
Keynesian liberals but that is because it is much closer to reality.
The anti-Keynesians still simplify the economy until it consists of
a multitude of Robinson Crusoes alone on their indifference
maps busily producing, exchanging and consuming, and believe
this can clarify all economic questions. The Keynesians, even
though many still accept the myths of marginalism, in practice
are obliged to throw them out in their analyses, and start from
the basic data of a capitalist economy – the fact of monopolistic
and oligopolistic market structures, the dominance of the world
market by a handful of great companies, the setting of wage rates
through collective bargaining and the existence of nations.

Once inflation is treated as a question of applied political
economy, remedies at once suggest themselves. Keynesians
acknowledge that more competition can help but do not place
much faith in it. It is far more important to alter the behaviour
of the corporations and the unions. If inflation originates from
administered prices, and if the wage–price spiral is a constant
expression of the struggle over the distribution of national income
between two sets of monopolists, then some alteration has to be
made to the procedures of collective bargaining that make this
possible. Thus the Keynesians propose institutional changes to
counter inflation rather than any policy that requires or implies
dismantling the oligopolistic structure of the advanced sectors of
industry and abolishing the trade unions. Optimists among them
used to believe that only some kind of *voluntary* incomes policy
was necessary. By stating 'norms' or guidelines which pay and
price increases should not exceed, governments hoped to influence the level of wage- and price-fixing decisions. In advanced
forms of incomes policies these guidelines could be entrusted to a
supposedly independent review body like the U.K. Prices and
Incomes Board (P.I.B.), which would also seek to wrestle with the
anomalies that were bound to creep in to any incomes policy that
awarded a fixed percentage wage increase to all categories of

employees. Significantly, new institutions like the P.I.B. also began to develop new criteria for setting wages and prices, according to what was 'just' and 'fair'. Fairness never had much to do with efficiency, and the effect was to underline still more the changed institutional realities of the economy.

Many Keynesians, however, do not believe that a voluntary policy based on exhortation, guidelines and attempts to inject consideration of 'national interest' into wage negotiations is strong enough to withstand the pressures and temptations that accompany the wage–price spiral. In their view the only solution is compulsory and permanent controls over wages and prices. Since wages and prices are fixed more and more independently of changes in demand and are influenced less and less by competition, governments are obliged to impose direct controls to smother inflation. These Keynesians reason that, if governments continue to maintain full employment, then given the structure of aggregate demand, there are no sanctions in a market economy to stop firms raising prices and unions demanding higher wages. Thus, a full-employment economy eventually requires that the government assumes responsibility for wages and prices and fix them at levels which are compatible with the growth of productivity.[36]

The admirable logic of these Keynesians, however, has dangerous political implications. No one doubts that wage and price controls can be successful if rigorously applied. They were used in the war economy (1939–45). Between 1942 and 1945 prices only rose 6 per cent – a remarkable record given the claims on resources. But to impose such controls in times of peace would mean the effective destruction of the market economy. All economic decisions would become directly political decisions – with incalculable consequences. Such controls would heighten class conflict, for the distribution of income would become directly a matter for political decision. Instead of reform-minded governments attempting to intervene in the market to influence its working, the state sector would have swallowed the market. Class struggle would now take place within the state and this would increase political confrontation and threaten the political power of private capital, which depends on the state remaining separate from the market. Wage and price controls, except for short periods or in exceptional circumstances, are thus only compatible with a capitalism that has acquired authoritarian political

institutions. Furthermore, such controls require either a remarkable degree of consensus and national unity or an army of spies
and inspectors – otherwise they are simply evaded. Economic
efficiency would suffer less under a regime of controls than many
economists imagine, and might even increase, but making
controls work is never easy.

To get even minimal consent to this, the control of wages, prices
and other incomes, particularly property incomes, profits, dividends and interest, have to be controlled too. Dividend restraint
is relatively painless except for small shareholders. So long as the
economy continues to grow, the big shareholders receive their
lost income back again in the form of the rising prices of the
firm's assets. Any restraint on prices and profits, however, is the
opposite of what is required, as most of the cost-push theorists
recognise. Decrying profits is one thing. Imposing an incomes
policy, however, that penalises them is no way to run a capitalist
economy, as social democrats often discover. To encourage a
rapid expansion of output and productivity high profits are
absolutely essential. This is because, as Keynesian economists
point out, profits are a quite different form of income compared
to wages and salaries. They are the motive force of the whole
system. Profits must be allowed to vary to encourage competition,
efficiency and innovation. The notion of a 'fair' or 'reasonable'
profit in a capitalist system is a nonsense. The only fair profit is
the highest that can be gained. Profits fuel the accumulation of
capital. It is useless expecting investment and growth if they are
curtailed. This is the dilemma of an incomes policy. It must be
fair for all sections of the community, but if it is equally fair to
wages and to profits it will defeat its main purpose. Permanent
controls on profits mean the erosion of the private sector and
the eventual socialisation of investment. The government would
be forced to step in more and more to provide the investment
and employment that private capital is unwilling to contemplate.

'MORTON'S FORK'

Certainly the experts have no easy solutions for inflation. In this
chapter we have emphasised the range of disagreement that is to
be found in their ranks. Yet in one respect the disagreement is
perhaps not so great after all. Like the economists debating the

causes of the slump in the 1930s, though they could agree on
nothing else, they could agree on the assertion that the unemployment did not have economic causes. The same applies to inflation.
Professor Harrod may declare : 'Wage rates, productivity,
profits : that is what we should be discussing around this table
instead of all this nonsense about money supply.'[37] Professor
Friedman may retort : 'Inflation is always and everywhere a
monetary phenomenon, produced in the first instance by an
unduly rapid growth in the quantity of money.'[38] But Professor
Robbins has the final word : 'In the last analysis, the solution of
the monetary problem, the solution of the problem of international inflation, is a political rather than an economic problem.'[39]
Whenever economists really get down to studying a pressing
problem of the actual capitalist economy, they are forced, just
as they were in the 1930s, to conclude that its causes and its
solutions lie for the most part beyond their science.

This is not so surprising as far as the anti-Keynesians are concerned. After all, they still identify the economy quite directly
with the market, and still subscribe to an individualist theory of
value and rationality that prevents any understanding of
economics in terms of political economy. But the Keynesian
achievement was to break with the assumptions of marginalism,
at least at the macro level of analysis. The reason so many of the
Keynesians are now stuck in the same impasse as their opponents
on the question of inflation is that they too have not moved
beyond the market. They have merely redescribed how it works.
They have achieved far more in terms of applied economics than
the marginalists ever did. But still they remain at the level of
appearances, the immediate form in which economic phenomena
can be observed. This was also true of Keynes. He showed how,
if investment was too low, aggregate demand would be insufficient to maintain full employment, and permanent unemployment might result. But he did not satisfactorily explain why
investment should be so low.

What both Keynesians and monetarists do is to throw much
incidental light on the process and character of permanent inflation. But they do not adequately explain it. Its causes remain
outside – they are 'political' or 'social'. Keynesians often talk
about an autonomous explosion of expectations that is fuelling
wage-push and has its roots in fundamental changes in social

structure and social attitudes. Anti-Keynesians blame inflation directly on government policy – maintaining full employment by continually expanding the money supply. It is a poor theory that must rely on *ad hoc* external factors to account for the principal problem under examination.

The Keynesians advocate more government intervention as the solution while the anti-Keynesians advocate less. Both are agreed that it is the government and the state sector that are the key to solving inflation. As yet they have no theory of this state sector and the growing role of government in the economy. For both schools, it is simply another intrusion of the 'political' into the 'economic'. Economists are prevented from developing such an analysis because all they fundamentally see in the 'economic' is the market, and all they are concerned to do is to analyse the 'economic' aspect of behaviour. That is why they generally show such little grasp of the political difficulties of their solutions to inflation.

Running a modern capitalist economy requires an ever greater degree of consent, particularly from certain key sections of the labour force which operate the huge capital-intensive installations and control the power supplies that keep the whole economy moving. The structure and division of labour of the modern economy cannot be wished away, as some of the anti-Keynesians appear to dream. At the same time, the government cannot simply control the situation by extending its power. To be exerted effectively power must eventually be transformed into legitimate authority. Hence the political problem. Capitalist governments are obliged to choose between the path of monetary correction and permanent control over wages and prices, at a time when output is stagnant or declining, living standards are falling, and struggles over pay tend to become struggles, not only over the distribution of income, but over the source of income from the process of production itself.

3

Monopoly Capitalism

Given the tendency to secular stagnation, the continued existence of monopoly capitalism depends on the existence or
creation of sufficiently strong and interacting forces to permit
the system to operate at a politically tolerable level of production and employment.

Paul Sweezy, *Modern Capitalism*
(New York : Monthly Review Press, 1972) p. 8.

Inflation has not only occupied orthodox economists. It has
been discovered by the Marxists as well. But most Marxists have
treated inflation not as the central economic problem of modern
capitalism but as the symptom and expression of much deeper
contradictions. Marxist and radical economics have burst into
new life during the last ten years. Critiques of orthodoxy and
critical analyses of capitalism have been restored and re-uphol-
stered.

This revival follows both the disarray of the Keynesians and
the growing difficulties of the world economy. In the 1930s
John Strachey argued in *The Nature of Capitalist Crisis* that there
were two competing branches of economic science – capitalist
and Marxist. Capitalist economics at that time was bankrupt. It
had nothing of importance to say about the most obvious and
most pressing economic reality – the fact of slump, depression
and unemployment. Its leading spokesmen were agreed that no
recovery could come until profits were somehow increased, but
they could not explain with the aid of economic theory why
profits were no longer sufficient to keep the economic machine in
motion, nor could they agree whether profit margins should be
raised by increasing demand or by lowering wage rates. They had
no economic remedies for overcoming the slump. To them it was

an unavoidable natural disaster which contradicted all the laws of economics.

Marxist economics had no such limitations. Reviled and scorned by most professional economists, consigned to the underworld of economic theory along with various monetary cranks, Marxism still retained its attraction and compelled attention whenever the comfortable optimism of conventional economics evaporated. The enduring appeal and relevance of Marxism is its insistence on political economy as the framework for its analysis. Furthermore, it has never imagined capitalism to be a system of steady, harmonious and uncomplicated growth. On the contrary, Marxists have always expected the progress of capitalism to be marked by crises and conflict. So, at times of general economic crisis in the past, Marxists always appeared to have far more to say about its causes and consequences than did the experts of the economic establishment.

Marxists insist that capitalism can only be understood as a whole. It is pointless to abstract the economic from the political. They have to be grasped together or not at all. Moreover, Marxist analysis is always historical. Universal economic laws have no meaning for it. This means that Marxists have always tried to understand how the capitalist order at different times can display extreme fragility and enormous strength, for they treated capitalism as one mode of production and one form of society among others in history, which was subject to change, decay and disappearance.

The Great Depression of the 1930s seemed to completely justify the Marxist analysis of capitalism, and Marxism attracted a host of new converts. The remarkable spectacle of men and machines idle on a vast scale, whilst millions lacked even basic necessities, hung over all countries in the capitalist economy. An economic crisis caused not by too little means of production but by too much was a cruel paradox, which marked out capitalism from all previous forms of economic society.

What was novel about the depression of the 1930s was the size of the interruption to production and the length of its duration. World production declined by one-third between 1929 and 1932. Unemployment reached three million in the United Kingdom, six million in Germany. In the United States, at the worst point of the slump, 23 per cent of its work force was out of work. The international monetary system based on gold that had been so painstakingly rebuilt in the 1920s by Montagu Norman collapsed. World trade fell sharply as different nations rushed to erect high tariffs in a vain bid to protect themselves from the consequences of the world slump. Recovery after 1932 was uneven, and nowhere complete, save in Nazi Germany. In the United States, in the New Deal era, output fell more sharply in 1937 than it had in 1930. The spectre of permanent stagnation permeated the decade.

Marxists had predicted that as capitalism developed its periodic crises would intensify, until a final economic breakdown would usher in the universal crisis – a crisis not merely of the economy, but of all parts of society, that is the entire social system. That point appeared to have arrived in the 1930s. The economy had fallen into a trough out of which it could not clamber. The rate of profit had fallen too low to generate a level of investment needed to keep the economy anywhere near full employment. Further accumulation under the direction of private capital seemed improbable. The contradiction between forces of production and social relations was stark and obvious. On the one hand, there was an immensely powerful apparatus of production, based on machinery and an ever-increasing division of labour, which constantly strengthened the interdependence of the whole society; on the other, a system of social relationships which gave to owners of capital and their agents the right, the power and the compulsion to direct the process of production with the aim of expanding their capital. 'Accumulate, Accumulate, that is Moses and the Prophets', wrote Marx. Accumulation of capital raised enormously the productivity of labour; at the same time it meant that all production had to contribute first and foremost to that end. The satisfaction of needs, the production of useful things was also essential, but still secondary. When production was no longer profitable, accumulation faltered, output was reduced, workers dismissed, machines stopped, whatever the level of human needs still unsatisfied. Capitalism was always an economic system of *production*, rather than of consumption. That was why it had advanced the productivity of labour and the productive potential of human societies so much. But any interruption to accumulation also plunged it into crisis in which consumption and the material needs of the great majority were ruthlessly sacrificed.

The possibility of permanent stagnation and unemployment as long as capitalism existed was recognised by Keynes as well as by Marxists. By full employment both Keynes and Beveridge meant a rate of unemployment of 5 per cent or, in starker terms, around one million people on the dole. That was the best they thought possible. Indeed, optimists about future growth in a capitalist economy were hard to find in the 1930s. Apostles of secular stagnation and zero growth were much more common. One of Keynes's leading followers in the United States, Alvin Hansen, developed a theory of secular stagnation in, for example, *Fiscal Policy and Business Cycles* (New York: Norton, 1941). He saw a vanishing of investment outlets caused by a declining rate of growth of population, the closing of the frontier, and a slowing down of technological progress. He was unable to explain why these external forces, which had plainly existed for a long time, should suddenly erupt with such devastation in the 1930s. But his gloom was widely shared. Others like Schumpeter believed the threat to accumulation was caused by the destruction of free enterprise and the entrepreneurial spirit. In *Capitalism, Socialism and Democracy* (London: Allen & Unwin, 1950) he described how an anti-capitalist ethos fostered by unions and government, the divorce of ownership from control, the routinisation of innovation, all spelt death to the confident buccaneering world of Schumpeter's entrepreneurs.

The Great Depression was not overcome by economic management. What ended it was re-armament and the war economy in all the nations of the capitalist economy. Nazi Germany led the way. The war demonstrated dramatically the enormous productive potential which had been built up by capitalism. Output, productivity and investment all raced ahead. Under the right conditions full employment and further growth were shown to be realisable. Yet, changing from a war to a peace-time economy was viewed everywhere with foreboding. Keynesians and Marxists alike assumed that the war was only a temporary interruption in the long-term decline of capitalism. Once the backlog of demand for consumption and investment built up during the Second World War had been wiped out in the usual post-war boom, then the powerful forces making for stagnation would reassert themselves. A new slump and a new depression would ensue. Keynesians thought a sufficient programme of pump-priming and public works could mitigate its effects. Marxists argued that a programme that was sufficient would not be politically practicable – the capitalist class would not consent to it. Both agreed that rapid, over-all growth was not a likely prospect. In the late 1940s, many Marxists took every downwards movement in economic activity as the first sign of the new slump they knew from their theories must eventually come.

Yet for thirty years no slump did come, and serious Marxists have been wrestling with the consequences ever since. Keynesians triumphed from a development which they had neither predicted nor expected, yet which seemed linked in some miraculous way to the new techniques of economic management which they advocated. Marxists were forced to reflect bitterly on the powers of recuperation which capital possessed. The final crisis was not appearing. Instead, the longest uninterrupted boom the capitalist world economy had ever experienced was under way.

The boom puzzled some in the economics profession too. As Andrew Shonfield asked at the beginning of his book *Modern Capitalism* : 'What was it that converted capitalism from the cataclysmic failure which it appeared to be in the 1930s, into the great engine of prosperity of the post-war Western World.'[1] Shonfield noted that the very question prompted many to deny that the post-war system was capitalism at all. Although he rejected this idea, he still felt a sneaking sympathy for it : 'It is hard for us to believe that the bleak and squalid system which we knew could, in so short a time, have adapted itself, without some covert process of total destruction and regeneration, to achieve so many desired objectives.'

Posing the problem in this way led Shonfield to an examination of the new institutional apparatus that maintained and promoted economic growth in modern capitalism. For most economists, however, no attempt was made to explain the long boom in political–economic terms at all. It remained as mysterious as the Great Depression had been. Marginalists who regarded the depression as an unwelcome aberration had no difficulty explaining how everlasting economic growth without hiccups was the natural course of evolution for a capitalist market economy. All techniques could be 'switched' and all factors of production substituted for each other in the long run. Diminishing returns in some fields would be offset by increasing returns in others. The sensitivity of the price mechanism, particularly the rate of interest, would ensure smooth adjustment of resources between different uses and different sectors. In this way capital would be accumulated, the different factors of production would be distributed with maximum efficiency, and productivity would constantly increase. Since they assumed full employment and a constant money supply, plus perfect competition in all markets, the conclusion was hardly surprising. The sources of growth came from outside – an autonomous increase in population or technological progress. The economy merely absorbed it and translated it into rising output.

Keynesian theories of growth that developed after 1945 were also optimistic. However, their optimism was not founded on the unrealistic assumptions of the marginalists – such as unlimited 'switching' of techniques and the perfect 'malleability' of capital. They were more interested in finding the conditions under which the two aspects of investment spending – the creation of production capacity and the creation of income – would be kept in balance. Given a rate of growth of capacity, what rate of growth of income would be necessary to maintain full employment? The Harrod–Domar model saw the actual rate of growth oscillating around the 'warranted' rate of growth, causing either severe inflation or severe unemployment. The problem of steady growth for the Keynesians was thus matching the growing productive capacity with adequate effective demand. They sought to achieve this through policies of stabilisation pursued by governments to iron out the fluctuations of the trade cycle, and so create a business environment which would encourage steady investment.

In general both schools viewed the modern industrial economy as the application of science and technology to production. Technological progress, like population, was an autonomous factor that determined long-run growth. Since scientific knowledge was constantly increasing, it followed that the potential output and productivity of the economy was increasing also. All that was needed to ensure everlasting growth was either an efficient price mechanism (the neoclassical marginalist school) or an institutional order (the Keynesians) that would remove obstacles, including cylical fluctuations, booms and slumps, and bottlenecks and shortages of all kinds, and so allow a smooth translation of increasing scientific knowledge into rising output.

All the orthodox theories of growth shared at bottom a common technological determinism, and this was paralleled in various sociological theories of the time. The problem of industrial society was seen as adapting social institutions and social attitudes quickly enough to the technological requirements of modern industry. The nature of these requirements overrode differences in cultures and political systems, and led naturally to ideas of convergence between all industrial societies, on both sides of the Iron Curtain.[2]

The only pessimists were those who thought they detected long-term cyclical patterns at work in the economy. Most famous of all of these was Kondratieff's long-wave cycle – one lasting fifty years, which, if projected into the future, predicted that the long upturn in the economy during the post-war boom would come to an end in 1971, to be followed by a period of decline. Other cycles – for building and for international trade – detected by Simon Kuznets and Arthur Lewis also pointed to increasing difficulties for the world economy in the 1970s, but the reasons for these cycles remained mysterious. Shonfield was undoubtedly right to see no good reason why they should hold in the future. (For further information on these cycles see S. Kuznets, *Capital in the American Economy*, Princeton University Press, 1961, and W. A. Lewis and P. J. O'Leary, 'Secular Swings in Production and Trade, 1870–1913', *Manchester School of Social and Economic Studies*, May 1955.)

Thus, despite Marxist predictions of eventual collapse, during the long boom the capitalist economy not only grew more rapidly than ever before but also more steadily. Economic activity still fluctuated, but the fluctuations were mild and rarely involved any major interruption of production or any fall in output or employment, only a temporary slackening in the rate of growth. Furthermore, the business cycles of the major nations in the capitalist economy did not tend to coincide, and this prevented a generalised recession, and speeded recovery. The causes of faster growth, Shonfield argued, were the sustained expansion of international trade – particularly the new pattern of trade in manufactured and capital goods between the industrialised states – and the great building boom of the 1950s. The steadiness of the boom was due to the new institutional apparatus, particularly Keynesian economic management of the cycle, and the new inter-

ventionist and spending policies of governments. The role of the
state was thus crucial, not merely in maintaining full employment,
but also in promoting growth. Shonfield showed how even those
governments to whom Keynes was a mystery and who brandished
a social market ideology had still developed an institutional apparatus, particularly a large public sector and instruments for controlling the economy, that achieved the same results as Keynesian
theory prescribed.[3]

For a time capitalism appeared not only to have discovered
within itself vast new energies and opportunities for expansion,
but also to have stumbled on the means for achieving growth
without periodic crises. The dreadful possibility which reformists
had been pressing on the orthodox ever since Marx's *Capital*
rolled off the presses, was voiced yet again. Capitalism had
evolved into something else, a new mode of production, a different form of economic organisation that had transcended the
contradictions and laws of motion that had formerly ruled it.
Industrial society, post-industrial society, post-capitalism, welfare
capitalism – whatever the terminology used all were agreed that
it was certainly a new capitalism, purged of the worst defects of
the old.

For Marxists a capitalism without crises was apparently invul-
nerable. If economic and political convulsions no longer shook
the citadel of capital, it could no longer be taken from within,
and there were only a handful of Marxists by the end of the
1950s who would have chosen to be 'liberated' from without by
Soviet tanks. The long boom thus announced an age of gloom
and pessimism for socialists. Faith in the Soviet Union had been
destroyed. No 'new civilisation' had emerged, only Stalinism. The
differences between the two great power blocs that divided up the
world market between them seemed less remarkable than the simi-
larities. The political and economic stability of both were overwhelming, reinforced by the competition in arms and space
between them. During the Cold War cultural critiques of capitalism greatly outnumbered economic analyses among Marxists.
Marxist humanism flourished and alienation was suddenly
discovered to be the major concept of Marx's theoretical
system.

Yet the Marxist tradition of political economy did not die. Apart
from certain 'doomwatchers' who perched high on their orthodox

mountain confidently predicting every year that the final crisis
was upon us, Marxist economists grappled with two central
problems during the 1950s and 1960s – explaining the long boom
and coming to grips with Keynes. During the boom it was capitalist economics in its new Keynesian guise that seemed relevant
and Marxism that had lost touch with reality. Yet both Keynesianism and the new western Marxism that emerged after 1945
had some things in common. Both were attempts to describe and
explain the new relationship between the state and the economy
that had emerged in all advanced capitalist countries. Marxists
and Keynesians often misunderstood the significance of Keynes's
work and often overestimated its practical achievements. The real
secret of Keynesianism was not its provision of techniques of
economic management that could rid the capitalist system of
periodic crises; it was its theoretical expression and ideological
justification of the new role of the state sector in the economy, a
role which assisted but did not by itself cause the great boom
and which carried within itself contradictions that Keynesianism
had no answer for.

From one standpoint all the Marxist explanations of the boom
can be taken as different attempts to account for this new stage
in the relationship between the state and capital, and to connect
it with a theory of capitalist crisis. Keynesians were happy to
forget about crisis and slump in the new post-war conditions,
and believed they had relegated them to economic pre-history.
Some Marxists believed it too, embraced Keynesianism, and
disappeared into the windy deserts of social democracy. But
for the steadfast, crisis and contradiction remained inseparable
from capitalist reality. The task was to show why crisis, slump
and breakdown were no longer appearing. Non-appearance, it
was believed, did not mean disappearance, only postpone-
ment. Patience and irony became the chief virtues of the
Bolsheviks.

Ever since Marx himself the economic writings of Marxists
have been marked by a strange paradox – a fierce hostility to
the mode of production based on the accumulation of capital is
combined with deep respect and appreciation for its enormous
energies, resilience and power, and its historic importance. Marx
and Engels panegyric to the bourgeoisie in *The Communist
Manifesto* is well known. They write, for instance that :

The bourgeoisie, during the rule of scarce one hundred years has created more massive and more colossal productive forces than have all preceding generations together. Subjection of nature's forces to man, machinery, application of chemistry to industry and agriculture, steam navigation, railways, electric telegraphs, clearing of whole continents for cultivation, canalization of rivers, whole populations conjured out of the ground – what earlier century had even a presentiment that such productive forces slumbered on the lap of social labour.[4]

As Marx studied the workings of capitalism more deeply, so he became still more impressed by the potential for growth within the straitjacket of capital accumulation. Yet he argued just as firmly that, in the final analysis, capital itself created the barrier to further production. The actual point at which it did so remained obscure. The riddle Marx left for others to decipher was contained in his famous *Preface* of 1859 : 'No social order ever perishes before all the productive forces for which there is room in it have developed; and new higher relations of production never appear before the material conditions of their existence have matured in the womb of the old society itself.'[5]

Marx had good reasons for making such confident statements. They lay in his detailed study of capital, part of which was published as *Capital*, part of which lay buried and unfinished in his manuscripts. For later Marxists a central question became, was there an inherent tendency for capitalism to suffer crises and would these become more severe as it developed? The idea that capitalism was heading for a certain and unavoidable breakdown from which it could not recover held considerable attraction and definite implications for politics. Some thought the revolution had best wait on the unfolding of capitalism's own urge to self-destruction. Capital, as Marx wrote, is its own grave-digger. These Marxists were ready to carry the coffin but others were less fatalistic. There were those who came to see no essential barriers to the progress of capitalism and argued that if it was to be replaced or modified, it would be by political means alone. Still others rejected the fatalism of the breakdown theory, yet foresaw continual crises and disorders arising from the organisation of the capitalist economy. Such crises continually resurrected the spectre of a revolution that could end production based on capital.

The immediate problem for Marxists during the long boom was that capitalism displayed no tendency at all to crisis, still less to breakdown. This had a profound effect on Marxist analysis. The change from the 1930s was dramatic. Keynesians argued that the stagnation and unemployment of the 1930s had been caused by too low a level of aggregate demand. Demand, made up of spending on investment and consumption, was inadequate in relation to productive capacity. The result was stagnation and permanent unemployment. Such ideas provided an underconsumptionist theory of crisis : too little demand and too little consumption caused by imperfections intrinsic in the markets of monopoly capitalism. The imperfections, particularly the degree of concentration in industry and the existence of trade unions, could not be removed, but they could be neutralised if the state used its taxing and spending powers to generate sufficient demand to achieve full employment.

Marxists rejected many aspects of Keynesianism, but it left a deep mark, particularly on their theories of crisis. The explosion of demand after the Second World War, the size and volume of government expenditure, the fuelling of the boom by mass consumption and exports − all this persuaded many that the crisis of the 1930s had been primarily a crisis of underconsumption, a crisis brought about by institutional blockages and rigidities which had now for the moment been overcome. Many Marxists, therefore, reflecting on the crisis of the 1930s, in the circumstances of the long boom and triumphant Keynesianism, came to view the chief cause of capitalist crisis as a crisis of markets, a crisis of realising surplus value. If capitalism could not create sufficient markets, sufficient demand, in which to sell its ever-increasing output, then production would be interrupted and the economy would stagnate. Explaining the post-war boom, therefore, became a matter of analysing the new markets which capital had discovered since 1945 and showing the barriers to their indefinite expansion. In this way the very strength of post-war capitalism could be shown to contain the seeds of a new crisis.

These Marxists, therefore, agreed with Keynesians that, left to itself, the capitalist system had a profound tendency to increase productive capacity faster than it could create markets to absorb the output profitably. It therefore was constantly tending to stagnate at a level of production far below its potential. This was certainly one way to interpret Marx's conception of the fundamental contradiction of the capitalist mode of production – the fetters placed by private-property relations on the increasingly collective nature of the economy. In this interpretation, the tendency for the rate of profit to fall was replaced by the tendency of capitalist production to stagnate.

Such an analysis of the long boom and the causes of the Great Depression has received its classic expression in the work of Paul Baran and Paul Sweezy. Building on two earlier works (Paul Sweezy's *The Theory of Capitalist Development*, and Paul Baran's *The Political Economy of Growth*) they produced in 1965 *Monopoly Capital*.[6] This book is regarded by many as the most important work in Marxist political economy to have been published since 1945. It is a sustained and systematic analysis, at once theoretical and empirical, of the nature of monopoly capitalism. The authors have no doubt that monopoly capitalism is a new stage of capitalism and can no longer be analysed with many of the theoretical concepts developed by Marx. The theory that they develop provides an explanation both of the Great Depression of the 1930s and of the long post-war boom. They also predict the return of crisis to capitalism on the basis of it.

UNDERCONSUMPTION AND THE 'ECONOMIC SURPLUS'

Baran and Sweezy's conception of monopoly capitalism is built on two supports – an underconsumption theory of crisis and the concept of the 'economic surplus'. The first was developed by Sweezy in his book, *The Theory of Capitalist Development*. In his discussion of the Marxist theory of capitalist crisis, he distinguished between the necessary form which every such crisis must take and its causes. The form of every crisis is a decline in the rate of profit. In his words: 'The specific form of capitalist crisis is an interruption of the circulation process induced by a decline in the rate of profit below its usual level.'[7] In discussing the causes of crisis, Sweezy argued strongly that there were two distinct theories of crisis in Marx, which in principle operated independently, although both might be found together. The first was the long-term tendency of the rate of profit to fall in the course of capital accumulation, due to the increasing proportion of machinery to labour in value terms (the rising organic composition of capital). The rate of exploitation could not be raised fast enough to offset the cost of investment in plant and machinery.

The second theory of crisis in Marx, according to Sweezy, saw crises arising from problems of realisation, that is from problems of markets. Surplus value, the unpaid labour-time surrendered to the capitalist in return for wages, is produced through the production of commodities. But it is only realised when these commodities are sold on the market. So, analytically, the accumulation of capital can suffer from crises that arise because capitalists are unable to extract sufficient surplus value from their workers to make production profitable, or because, having extracted sufficient surplus value, they are unable to realise it because the goods cannot be sold. There are insufficient markets. These can take two forms. It may be that there arises a disproportion between different sectors of the economy, the capital-goods sector on the one hand, and the consumer-goods sector on the other. Output and capacity in one was ahead of output and capacity in the other, because economic production as a whole is unplanned and chaotic. Or it may be because there is inadequate effective demand, too little credit, in the Keynesian sense. There is no one who can buy the goods that have been produced at the price which makes production profitable.

Sweezy argues that crises arising from the tendency of the rate of profit to fall do not occur in monopoly capitalism.[8] The organic composition of capital, he says, only tended to rise sharply when there was a switch in early capitalism from labour-intensive methods of production to production based on machinery. Since then the tendency of the rate of profit to fall has been more than offset by the increase in the rate of exploitation which technological innovation has permitted. Realisation crises arising from unevenness between sectors he tends to discount. In monopoly capitalism the rise of new conglomerates and holding companies spanning many industries tend to increase co-ordination.

The real cause of crisis that still afflicts the accumulation of capital in its monopoly stage is, according to Sweezy, the crisis of underconsumption, that is of ineffective demand. The cause of the Great Depression, he argues, was the unfolding of the strong tendency within monopoly capitalism to stagnation and overproduction: 'The real task of an underconsumption theory is to demonstrate that capitalism has an inherent tendency to expand the capacity to produce consumption goods more rapidly than the demand for consumption goods.'[9] Given such a tendency, which both Sweezy and the Keynesians believed they could demonstrate, then crisis would take the form either of literal over-production – in which goods would pile up in shops and ware-houses awaiting purchasers – or of excess capacity. Industries would tend to produce at lower and lower levels of their total capacity.

To round out his theory of underconsumption which he now regarded as the most relevant of Marx's crisis theories for the analysis of monopoly capitalism, Sweezy listed the various counteracting forces that might prevent the tendency to stag-nation from becoming reality. 'New industries' for instance, such as the car industry and the railways, allowed the absorption of enormous amounts of capital without adding to the output of consumption goods. 'Faulty investment' meant that large amounts of capital could, in effect, be wasted, and fail to raise the output of consumer goods. 'Population growth', if it were rapid enough, could mean an expanding work force, hence a growth in wages and effective demand. These three factors had been important at various times, Sweezy judged, in checking the tendency to stag-nation, but were generally of declining significance. No new industries on the scale of the railways, for instance, were on the horizon. Faulty investment was becoming less rare as marketing and planning procedures within big companies developed. Popu-lation growth in the capitalist countries was markedly slowing down and so were opportunities for drawing groups like women into the labour force.

There remained two counteracting forces which Sweezy reckoned were increasing in importance – unproductive consump-tion and public expenditures. Unproductive consumption meant the growing army of occupations that did not add directly to pro-duction, but were maintained out of the proceeds of production. It was, therefore, a way in which capitalists' surplus value could be safely absorbed and could, at the same time, create demand for consumer goods. The unproductive consumers were primarily the new middle classes – especially those employed in such occu-pations as advertising, banking, insurance, retailing, teaching, and the like. Still more important, however, were expenditures by the state, including spending on capital formation, transfer payments – such as welfare benefits of all kinds – and current consumption of goods and services, particularly of arms. The growth both of unproductive consumers and of state expenditures added enormously to the total effective demand in the economy, and therefore markedly reduced the tendency for the capacity to produce consumer goods to outrun the ability to sell them. By creating extra markets the tendency could be suspended.

It is noticeable how close, in some respects, Sweezy's analysis is to that of the Keynesians. The problem of capitalist crisis is once again described in terms of demand and markets, not in terms of production as such. Where Sweezy differs from the Keynesians is (1) in his assessment of the political possibilities of increasing effective demand in a capitalist economy, and (2) his analysis of why there should be a permanent tendency to stagnation in a capitalist system.

He argues that this tendency arises in the stage of monopoly capitalism. The compulsion to maximise profits and accumulate capital as fast as possible means that capitalists invest in machinery to raise the productivity of labour. Economies of scale, techno-logical innovation and price competition allow a few firms to survive and prosper at the expense of others. Competition wanes as capital is both concentrated at the point of production and centralised at the level of ownership and control. The new cor-porations are able to ensure both that their costs are minimised and that, therefore, the surplus value is constantly rising as pro-ductivity advances. It is in the interests of the corporations to use as great a part of the rising surplus as possible to expand their capital by new investment. So every increase in surplus will add proportionately more to investment than to consumption. Capi-talists will spend more on improving and renovating their plant and equipment from their increasing surplus than they will on current consumption. From this Sweezy deduced that for the economy as a whole, assuming no counteracting factors, there was an inherent tendency for the rate of growth of consumption to be outpaced by the rate of growth of the means of production. Since the nature of the production process meant that the rate of growth of the output of consumption goods must balance the rate of growth of the means of production used to produce them,

D

it followed that the balance could only be maintained either by
overproduction or by productive capacity lying idle.

'ECONOMIC SURPLUS'

The other main strut of Baran and Sweezy's analysis of monopoly capital was developed by Paul Baran in *The Political
Economy of Growth*. This was the concept of 'economic surplus'.
Marx had not talked of surplus as such when he analysed capital,
but of surplus value, that is he tied the notion of surplus very
clearly to his analysis of capital accumulation in terms of the
labour theory of value. We shall examine the value analysis
in detail in Chapter 4. Baran was therefore aware that he was
breaking with a fundamental tenet of Marxist theory and usage
by introducing the concept of economic surplus, but again he
felt the need to do so in order to explain the specific characteristics of monopoly capitalism.

His analysis, in fact, was aimed primarily at explaining the
economic structure of underdeveloped countries, but to do this
properly he developed a general theoretical analysis which could
explain and compare the facts of both developed and underdeveloped systems, and devoted two chapters to 'Standstill and
Movement under Monopoly Capitalism'. The hinge of his whole
analysis is the distinction between the actual and potential surplus of an economic system.

The actual surplus was simple enough and could be measured
in conventional Keynesian terms – that part of the national
income that was not currently consumed but spent on raising
productive capacity for the future. The potential surplus was
somewhat more tricky. Baran himself defines it as 'the difference between the output that could be produced in a given
natural and technological environment with the help of employ-
able productive resources, and what might be regarded as essential consumption'.[10]

From this definition it is obvious at once that the potential
surplus of an advanced economy is far greater than its actual
surplus. The actual surplus reflects what does exist, whereas the
potential surplus reflects what could exist if there was a 'drastic
reorganisation of the production and distribution of the social
output'. To get some estimate of the size of the potential surplus

in Baran's terms, would mean calculating the amount of excess consumption, the number of unproductive workers, the extent to which the existing organisation of the productive apparatus is 'irrational and wasteful' and the degree of unemployment of productive resources.

The notion of a potential surplus is thus intended to supply a weapon of criticism against existing conditions, a yardstick against which to measure the achievements and shortcomings of the economy's performance. Baran's criteria are historical criteria of what is essential, productive and rational. He justifies his rationalist stance – applying the pure standards of reason to con-crete circumstances – by invoking classical political economy. The classical political economists, as he points out, were not afraid to lambast established economic arrangements for preventing the possibility of much faster economic progress and much greater economic welfare. In particular, they attacked the unproductive class – those who consumed without producing. In Adam Smith's famous words :

> The labour of some of the most respectable orders in the society is, like that of menial servants, unproductive of any value. . . . The sovereign, for example, with all the officers both of justice and war who serve under him, the whole army and navy, are unproductive labourers. . . . In the same class must be ranked, some of the gravest and most important, and some of the most frivolous professions : churchmen, lawyers, physicians, men of letters of all kinds; players, buffoons, musicians, opera singers, opera dancers.[11]

This attack was not merely a piece of economic analysis but also a political challenge, on behalf of the real producers of wealth to the class that held political power. The idea that economic analysis could be used as a basis and buttress for political argu-ments was novel but soon spread. Malthus, putting forward one of the first statements of the underconsumptionist position, argued that the landowning and professional classes were indeed unproductive, but were still vital to the economy which would founder without their consumption. Economic thought is like a merry-go-round. The same ideas always come round again. Keynes, for instance, saw Malthus as one of his forerunners because of the emphasis he put on eective demand. Baran, although agreeing with Malthus's formulation of the economic problem, disagreed with how he solved it. He argues that there are more rational ways of creating a high level of effective demand to keep the economy fully employed than maintaining an upper class of social parasites, and he similarly castigates the Keynesians for their 'irrational' solutions to the problem of inadequate effective demand – employing men to dig holes, build pyramids, manufacture arms, and so forth.

Baran therefore claims that any economic system can be investigated to see how large is the potential compared to the actual surplus. Knowing the size of the real surplus permits a description and analysis of the essential features of that economy. As Baran says, 'the rate and direction of economic development in a country at a given time . . . depends on both the size and the mode of utilisation of the economic surplus'.[12] This statement is both a key to his thought and to the analysis of monopoly capitalism that he and Sweezy developed.

'MONOPOLY CAPITAL'

Sweezy's notion of underconsumption and Baran's notion of surplus are combined in *Monopoly Capital* published shortly after Baran's death in 1965. They supply a framework within which is developed a rigorous and well-documented examination of the long boom and the nature of contemporary monopoly capitalism. Combining the underconsumptionist theory of crisis and the concept of economic surplus leads to the following hypothesis which is repeated many times in the book: 'The growth of monopoly generates a strong tendency for surplus to rise without at the same time providing adequate mechanism of surplus absorption.'[13] Its implications we shall examine in a moment.

Baran and Sweezy maintain that, in several significant respects, monopoly capitalism is unlike competitive capitalism. These differences concern, above all, how prices are determined. Indeed, true to their location of the cause of crisis in the realisation rather than in the production of surplus value, they describe the main difference between competitive and monopoly capitalism as a difference in the way their markets are organised: 'Since market relations are essentially price relations the study of monopoly capitalism, like that of competitive capitalism, must begin with the working of the price mechanism.'[14] The price mechanism works differently in the two systems because of the existence of what the Keynesians call oligopolistic market structures in many industries. This divides the economy into two sectors – a competitive sector, still made up of numerous small firms, none large enough to control the price set by the market, and a corporate sector, in which economic power, investment and employment are increasingly concentrated. Here are the corporate giants, whose operations span industries and continents. They have become the main agents of the accumulation of capital, the powerhouse of the whole system, and the competitive sector, though not without its use to corporate capital, especially innovation, has sharply declined in real importance, though it has retained an ideological significance as the arena of the small man, free competition and self-help.

Baran and Sweezy study corporate capital. They argue, like many of the Keynesians, that its behaviour cannot be described at all adequately using the models of perfect competition and price formation as developed by marginalism. Indeed, they state bluntly that there is no way of analysing precisely how prices will be determined in a monopoly-capitalist system. There are no general rules, because prices are no longer variable. They no longer respond in any predictable way to the forces of demand and supply or to the forces of competition. This is also the basis for their revision of many of Marx's concepts, particularly the notion of an average profit brought about by competition between capitalists which equalises the rate of profit between industries. They argue that this no longer applies. (This is a further nail in the assertion that the tendency of the rate of profit is to fall.)[15]

Freed from the constraints of competitive-market pricing, corporate capital moves according to its own laws. Baran and Sweezy stress, however, that although price competition is mostly dead in the corporate sector – firms fix their own prices, follow price-leaders, use mark-ups on costs – all of this does not mean competition between capitals is dead. But it finds new expressions. To protect and enlarge its share of the market becomes a major objective for each firm. It seeks to achieve it through its marketing policies – in which packaging and advertising loom large – and through general development programmes and forward planning, particularly as regards technological progress, training its labour force, and securing its raw materials. Such firms develop a concern for long-term expansion of their operations which is not only compatible with maximising profits but virtually identical with it. Baran and Sweezy swiftly demolish the myth of the managerial revolution which is supposed to see a new class of managers emerge, who are divorced from ownership, and no longer attempt to maximise profits, but other goals they happen to set themselves. That imaginary beast the Soulful Corporation, first glimpsed by Carl Kaysen, has even flitted through the glades of some economists' imaginations. Baran and Sweezy show convincingly that the modern corporation is not less but more orientated to profit maximisation. Profits are the life-blood of the corporation and the motor of the accumulation process, and modern corporations are in a far better position than the small firms to calculate their costs and their pricing and marketing strategies in order to generate a level of profits and a cash flow that enables them to achieve all their objectives.

The rise of the corporate sector and the demise of price competition together with most of the conditions for the effective functioning of free markets – such as no barriers to entry and no product differentiation – leads to the tendency for the surplus to rise. Surplus, in the sense used by Baran and Sweezy, means the potential surplus, the amount the economy could produce, minus essential consumption. That this surplus will rise follows from their description of monopoly capitalism. If corporate capital exercises a considerable degree of monopoly power and control over market share and price, then it will use this power to assure that most, if not all, of the gains from increasing productivity accrue to it in the form of higher profits. Hence, there will be a secular tendency for the total amount of potential surplus to increase.

Baran and Sweezy consider three possible objections to their hypothesis. First, there is Schumpeter's view, developed in *The Theory of Economic Development* (Harvard University Press, 1934). He argued that monopoly profits were only a transitory phenomenon in the process of capital accumulation. They came about following a wave of technological innovation – the 'perennial gale of creative destruction', as he called it. Many established firms, unable to adapt, go to the wall. Those that survive, with new ones that spring up alongside, do so by developing and exploring new techniques and processes. As a result, such firms earn monopoly profits for a time, but then competitive pressures reassert themselves, other firms emerge, and monopoly profits disappear. Against this, Baran and Sweezy point out that however much Schumpeter was accurately describing some aspects of the process of capital accumulation in the competitive phase of capitalism, it is no longer applicable. The perennial gale has subsided to a 'mild breeze'. Shake-ups in industry rarely affect the corporate giants. Technological innovation is firmly under their control, either because it is carried on in their own research and development departments, or because they allow small firms to experiment with new techniques, thus allowing them to bear all the initial costs, and step in to buy out those that are successful. The process of technological innovation therefore no longer supplies any check to the earning and maintaining of monopoly profits by corporate capital.

The second objection to the idea of a rising surplus that is considered emanates from Kaldor, one of the leading post-war Keynesians. He states that a Marxist analysis of the accumulation process would predict that the competitive phase of capitalism would give way to a monopoly phase by causing concentration and centralisation of capital, and that this should lead to a rising proportion of profits in national income. However, Kaldor notes that this has not happened. The share of wages and of profits in the national income has remained remarkably constant for almost one hundred years.[16] Baran and Sweezy retort that Kaldor's analysis is right but his conclusion wrong. His mistake is to identify the share of profits in national income with the surplus. Clearly, profits that are declared and taxed within a given year do not begin to measure the real level of profits in a monopoly-capitalist economy, partly because so many other kinds of expenditure are paid for out of profits but are classified as costs. So an accurate measure of profit (difficult to obtain) would have to be used in order to really test the Marxist prediction.

The third objection is that of John Strachey, but it has also been put forward more recently by Andrew Glyn and Bob Sutcliffe.[17] Strachey argued that political changes and Keynesian economic politics had created a situation in which trade unions could increase real wages and grab for themselves the greater part of any increase in productivity. This theory then accepts the imperfect nature of modern markets and the idea that prices are determined in labour markets not by the impersonal inter-action of demand and supply but by the degree of monopoly power that unions and employers can bring to bear. Its pro-ponents argue that since 1945 full-employment policies and the capital-intensive nature of modern industry tip the balance towards labour. Faced by union militancy, companies may prove unable to raise prices sufficiently to protect profit margins, par-ticularly if they are facing severe international competition. The consequence is a growing squeeze on profits – both the rate of profit and the share of profit in national income begin to fall. This Marxist theory of wage-push has been put forward to explain developments in some of the weaker nations of the capitalist economy such as the United Kingdom. Baran and Sweezy's whole focus is on the United States, the most developed and largest of the monopoly-capitalist countries. They argue that control over prices is one of the most important instruments of the economic power of corporate capital. Companies can always raise prices to cover any increase in wages which unions demand or which employers themselves offer. In the inflationary process companies become adept in their public relations techniques and learn how to announce price increases just after wage settlements. In this way, higher prices can be blamed on workers' wages. When investigated, however, the reality usually turns out to be rather different. A notorious case in the United States in the 1950s was United States Steel which consistently raised its prices after every wage settlement to cover the increased costs and to raise its profit margins at the same time.[18]

Baran and Sweezy's central point is clear. The markets of monopoly capitalism are different from the markets of competitive capitalism. Permanent inflation is built into the administered pricing practices of corporate capital. Surplus has a tendency to rise both absolutely and as a share of total output. But this very sign of the strength of corporate capital also displays its weaknesses. For as surplus rises, as the share of national income that potentially can accrue to capital increases, so the problem of absorbing the surplus grows, of finding sufficient outlets for consumption and investment by capitalists that can dispose of the surplus without threatening the institutions of the capitalist order and the process of capital accumulation. Much of the analysis of *Monopoly Capital* is devoted to this problem – in what ways is the rising surplus absorbed?

The first way in which it could be absorbed is by increasing the consumption and investment of capitalists themselves. The former is dismissed as totally inadequate. Even the most extravagant luxury would not suffice. The possibility of accelerating investment, however, is taken more seriously. In principle, there is no reason why there should be any hitch in the accumulation process if capitalists re-invest all the surplus they obtain from production, provided the investment was not directed at increasing the output of consumer goods but only at increasing the output of capital goods. In this way, provided production was properly synchronised and capitalists bought each other's capital goods, no problem of 'surplus absorption' would arise. Such was the argument of Tugan Baranowski. Baran and Sweezy, however, argue that such accumulation is a fantasy. Apart from the extreme irrationality of an economic system in which production and productive capacity is always increasing, but consumption never, the degree of co-ordination that would be needed would be far too great for any system with competing capitals. Even in the Soviet Union such accumulation was not at all smooth. So, in general, Baran and Sweezy discount this extreme theoretical possibility.

Investment by capitalists is, however, still important. What has to be ascertained are its limits. Baran and Sweezy claim that the whole profitability schedule of corporate capital tends to shift upwards over time. Actual profits earned, however, depend on what proportion of capacity is employed. In general, the higher the utilisation of capacity and therefore the greater the output, the higher the level of profits, if only because of the reduction in overhead costs. High profits in the short run, however, mean even higher amounts of surplus to re-invest in the long run. So capacity utilisation shows a persistent tendency to drop. This makes profits much lower than they would otherwise be. Some of the problem of surplus absorption is thus solved by the creation of excess capacity. Part of the surplus is just not produced.

New investment is a major way of absorbing surplus, but in so far as it increases capacity, it raises the potential profits at full-capacity working, thereby increasing potential surplus. Invest-

ment that absorbs current surplus is listed by Baran and Sweezy
under three main headings: the needs of an expanding population; investment in new methods of production and new
products; and foreign investment. All these have obvious limits
– those on the first two have already been mentioned. Foreign
investment helps develop the world market and draw all nations
into the capitalist system. But its indefinite expansion is obviously
limited by its very success in industrialising the rest of the world.
If foreign investment does not promote industrialisation, then the
only outlets are in primary-good extraction and processing. If it
does promote industrialisation, then it creates new markets, but
also new competitors. In addition, whole areas of the world have
been lost to the capitalist world market by being incorporated in
the communist bloc. A further problem with investment as an
absorber of surplus, which Baran and Sweezy note, is depreciation. Depreciation allowances to cover the replacement of existing plant form a major item in company accounts. But in terms of
the theoretical analysis of monopoly capitalism, new investment
must at least equal depreciation before any absorption of surplus
can take place. Yet, depreciation allowances are now so large that
companies are often able to finance from these funds alone any
investment in innovations which it considers will be profitable.
They do this simply by introducing capital-saving innovations to
replace the old equipment that needs scrapping.

Given the framework of the analysis, Baran and Sweezy can
reasonably conclude that capitalists' own consumption and investment will never be sufficient to absorb the growing amount of
surplus that is constantly generated through the workings of
modern monopoly capitalism. Unless the whole economy is to be
plunged into chronic and permanent stagnation, at least as serious
as the 1930s, and suffer from ever-increasing excess capacity,
then other 'modes of surplus utilisation' have to be found. For
Baran and Sweezy the typical problem of accumulation in competitive capitalism was a shortage of surplus value. Periodically
capital found that it could not wring enough from its labour
force to make continued production profitable. But for monopoly
capitalism the shadow over accumulation is not too little surplus
value, but too few ways of disposing of it. It is a market problem.
The tendency of surplus to rise actually replaces the tendency
of the rate of profit to fall. Left to itself the economy would be

permanently depressed. Yet actual experience since the 1930s has
been very different. So where has capitalism discovered sufficient
additional outlets to absorb the growing surplus?

THE 'SURPLUS EATERS'

Baran and Sweezy identify two main additional outlets : the sales
effort and government spending, particularly on arms. The first
is one of the most evident characteristics of modern industry.
Marketing has become so important to firms that it often rivals
production itself. In Baran and Sweezy's account it has two
central aspects – advertising and packaging. Spending on advertising has grown enormously as corporate capital has developed
and price competition has declined. It is one of the conditions of
monopolistic competition. Firms seek to make their product different from their rivals by establishing brand names and trying
to get the consumer to feel that their product is somehow unique
or special. The bulk of advertising long ago ceased attempting to
supply information to consumers about the range of goods on the
market and became an instrument in creating and protecting
market shares. This was espcially important as real incomes of
workers rose, and new groups of unproductive workers, the new
middle classes, were spawned. It created a mass of consumers
outside the ranks of the capitalists and the upper class, with dis-
cretionary spending power. It became essential that these rising
incomes be diverted into consumption. Saving was no longer a
problem for capitalism, and therefore no longer a virtue, since
corporate capital conducted its own saving through depreciation allowances and undistributed profits. Modern advertising
thus also became a means of implanting new needs and new
consumption habits on the middle-income groups. The age of
high mass consumption would hardly have been possible without
the regular discovery and promotion of new needs. In an ironic
reversal of its ascetic origins, monopoly capitalism waged a relentless war against saving. Indeed Marx had noted that this was
already a tendency within competitive capitalism :

> Although every capitalist demands that every worker should
> save, he means only *his own* workers, because they relate to
> him as workers; and by no means does this apply to the

remainder of the workers, because these relate to him as consumers. In spite of all the pious talk of frugality he therefore
searches for all possible ways of stimulating them to consume,
by making his commodities more attractive, by filling their ears
with babble about new needs.[19]

Monopoly capitalism had succeeded in overcoming this contradiction. Now consumption was all it demanded, and indeed consumption in excess of current income. The multiplication of credit
and private debt paralleled the compulsion to consume.

The second aspect of marketing that helped devour the surplus
was packaging of all kinds. The growth of packaging is hard to
estimate at all accurately because it is no longer an activity that
takes place alongside the production process and supplements it.
Marketing needs now 'reach back and dictate the arrangement
and grouping of production facilities'. Real costs become impossible to calculate. As Veblen argued in *Absentee Ownership and
Business Enterprise in Recent Times* (1924), the distinction
between salesmanship and workmanship becomes blurred. It
becomes increasingly difficult to separate the appearance and the
quality of the goods that are produced. But, to show the order
of magnitude that is involved, Baran and Sweezy quote the study
by Fisher, Grilliches and Kaysen,[20] of the cost of car-model
changes since 1949. Taking the 1949 model as their base, they
try and estimate the cost of the resources that would have been
saved if 1949 model cars had been produced every year, instead
of new models being introduced. They calculated that the cost
amounted to $700 per car (25 per cent plus purchase price) or
$3·9 billion per year over the 1956–60 period. When the addi-
tional petrol costs of model changes and the huge profits of the
companies and retailers are also deducted, Baran and Sweezy
conclude that the final price of a car in 1960 need not have
exceeded $700. Car-model changes in the late 1950s were costing
the United States $11 billion a year, equal to 2·5 per cent of
its G.N.P.

The second great eater of surplus that is analysed in *Monopoly
Capital* is the state. It is an even bigger consumer of surplus than
the sales effort. Baran and Sweezy argue that it is only able to
play this role because of the nature of monopoly capitalism.
Classical political economists and marginalists assumed full em-

ployment of resources. So any state expenditure had to be at the expense of part or all of the population. Since it was also assumed that wages would fluctuate around the subsistence level, it followed that taxation had to be borne by the property-owning classes, the classes that controlled and received the surplus. In these circumstances it was hardly surprising that there should have been general agreement amongst liberals that that government is best which governs least.

The drive of competitive capitalism into monopoly capitalism created a new situation. Full employment of resources was no longer even an approximate characteristic of the economy. Instead, excess capacity and a tendency to stagnation became the rule. It became possible for the state, by increasing its own spending, to raise the level of effective demand, and hence the level of output and national income. State spending in the Keynesian manner could thus greatly improve economic performance without taking income away from anyone. Higher taxes on capital and on labour would be more than offset by the higher profits that would come from increased capacity working and the higher employment incomes.

As in Sweezy's earlier formulation, state spending that raises effective demand (and so consumers' surplus) has three main categories: fixed capital formation, transfer payments, and current spending, mostly on arms. Central to this whole theory of the state is the idea that far from being an encroachment on funds that could be used for private accumulation, state spending in fact is always additional to spending by capitalists. In the words of Baran and Sweezy, 'The vast and growing amounts of surplus absorbed by government in recent decades are not, we repeat, deductions from what would otherwise be available to corporations and individuals for their private purposes.'[21] If the surplus cannot be consumed, then it will not be produced. Only if capacity is fully utilised will government spending encroach on private accumulation, and Baran and Sweezy produce figures to show that that is far from the case in the United States, where unemployment and excess capacity remained a permanent aspect of the economy even during the long boom.[22]

Having posed the problem of the state in monopoly capitalism in these terms, the question for Baran and Sweezy is what limits there are to state spending. For if one accepted their view that monopoly capitalism had a permanent tendency for the surplus to rise faster than could be absorbed, and therefore was doomed to perpetual stagnation unless rescued from without, it could still be argued, in orthodox Keynesian terms, that a saviour was indeed at hand – the modern state. What is to prevent the state from raising its expenditure continually in order to create the effective demand that will allow the economy to run at full employment and absorb all the surplus that is produced?

The answer that Baran and Sweezy give is perhaps the least satisfactory part of their theory, in the sense that it relies on institutional factors that are brought in from outside and are not themselves explained in terms of the theory of monopoly capital. Sweezy has criticised Keynes for treating the state as a *deus ex machina* that could be brought in to solve the problems of capital accumulation.[23] But Baran and Sweezy treat it in similar fashion in order to explain why state spending cannot permanently solve these same problems. They note that following the New Deal era U.S. government spending rose 70 per cent, mostly on welfare. But this they argue was by no means sufficient to counter the powerful drift to stagnation. The economy relapsed into deep unemployment in 1937–8. Baran and Sweezy explain the failure of the New Deal as follows : 'Given the power structure of United States monopoly capitalism, the increase of civilian spending had about reached its outer limits by 1939. The forces opposing further expansion were too strong to be overcome.'[24] They are able to conclude, therefore that what really ended the Great Depression was also what ended it in every other major capitalist country, starting with Nazi Germany – re-armament. The wartime military budget and its retention afterwards is the principal contribution of the state to solving the problems of surplus absorption which are inherent in monopoly capitalism. The arms budget is thus the key to the much higher levels of employment and capacity utilisation of the 1950s, as compared to the 1930s. If the military budget were reduced to 1939 proportions, then unemployment would also revert to 1939 proportions.[25]

For Baran and Sweezy, the fundamental question concerning the state is how the budget is drawn up : 'The big question . . . is not whether there will be more and more government spending but on what. And here private interests come into their own as the controlling factor.'[26] The actions of the government are closely confined and restricted by the structure of interests within the state. These interests derive, in the main, from the class nature of society, the division into owners and non-owners, propertied and propertyless. The existence of such a restrictive structure normally prevents any major extension of government expenditure in such fields as health, education and welfare. The New Deal was a period when these interests were temporarily superseded by the seriousness of the crisis and the need to make concessions to a mutinous populace. But the success was short-lived. Further increases were blocked. Arms spending became the only major channel that the dominant private interests could tolerate. It did not compete with existing firms, nor did it undermine the position of vested interests. On the contrary it was a lucrative source of profits for many industries. Yet arms spending itself could not be increased fast enough to absorb the ever-growing surplus. The composition of military demand began to change as arms became more sophisticated, requiring less massive doses of heavy investment. As the arms industry itself became a less efficient waste-bin for surplus, so ever-increasing arms bills were blocked in the budget by coalitions of other political forces opposed to increased military spending.

BOOM AND BUST

The picture Baran and Sweezy draw of monopoly capital is thus a grim one. The nature of corporate capital has gradually unfolded during its development out of competitive capitalism. Secure in its monopolistic markets, no longer subject to the same constraints as competitive capital, corporate capital constructs an economic system in which the surplus is always rising, but in which ways of disposing of the surplus fall behind. The result is a chronic tendency to either stagnation or overproduction. The dilemma for monopoly capital is that every new way of disposing of the surplus, which does not infringe on dominant class interests, only increases the surplus even faster. For it raises the level of effective demand, and so capacity utilisation and employment rise too. This means faster growth of output, higher profits and an increase in productive capacity. So every attempt to absorb surplus now only increases the amount of surplus that will have to be absorbed in the future. The absolute disposal of surplus must constantly accelerate in order to cope with the increasing value of surplus it is itself helping to generate. Clearly this is a race monopoly capital cannot win. Sooner or later the system must collapse once more into depression and slump.

This is Baran and Sweezy's prediction. They argue that if even the enormous waste-bins represented by the sales effort and the arms budget are still not sufficient to prevent unemployment and excess capacity in the U.S. economy, then the tendency to stagnation must be powerful indeed. They claim that this has indeed been the law of motion of U.S. capitalism throughout this century. Only two counteracting forces have been strong enough to offset it, one being 'epoch-making innovations', the other being wars and their aftermath. Capitalism has only known three epoch-making innovations – innovations that generated a vast amount of subsidiary investment. They have been the steam engine, the railways, and the internal combustion engine. Baran and Sweezy point out that the railway boom in the United States lasted from 1870 to 1907. From 1907 onwards, a marked trend towards stagnation asserted itself. Unemployment and excess capacity began to rise sharply – registered unemployment reached 9·7 per cent in 1915. Only entry into the First World War prevented a major depression. In the 1920s the first stage of the car epoch resulted in a sustained boom, but then the economy relapsed into the worst depression it had ever experienced.

The explanation therefore that Baran and Sweezy offer for the long boom should by now be apparent. The depression of the 1930s was ended not by the New Deal but by re-armament. After 1944 there was the usual post-war boom, which was maintained and perpetuated by the enormous peace-time military budget for the Cold War, and by the second stage of the epoch of the car. The latter produced a wave of secondary investment – the whole growth of suburbs for example – and was propelled by an enormous growth in credit and consumer debt. Towards the end of their book, Baran and Sweezy state that 'at the time of writing, nearly two decades after the war, it is still not possible to say when the whole movement will lose its momentum'.[27] Yet if their analysis is correct, lose its momentum it must.

Baran and Sweezy's theory of monopoly capital and their explanation of the long boom is certainly one of the most coherent and searching Marxist treatments that has appeared since 1945. No other explanations are nearly as complete or as detailed. This success is in part due to the incorporation of many Keynesian insights and concepts into their analysis. They are often described as Marxist Keynesians, although their analysis goes far beyond that of Keynes. Yet they do share one of Keynes's decisive limitations – they concentrate on the market and they have no real theory of the state. One way of describing Keynes's achievement is that he made realistic assumptions about the nature of modern monopolistic markets the cornerstone of his analysis. But his realism evaporated when it came to the state. For Keynes and for most of his followers the state merely supplied neutral technical instruments which could be employed to pull capitalism out of its stagnation. Baran and Sweezy make more realistic assumptions about the role of the state, and what kinds of expenditure it is in fact possible for governments to undertake. But the state still materialises from outside the economic process to provide the largest dustbin of all for the system's unwanted surplus. They can do this because their starting point for analysing capitalism is class ownership and control of the means of production. Yet they do not, as Marx himself did, concentrate on how the classes are established in the process of production itself and how the class relationships of production both determine and set limits to the accumulation of capital. The decisive limitation that Baran and Sweezy see resides in the markets of monopoly capitalism and nowhere else.

In this they reflect a strong current of thought that was present in the United States during the 1950s. Joseph Steindl's *Maturity and Stagnation in American Capitalism* and Joseph Gillman's *The Falling Rate of Profit* were typical of this school of Marxism. Both books emphasised the crucial difference between monopoly and competitive capitalism. Gillman attempted to derive measures of the organic composition of capital to see whether or not it rose historically, and so whether there was a tendency for the rate of profit to fall. His conclusion was as follows :

The results show that whereas for the years before about World War I the historical statistics seem fully to support these theories of Marx, after that war theories studied appear generally to behave in contradiction to the Marxist expectations. The explanation could be that our statistics or our procedures or both are wrong. Or Marx was right for the period of competitive capitalism, but wrong for the period of monopoly capitalism, which began to dominate the capitalist mode of production at about the time of the First World War. Or again, the terms in which Marx formulated his theories were too narrow to encompass the conditions of monopoly production.[28]

Steindl's book is a rigorous statement of the underconsumptionist position. He dismissed the falling rate of profit argument in Marx as a relic of views Marx would have been sure to reject had he lived to complete his work and develop the underconsumption approach which is implicit within it. Steindl's formulations of the underconsumptionist theory foreshadowed Baran and Sweezy's later exposition.[29] He argued that growing oligopoly in capitalist markets meant there was a tendency for gross profit margins and for the capitalists' share of national product to increase. But this did not mean that the actual share of capitalists in net incomes need increase at all. Increased profit margins could be compensated by a reduced degree of utilisation. So there need be no shift of actual income from wages to profits, only a shift of potential income of workers to become wastage in the form of excess capacity. Oligopoly thus caused the rate of exploitation to rise, but since the increase in surplus value could not be realised the result is an increase in excess capacity. Insufficient markets, not sufficient surplus value, are the curse of monopoly capitalism in Steindl's view.

This view also became, as we now know, Baran and Sweezy's view. It is this view which has attracted most criticism. By concentrating on the change in the markets of monopoly capitalism, Baran and Sweezy focus attention on the level of appearances only. They neglect the real laws of motion of capitalism, rooted in the production not the realisation of surplus value. As Martin Nicolaus points out,[30] presenting the tendency of surplus to rise as the antithesis of the tendency of the rate of profit to fall is a false antithesis. Marx predicted that the rate of profit would have a tendency to fall *and* that this would be accompanied by a tendency for the mass of profits to rise. Baran and Sweezy are wrong to suppose that the tendency of the rate of profit to fall depends upon price competition between capitals.

Ernest Mandel has developed this criticism further.[31] He argues that all the laws of motion of the capitalist mode of production arise from the process of capital accumulation. Thus, in the process of accumulation there is an inherent tendency towards the concentration and centralisation of capital which eventually means that competitive capital gives way to monopoly capital and, secondly, the organic composition of capital rises. These two laws or tendencies are brought about by two kinds of competition – competition between capitals, which drives out the weak and allows the strong to grow, and competition between labour and capital, which forces capital to increase its outlay on constant capital (plant, equipment and raw materials) relative to its outlay on variable capital (living labour power). According to Mandel, a change in the way markets are organised does not alter the way these laws operate. They are not dependent on 'free competition'. The basic problem of capital accumulation remains the same – how to raise the rate of exploitation, or how to increase relative surplus value. The problem for capital is always that there is insufficient surplus value to keep production and accumulation profitable. All income in capitalist society has only two sources – either variable capital or surplus value. The total quantity of surplus value produced in a given period of time is fixed – the barrier is variable capital in two senses; first because wages have to be paid in exchange for labour power and, secondly because the surplus value that is then extracted from labour power will depend either on how long and how hard the capitalist can make his workers work, or on how much he can increase their output by investing in machines for them to work with.

In such an analysis, Baran and Sweezy's calculation in terms of national income is out of place. A given sum of surplus value can circulate many times. To obtain their total of economic surplus Baran and Sweezy count the same surplus value several times over. What appears to them as a problem of absorbing surplus and insufficient markets appears to Mandel as too low a rate of exploitation – not too much surplus but too little surplus value. Baran and Sweezy offer a highly sophisticated interpretation of the crisis of monopoly capitalism from the standpoint of markets and realisation. It can thus incorporate and develop many of the principal insights of Keynesian economics. That is its strength. But it is also its weakness. The explanation remains partial, particularly as concerns the role of the state. It is therefore necessary to turn to examine Marx's value analysis of capitalism, and to those Marxists such as Ernest Mandel and Paul Mattick, who have attempted to use it to account for the role the state now plays in accumulation. Despite this, the sweep and rigour of Baran and Sweezy's theory has not yet been equalled by other Marxists in their explanation of the long boom. Some stress the role of credit, others the role of arms, but rarely develop their insights into a comprehensive theory. It is the vision of *Monopoly Capital* that impresses and which set it apart from most other Marxists books of the period and from the works of orthodox economists.

4
Value, Price and Profits

Every beginning is difficult, holds in all sciences. . . . The value-form, whose fully developed shape is the money-form, is very elementary and simple. Nevertheless, the human mind has for more than 2000 years sought in vain to get to the bottom of it. . . . With the exception of the section on value-form, therefore, this volume cannot stand accused on the score of difficulty.

Karl Marx, *Capital*, Preface to the First German Edition (Moscow: Foreign Languages Publishing House, 1967) pp.7–8.

Many people assume that Marxism is so dogmatic and outdated in its methods of enquiry and conclusions that it has nothing of interest to say about the modern world. In part this is due to widespread misconceptions and ignorance of Marx's own work. In part it is due to simple ignorance of the work of modern Marxists. In recent years controversies among Marxists have ranged over the most important questions about the nature of the modern capitalist economy and the causes and consequences of the present crisis. In contrast to Baran and Sweezy, who focus particularly on the nature of markets in modern capitalism, an alternative tradition has continued to stress the relevance and importance of Marx's value analysis of capital and the production process. There have been important contributions in Japan,[1] Europe[2] and the United States.[3] It is this kind of approach with which we shall be concerned in this chapter.

In recent years too the publication and translation of long-buried manuscripts, particularly the *Grundrisse*, has brought greater understanding of Marx's work.[4] Many myths about Marx's

work have been exploded, for example the idea that he was a technological determinist, or belived in some kind of inevitable polari-
sation of classes or progressive fall in the standard of living of
the working class. With the aid of *Grundrisse* it is again possible
to reconstruct Marx's system of thought and acknowledge its
profundity. Though Marx never completed the great work he
planned, he left behind its essentials and his method of analysis.
We believe that Marx's approach provided the means for understanding the development of capitalism, not merely in its early
laissez-faire stage, but in its late monopoly stage as well. Marx
foresaw the concentration of production, the divorce of ownership from control, the creation of the world market, the approach
to automation, the rise of the new middle classes.[5]

One of Marx's greatest achievements was to leave formulated
in general terms the limits to capitalist production and the cause
of crises. His method was to analyse capitalism as a system of
production and a system of circulation and markets. Both are
necessary to understand its development fully, but they require
different approaches. The market is the moment of exchange,
the sphere of money and price. It is through the market that all
exchange relations must be expressed and realised. It is not,
however, fundamental to the capitalist mode of production. At
the level of the market and competition everything appears back-
wards. To understand market phenomena it is necessary first to
analyse the sphere of production and the social basis of capitalism.
Only in this way can the inexplicable events of the world market
– inflation, crises, monopoly and cycles – be explained. Marx's
analysis, therefore, starts with production and a discussion of the
concept of value. It is, as he acknowledged, the most difficult
part of his analysis, but, unfortunately, also the most essential.

MONEY AND VALUE

In presenting his findings in *Capital*, Marx chose to start with
the most simple analytic categories of all and show how the
complex concrete phenomena of actual economies had to be
explained in terms of them. His analysis moves from the abstract
to the concrete by steadily relaxing the highly restrictive assumptions that are made at the outset. In this procedure Marx followed the characteristic form of analysis of economics – the

building of analytical models on the basis of highly simplified assumptions. Where he differs from the economists is, first, in the correctness of the assumptions that he makes and, secondly, in his method – the way in which he moves from the abstract to the concrete.

Marx's starting point is the analysis of value under the conditions of commodity production. His basic questions are what gives value to commodities and how can this value be measured. The marginalists, it will be remembered, pushed the problem away by defining value as whatever individuals placed 'value' upon, and measured that by whatever was 'demanded' in the market. So the value of a commodity could never be other than its price, and this sense of value – the price an article can fetch – corresponds to the everyday use of the term. Marx and the classical political economists before him were not interested in such a tautology. It explained nothing. They wanted to know if some objective measure of value, independent of market price, could be discovered which would throw light on the whole process of production and distribution in a capitalist economy.

They found this objective theory in labour. Despite endless confusions and misrepresentations the basis of the labour theory is straightforward enough. Marx expressed it bluntly in a letter:

The nonsense about the necessity of proving the concept of value arises from complete ignorance both of the subject dealt with and of the method of science. Every child knows that a country which ceased to work, I will not say for a year, but for a few weeks, would die. Every child knows too that the mass of products corresponding to the different needs require different and quantitatively determined masses of the total labour of society. That this necessity of distributing social labour in definite proportions cannot be done away with by the *particular form* of social production, but can only change the *form it assumes* is self-evident. No natural laws can be done away with. What can change, in changing historical circumstances, is the *form* in which these laws operate.[6]

The basic insight of the labour theory is that historically in all forms of society it is labour that is the active creator of wealth. All other factors of production – land, raw materials, and tools of all kinds – are only the means through which wealth is created.

Understanding the way in which the labour process is organised
in a society is thus the key to understanding its economy because
it provides the material basis of its life. Every society is obliged
to establish some means of allocating the total labour of its members between different uses and of distributing the proceeds of
labour among them. From the standpoint of the whole society
the only possible social measure of its labour is time – the number of hours of average skill and intensity that the whole population can work. Economics is thus ultimately concerned with
economy in time. Understanding any actual economy means
understanding how the labour-time available to it is employed
and exchanged; what social forces and institutions determine
what is to be produced and to whom it is to be distributed.

Historically there exist different solutions to such questions.
Marx characterised such differences as differences in the mode of
production. Capitalism was one such mode of production but was
also seen by him as different in significant respects from previous
modes of production. In earlier economies the meaning and
measurement of value was straightforward. Something was valu-
able that was useful. The value of an article meant its value in
use, and production consisted of the production of useful goods
and services. The apportioning of social labour-time between different branches of production and the distribution of the output
was relatively clear and transparent. Under feudalism, for
example, the labour process was directed by the landowners whose
monopoly of land enabled them to determine both what was produced and to extort a surplus from the direct producers, the
peasants, by forcing them to work so many hours directly for
them.

With the rise of capitalism the social relationships of feudalism
were transformed. The major institutional change that distinguished the capitalist economy from its predecessors was the
market. In a developed market economy, people came to live by
exchanging through the medium of money all or part of what
they produced for the products of others. This encouraged
specialisation and a growing division of labour. Markets, of course,
had existed in many previous societies, direct barter being the
earliest and most common type of exchange. But it had always
been limited in extent and significance. Only under capitalism
were exchange relationships made universal becoming the

characteristic form of economic production. In a capitalist market not only are goods and services bought and sold on the market, but the factors of production themselves, in particular labour, are bought and sold too. The direct 'compulsory' labour of feudalism is replaced by 'free' labourers who have to sell their labour on the market to the highest bidder in return for money wages. They sell their labour either in the form of goods they have themselves produced with their labour or in the form of their labour-power itself. The capitalist market appears as a vast conglomerate of free and sovereign individual producers who exchange their goods and services for money. Their mutual competition forces them to sell at the highest price and buy at the lowest. Competition was, and still is, praised for maximising efficiency, output, imagination and initiative.

The market place, the moment of exchange, became for the classical political economists, and for most economists since, the central focus of attention. The market economy became synonymous with the capitalist economy. Marx took a very different view. To understand the market was to understand only the superficial appearance of the capitalist economy. It was necessary to look deeper and it was the labour theory of value that was the indispensable first step.

The first thing to be noted about the market is that the goods and services produced in the economy appear on it in the form of commodities, that is they are not only useful objects and so possess a use-value; they also must appear useful to others and so have an exchange-value. Production occurs not directly for use but for the exchange of commodities. It is not enough for someone to produce articles that have obvious use-value like oxygen tents or kidney machines. Unless they can be sold on the market they have no value in exchange and so are of no value in the capitalist sense of value, that is price. This schizophrenic nature of commodities in a capitalist market was ignored or confused by the classical political economists and their successors. It was Marx's genius and inspiration which made the distinction the foundation of Marxist economics. His analysis was devoted to showing how commodities under capitalism must possess both an exchange-value and a use-value. He argued that for any understanding of economics it was necessary to grasp the nature of value and how it can be measured in terms of labour-time.

Imagine a society of individual producers all busy labouring to produce commodities which they can then exchange on the market. The exchange-value which these commodities can command in a perfect market will reflect the portion of total social labour-time that has gone into their production. If we further assume all labour is of average skill and intensity, the value of any article would be its socially necessary value. A table that took six hours to produce will have twice as much exchange-value as a coat that took three. Production and exchange are regulated in such an economy by the labour-time that is socially necessary to produce commodities, that is the number of hours that is necessary to produce a commodity under the normal conditions of production and with the average degree of skill and intensity that prevail at the time.

Such a simple exchange economy is an economy of barter. Commodities are exchanged according to the labour-time embodied in them. The market is here a mechanism for bringing the labours of individual isolated producers into harmony with one another and making possible the division of total labour-time available to society. It is this individualistic barter model of an exchange economy that underlay the classical political economists' understanding of how a capitalist market works. Marx's approach is, however, quite different. He does not try to grasp reality by assuming it is a direct reflection of the model. He uses the model as a stage in the elaboration of more complex and realistic concepts. This is the essential difference between his method and the method of orthodox economics. It is particularly clear in his analysis of money.

The market is one of the most obvious and distinguishing characteristics of a capitalist economy. The role of money is another. Under capitalism money is the form through which all exchange relationships take place, and there is a sense in which all the phenomena of exchange relationships, not just inflation, are monetary phenomena. Any meaningful theory of capitalism must possess a theory of money. Economists have generally adopted one of two approaches to money. In simplified terms these are either that 'money does not matter', that it is simply a veil over real economic relationships; or that 'money does matter', and has its own independent influence on the economy. This debate is, as usual, as old as the history of economics.

The great advantage of Marx's approach is that it cuts across the false distinction that bedevils orthodox theories. Marx placed great importance on the analysis of money for an understanding of how capitalism worked. But like his analysis of the capitalist market he did not regard money merely in its simple obvious character as a medium of circulation; rather he demonstrated the way in which it was related to value.

The emergence and adoption of money means that the barter model of an economy was no longer appropriate for analysing a capitalist exchange economy. In a barter economy, commodities roughly exchange according to the labour-time embodied in them. In a market economy commodities exchange according to their price. Exchange-value takes the form not of labour-time but of money. Classical political economists, like Ricardo, held fast to their barter model and argued that money prices generally reflected and were determined by labour-time values. Marginalists rejected the barter model and argued that prices were not in fact determined by labour-time values but by the interplay of demand and supply on the market. Value for them became indistinguishable from its money form, price. Marx rejected both notions. He attempted to grasp the actual nature of money and its contradictory role in a market economy. From one angle, all Marx's researches were aimed at forging concepts that could explain the two essential aspects of the capitalist economy – production and exchange on the market – and their interrelationship without reducing one to the other. Economists tended to make just this mistake – either explaining the market in terms of production, or production in terms of the market.

The existence of money is essential, not optional, in a market economy. It is not simply a means of making exchange more efficient and convenient. It is necessary if a capitalist market is to exist at all. In a market economy commodities have both use-value and exchange-value. The use-value of each commodity is unique, different in quality from every other. There is no means of comparing and ranking use-values. It is quite different with exchange-value. This must be expressed quantitatively in terms of a common standard, otherwise goods cannot be exchanged at all. The only possible objective standard is the labour-time used up in their production. This does not ensure exchange, however, because there is no clear and unambiguous way of reckoning labour-time. Labour varies in skill and intensity, and besides, since no invisible hand guides production, merely to expend labour power in producing a commodity does not mean that *on the market* that commodity can be exchanged for its full labour-time value. The individual labour-time actually embodied in a commodity and the socially necessary labour-time seen from the standpoint of society may diverge. What is then required so that exchange may take place at all, individual conflicts resolved, and production and distribution regulated in an orderly way, is one commodity in terms of which all other commodities can be expressed, and therefore exchanged. Such a commodity must act as the universal equivalent for all other commodities and so becomes the measure and reflector of social productivity. This commodity, whether it be salt, beads, cattle, silver or gold, is money. Due to their obvious advantages, for example durability and divisibility, the precious metals had already ousted all other forms of money in Europe before the rise of capitalism. But the form of money is much less important than its function. The function of money is to express the exchange-value of commodities and so co-ordinate, by establishing relative prices in the market, the whole process of production and distribution in a society of individual commodity producers.

Grasping this led Marx to one of his most important insights. On the market all that can be observed are commodities (C) with a definite price being exchanged for money (M), money then being exchanged for other commodities – a perpetual process of $C \rightarrow M \rightarrow C$. At this level the only thing that seems important about commodities is their price – their value in terms of money. What really gives these commodities value, however, and allows them to be exchanged is not money – that is only the superficial form of exchange – rather it is the fact that each commodity represents a part of the total labour-time of society. This is the anchor on which the market moves. The result is that the social relationships between the individual producers are never revealed in the market. All that appears is the exchange of commodities at given prices. This is what Marx meant. Thus :

A commodity is a mysterious thing, simply because in it the social character of men's labour appears to them as an objective character stamped upon the product of that labour; because the relation of the producers to the sum total of their own labour is presented to them as a social relation, existing not between themselves, but between the products of their labour . . . a definite social relation between men . . . assumes, in their eyes, the fantastic form of a relation between things.[7]

It followed from this analysis that to remain at the level of the market and study only the movement of prices was to fail to understand the specific form of social relations that distinguishes capitalism from other societies. Yet this is precisely the way economists proceed, and by so doing they empty history of its content, for they do not understand different economies in terms of their social organisation at all but in terms of the ahistorical timeless, reified categories of the capitalist market economy, like price and profit.

CAPITAL

Coming to grips with the capitalist market economy, therefore, means understanding how production and the market are related to one another. Exchange-value expressed in the form of money appears to belong to the commodity as such, that is as its price. Prices seem to be determined by the fluctuation of the market, the constant interplay of supply and demand. Unless refuge in mysticism is sought, however, the real basis of price movements is what gives exchange-value to commodities in the first place – the socially necessary labour-time which expresses the social relations between the producers. Value, however, is not the same as price and it makes no sense to calculate prices in terms of values. Despite belief to the contrary Marx never tried to reduce price to value. That was not his method. He always stressed that one could not be reduced to the other. For the purposes of analysis, however, he assumes throughout Volume 1 of *Capital* that all commodities exchange at their labour-time values, but he never imagined that such an assumption would furnish a theory of relative prices in the market. Its purpose was different – to permit an examination of the origins of capital and the process of its accumulation. Marx always insisted that capitalism was a contradictory mode of production and that to explain it required a twofold analysis – in terms of value and in terms of money. The former was the sphere of production and social relations, the latter the sphere of the market and price. Only by grasping both together could the actual nature of capitalism, its origins, development and ultimate limits, be understood.

The simple categories of the commodity, use-value, exchange-value, and money, only describe a simple society of commodity producers, in which production, controlled and disciplined through the market, is directed towards consumption, to the production and distribution of use-values. Capitalism is, however, a very different kind of economic system. It is orientated not to consumption but to production. The accumulation of capital is its driving force. But where does capital itself come from? How does it arise in a simple market economy of independent sovereign producers? If all men are free to buy and sell goods and services on the market in the form of commodities, is this not the best, most just and most efficient form of economic system?

Certainly the political economists themselves thought so. They regarded the market as the most important institution of the capitalist economy and they emphasised that all exchanges on the market were exchanges between free sovereign individuals. Such a description, however, is only true of the simplest kind of market economy, the society of independent producers. It is not true of capitalism. In place of independent producers are two highly stratified social groups, a class of capitalists who own the means of production and a class of workers who are employed by them. Using the model of the simple commodity-producing economy, economists describe the capitalist labour market as though it were no different in principle. Workers sell their labour to employers at the going market rate. It is a free and equal exchange like any other.

This equality is, however, only how it appears in the market. Marx's analysis penetrates deeper. What the workers sell to the capitalist is a commodity, not their bodies directly as labour, but labour-power. This commodity like any other in a market economy has a use-value and an exchange-value. Its exchange-value is obvious enough. On the market it is the money price that capitalists are prepared to pay. From the production standpoint, it is the socially necessary labour-time for producing the commodities that keep a worker alive and enable him to repro-

duce the commodity that he sells, his labour-power. But what is
the use-value of this commodity? Merely stating the question
makes it plain that this is no ordinary commodity – it is in fact
a unique commodity. All other commodities that are exchanged
have a use-value that can satisfy particular material needs.
Labour-power is unique because its use-value is to create value –
the activity of labouring produces articles that are useful and by
embodying labour-time in them it confers exchange-value upon
them. So what capitalists buy is not simply another commodity
that satisfies a specific individual need that they have. They buy
the activity that creates and confers value on commodities. If
they can ensure that the labour-power that they buy creates more
exchange-value than they paid for it in wages, they reap a
surplus value. This is the origin of all property income under
capitalism. By consuming labour-power in the process of production capitalist turn themselves into capitalists. To remain capitalists they must always repeat it. Buying labour-power at its
exchange-value and consuming it to yield new value is the social
relation that underlies the capitalist market economy. As Marx
scornfully pointed out, 'nature' does not produce on one side
owners of money and means of production, and on the other
men who possess nothing but their own labour-power. Such a
division of society into property-owning and propertyless classes is
not natural but social in origin, and its specific social basis is
not common to all historical forms of society. It is peculiar to
capitalism.

Capital springs into life only when the owner of money meets,
in the market, free workers selling their labour-power. What the
capitalist possesses is money which represents generalised exchange-value. Money being the common standard and measure
of all other commodities can normally be transformed into any of
them at will. From this viewpoint money is the first, most liquid,
and most general form of capital. Serving as the general index of
exchange-value, it gives access to the great mass of commodities
that appear on the market. In the society of simple commodity
producers the economic production takes the form of a constant
circulation of commodities – $C \to M \to C$. In the capitalist
market economy production is characterised instead by the circulation of capital – $M \to C \to M'$. The capitalist possessing
money (M) exchanges it for labour-power on the one hand and

raw materials and the technical means of production on the other. By consuming both in the process of production the capitalist creates commodities (C) that contain more value than the value paid for them. When these commodities are sold on the market the capitalist receives back a sum of exchange-values in the form of money (M') that is greater than the sum he had at the beginning. The difference results from the unequal exchange between capital and labour. It is the surplus value that was first *produced* in the process of production and then *realised* on the market.

Under capitalism, economic production is directed unceasingly towards increasing value. Production is only undertaken in the expectation that the money capital of the capitalist will be enlarged in the course of it. It is quite otherwise in the society of simple-commodity producers. There production is orientated to consumption. Each worker controls his own labour-power and disposes of the product of his labour. No surplus value arises. If the society grows richer it will be because the individual producers are able to raise their productivity. Under capitalism the labour process is directed by the capitalist class, because they purchase, in the market, the great bulk of all labour-power. In setting production in motion their aim is not *primarily* the production of use-values nor is it the profit that can be gained on any single exchange. It is the 'restless never ending process of profit-making' that rules the capitalist and must rule if capitalists are to remain capitalists. Production is therefore at the same time accumulation. Expanding value becomes its blind purpose.

ACCUMULATION

For Marx there are three essential aspects of capitalism: production of commodities according to socially necessary labour-time; their realisation or exchange on the market through the medium of money; and the accumulation of capital through the extraction of surplus value by the capitalist class. The consequence is an economic system which has an inner compulsion to expand production and raise productivity, yet which is at the same time ruled by certain laws that are inherent in its social basis, and which provide barriers and ultimate limits to its expansion. Marx's claim throughout his work is that, by understanding the real social basis of capitalism and analysing it in value terms, it becomes possible to move to a clear conception of the actual workings of capitalist economies. If the real social basis is not grasped and a false one, like the marginal utility theory, substituted, then economists can only analyse the economy at the level of immediate appearances, that is the phenomenon of price in the market. As in the case of inflation, they have either to leave out or introduce in an *ad hoc* and arbitrary fashion, the factors that alone can explain economic developments. The former course is followed by monetarists, the latter by Keynesians.

Capitalism is distinguished from all previous modes of production not by the use of machinery, or the application of science to production, but by the social relations in the process of production. Under capitalism the social surplus – whether measured in terms of output or labour – acquires a new form. It is no longer a sum of use-values in the shape of goods or services that are directly appropriated by a ruling class, as in feudalism; it is a sum of exchange-values that arise through a double process of exchange – first, in the exchange of money for living labour which creates the wage labourer and, secondly, in the exchange of the commodities produced by this living labour, with the aid of raw materials and tools, for money. The increase in money, the sum of exchange-values that accrues to the capitalist, is surplus value and represents the unpaid labour-time that the worker is forced to work for the capitalist. Surplus value is really the difference between the time the workers work for themselves (this replaces the value of their wages) and the time they have to work for the capitalist. Workers can only live by selling their labour-power to the capitalist class in exchange for a money payment – wages. Exploitation is an objective not a subjective aspect of the capitalist system. If there is no exploitation, there can be no capitalism. Every capital must exploit the workers it hires in order to wring from them a surplus value. Surplus value is at once the form which surplus labour takes under capitalism and it is the driving force of production. Since production is only undertaken to increase the value at the disposal of the capitalist, capitalists are compelled constantly to seek out new ways to increase the exploitation of their labour force in order to expand their capital at the fastest possible rate.

E

There are two main ways of increasing exploitation open to capitalists. Marx calls them the absolute and the relative extraction of surplus value, and exhaustively documents in *Capital* how they first appeared at different historical moments in capitalist economies. Absolute extraction means raising exploitation by squeezing more output from workers at a given wage. This can be done by either lengthening the hours they work, or by increasing the speed and intensity of the work. So workers come to work less reproducing the value of their own wages and more reproducing surplus value for the employer. Such methods were widespread in early capitalism, and remain the only effective way of raising the rate of exploitation where the industry is labour-intensive. They are crude and clearly subject to physical limits – the working day cannot be increased indefinitely, nor can the speed at which workers work. But the relative extraction of surplus value is different for it is not subject to such limits. Here the rate of exploitation is raised not by making the workers work harder or longer, nor by reducing wages, but by raising productivity, typically by investing more in means of production, in machines particularly. In this way workers' wages and conditions can constantly improve, so long as the productivity of labour and the rate of exploitation are increasing even more, and so long as the goods can be sold. This way of increasing the rate of exploitation has, of course, become the dominant form in modern capitalism, and accounts for the amazing growth in output and productivity which has been unleashed during the last one hundred years.

It is important to understand, since it is so often forgotten, that raising the rate of exploitation is not the same as depressing the standard of living of the working class. Marx merely asserted that raising the rate of exploitation was a constant necessity for capitalist expansion, and that this led to growing dependence of labour upon capital and a growing impoverishment of productive labour relative to the value appropriated by the capitalist class. This did not rule out rising real wages.

Despite the much greater scope for increasing the rate of exploitation through raising the productivity of labour the actual course of capital accumulation is never smooth. Marx expected it to oscillate violently. The contradictory nature of capitalist society would precipitate constant crises, which would appear as interruptions to production. In each such crisis certain barriers to further accumulation of capital would be revealed, and they would first have to be overcome before accumulation could resume. Marx predicted that as capitalism developed so the barriers to further accumulation would increase. Each major crisis would be more severe than the last, because of the size of the barriers to be removed. As capital pressed on towards its limits, developing the productive forces to unimaginable heights, so its social basis, its attempt to confine the productive potential of society within the narrow bounds of exchange- and surplus-value creation would increasingly become fetters on further economic development.

CRISES OF ACCUMULATION

A. The trade cycle and the industrial reserve army

Marx makes his analysis of crises under capitalism in two stages. He does not, however, have two theories of crisis, as Paul Sweezy argues.

At the most formal level the possibility of crisis is present in the way a market economy is organised. In such an economy purchase and sale are separated by the intervention of money. Since commodities are not directly bartered for one another but are produced and exchanged for money, a crisis is possible if some of the money is not used to buy other commodities, but is hoarded instead. This possibility was denied by Say and most other economists on the grounds that every sale was simultaneously a purchase, and generated enough effective demand to clear the market at the ruling price. Say's Law was a reasonable assumption to make for a society of simple-commodity producers, particularly if they regulated their affairs through barter. If they bartered their commodities, every sale was indeed simultaneously a purchase. If they exchanged for money then here too every sale could be assumed to be a purchase, since production was orientated to consumption, and commodities were only produced and sold for the purpose of buying other commodities. Say's mistake was to suppose that what was true of a barter economy and a monetary economy of simple-commodity producers was also true of a capitalist market economy. Marx showed it was not. There was no inherent reason for supply and demand to balance. Since production and exchange were orientated not to consumption but to profit there might very well be insufficient demand to clear the market if for some reason production became unprofitable. In such a situation, capitalists had every reason to hoard money, storing exchange-value, and not spending it. So the formal possibility of a crisis in any money-using market economy is a real possibility in capitalism. A situation of overproduction, slump and unemployment of resources is not an aberration but a perfectly natural expression of that economy's basic relationships.

Although he demonstrated that Say's Law did not hold for capitalism Marx did not base his theory of crisis upon that. On the contrary, throughout much of *Capital* he assumes that Say's Law does in fact hold, that is to say capitalism encounters no market problem, no problem of insufficient effective demand or excess capacity. Like the assumption that commodities sell at their labour-time values it is a simplifying assumption to lay bare the skeleton of capital accumulation, but which then has to be removed at a later stage of the analysis. While he is analysing crises that beset the accumulation of capital Marx conducts his analysis in value rather than price terms, and analyses capital in general, not individual competing capitals. The phenomena of competition, credit, prices and the market belong to the concrete analysis of capital. Again, failure to understand this has produced much confusion about Marx's method and his findings.

There are two reasons for crisis which are inherent in the accumulation of capital. One is the trade cycle through which capital accumulation moves; this is essentially short run. The second is the tendency for the organic composition of capital to rise in the course of capital accumulation and which causes the rate of profit to fall. This means that there are ultimate limits to production based on capital and its continual expansion. At some point capital finally exhausts its ability to expand production any further. Marx seeks to show that capitalist crisis is not some outside interference with the workings of a harmonious, felicitous system : it is inherent in the way the system works.

His initial analysis revolves around why the trade cycle, which was a noted characteristic of capitalism and normally covered a

period of ten years, was not an accidental but a necessary
feature of capitalist development. His explanation ran in terms
of the movement of real wages and the tendency of capital accumulation to create unemployment and an industrial reserve army.
The creation of surplus population is a necessary consequence of
accumulation. Once the point is reached in capital accumulation
where the development of the productivity of labour (that is the
relative extraction of surplus value) becomes the most powerful
lever of accumulation, then fewer productive workers need to be
employed, while the mass of the means of production with which
they work grows. Workers are made unemployed and go to
swell the numbers of the industrial reserve army. This population which is surplus in relation to the needs of capital accumulation is the 'pivot upon which the law of demand and supply
of labour works'.[8] It makes the part of the working class in employment still more dependent upon capital and thus tends to
keep down real wages. Marx commented that 'the greater the
social wealth, the functioning capital, the extent and energy of its
growth, and, therefore, also the absolute mass of the proletariat
and the productiveness of its labour, the greater is the industrial
reserve army'.[9] At the same time, capital, in order to accumulate
and maintain itself *as* capital, has to constantly produce on an
extended scale. It does so not merely by raising the rate of
exploitation of its existing labour force but by employing new
workers, searching out extra reserves of labour-power from which
to wring more surplus value. This tendency is especially marked
when times are prosperous and accumulation is proceeding
rapidly. Engaging extra workers will not harm the accumulation
of capital at all provided their wages do not encroach too far
on the surplus value that can be realised from their labour-power.
Increasing demand for labour during a boom can therefore mean
accelerating accumulation and rising real wages. But beyond a
certain point rising real wages will encroach on surplus value and
so 'blunt the stimulus of gain'. Accumulation at once slackens,
the industrial cycle moves into the phase of crisis, unemployment
rises sharply and real wages fall. When accumulation starts
again, it has to be with lower real wages and a reduced labour
force. Capitalists take the opportunity of the crisis to introduce
new machines and reorganise production. The crisis is the
crowning point of the cycle. It permits major structural changes

in the economy to be pushed through, changes which the ordinary workings of the market cannot achieve. It makes accumulation possible once more, by improving profit expectations. Expectations improve because many individual capitalists are bankrupted in the crisis and costs are lowered.

B.   *The organic composition of capital*

Of all Marx's concepts the organic composition of capital has been perhaps the most mysterious and most disputed. Yet Marx himself attached the greatest importance to it. Once accumulation was powered by rising productivity or relative extraction of surplus value, the organic composition of capital would rise and there would be a tendency for the rate of profit to fall and consequently creating an ultimate limit to further accumulation.

The concept itself is straightforward. At the outset of the production process capital exists as money in the hands of the capitalist. To become capital it must be exchanged for labour-power on the one hand and means of production on the other. What the capitalist parts with is money, which is in reality a sum of exchange-values. What he gains is the right to consume the use-value of labour-power by employing it to produce commodities. In the production process capital therefore has two forms – constant and variable. The capitalist must divide his money between outlays on raw materials and tools, and outlays on labour-power. The former represents his constant capital – constant because its value does not change in the production process. It is simply consumed by labour-power and its value preserved as part of the value of the new commodities that are produced. Outlays on labour-power represent variable capital. It is variable because, although the capitalist buys it for a specific sum of exchange-values (wages), labour-power not only reproduces the value of its wages but creates new value as well. How much new value depends on how high the rate of exploitation can be raised. So this part of capital is the variable part.

For the purposes of analysis Marx divides capital into two parts – constant and variable. Both parts appear as commodities, as must all goods and services in a market economy. As commodities they have both a use-value and an exchange-value. It follows that the composition of capital has two aspects – one is its *value composition*, the division into constant and variable capital, which is measured by exchange-value. The second is its *technical composition*, the proportion of machines and raw materials in relation to workers employed in production. Marx called the value composition 'in so far as it is determined by its technical composition and mirrors the changes of the latter, the organic composition of capital'.[10]

The organic composition of capital therefore expresses the relationship between living labour and the means of production in the process of production in terms of value (exchange-value) and of use. Marx believed that as soon as raising the productivity of labour through technological advance became more important for increasing the rate of exploitation than lengthening the working day or forcing the workers to work harder, then there is an inherent tendency for the organic composition of capital to rise. For, in order to raise productivity, capitalists are obliged to invest more of their capital in machines and raw materials in relation to labour-power. In this way the absolute number of workers employed by capital might rise as the scale of production expanded, but the number employed relative to the constant capital they set in motion would decrease. Such a development would have two contradictory consequences. On the one hand, it would steadily raise the productivity of labour and therefore the rate of exploitation. On the other hand, the variable part of capital, the only part that created new value, surplus value, would be burdened by an ever-increasing constant capital whose value had to be preserved before any net surplus value could be produced.

Marx predicted on the basis of this model of capital accumulation that in the long run the rise in the organic composition of capital brought about in order to raise productivity and the rate of exploitation would be faster than the actual increase in exploitation that it achieved. If this turned out to be the case there would be a tendency for the rate of profit to fall. The rate of profit is here understood in value rather than in price terms, that is it is the total surplus value which is earned on total social capital, before it is divided into its price components of profits, interest, rent, dividends, and unproductive consumption. In the extreme case of the rate of exploitation not rising at all, the fall in the rate of profit follows inexorably. If s is total profit, c is constant capital and v is variable capital, then the rate of profit is $s/(c + v)$. It follows that if c rises, then $s/(c + v)$ must fall.

Such an extreme case is inherently unlikely since the very purpose of increasing constant relative to variable capital is to increase the ratio s/v, the rate of exploitation. Marx posed the central dilemma of capitalism as a race between an increasing organic composition of capital and an increasing rate of exploitation. If the former rose faster than the latter the rate of profit would fall and beyond a certain point further capital accumulation would be impossible. In his analysis of the trade cycle and the industrial reserve army, Marx had noted how capital constantly tended to expel living labour from the production process by employing fewer productive workers in order to secure the greatest possible amount of surplus value from those that remained. He regarded the obstacles to constantly raising the rate of exploitation to offset the rising organic composition to be too great : 'With the development of capitalist production the mass of values to be simply reproduced or maintained increases as the productivity of labour grows, even if the labour-power employed should remain constant.'[11] Even before considering competition and the market and all the problems of realising surplus value once it had been produced, Marx showed the long-term course of capital accumulation was riven by a fatal contradiction. The real barrier of capitalist production is capital itself. Its social basis is at once the condition for enormously developing social productivity but, at the same time, it confines this development within narrow limits – the expansion and preservation of already existing *values*. As Marx wrote in one of the most famous passages from *Grundrisse* :

Capital itself is the moving contradiction, in that it presses to reduce labour-time to a minimum, while it posits labour-time on the other side as sole measure and source of wealth. Hence it diminishes labour-time in the necessary form so as to increase it in the superfluous form; hence posits the superfluous in growing measure as a condition – question of life or death – for the necessary. On the one side, then, it calls to life all the powers of science and of nature, as of social combination and of social intercourse, in order to make the creation of wealth independent (relatively) of the labour-time employed on it. On the other side, it wants to use labour-time as the measuring rod for the giant social forces thereby created, and to confine them within the limits required to maintain the already created value as value. Forces of production and social relations – two different sides of the development of the social individual – appear to capital as mere means, and are merely means for it to produce on its limited foundation. In fact, however, they are the material conditions to blow this foundation sky-high.[12]

THE REAL CRISIS

As the process of accumulation really gets under way and production takes place on an ever-expanding scale, so certain other tendencies assert themselves. Production is concentrated in increasingly fewer hands, labour is organised into social labour through growing co-operation and division of labour, and production is expanded until it covers the whole world and so creates the world market :

> The stupendous productivity developing under the capitalist mode of production relative to population and the increase, if not in the same proportion of capital values (not just of their material substance), which grow more rapidly than the population, contradict the basis, which constantly narrows in relation to the expanding wealth, and for which all this immense productiveness works. They also contradict the conditions under which this swelling capital augments its value. Hence the crises.[13]

But no actual crisis is confined to the realm of production. Under capitalism all economic developments must assert themselves through the market. The market is neither a simple reflector of a deeper reality nor is it the only reality. Marx's value analysis of capital accumulation is only the first step in the analysis of capitalist crises. The actual unfolding of crises in and through the market has still to be examined. It is not true, as some critics allege, that Marx had one theory of crises arising from production and the accumulation process and another of crises arising from realisation. This may be a way of presenting the problem for analysis, but it is misleading for it suggests that the two kinds of crisis can be separated empirically and can be tested independently of one another. At the level of the market, what has to be analysed are not value but price relationships. Capitalists do not, for example, make calculations in terms of labour-time values but in terms of money costs. They do not divide their capital into constant and variable components. For them, all costs are in principle the same, and profit is merely the surplus of revenue over costs. What concerns the capitalist, therefore, is the relationship between his 'price of production' and the market price. Turnover and the level of demand are as important as the level of costs in determining profits, because if there is no sale there can be no profit, and if turnover is low, then overhead costs will be more of a burden. Any actual collapse of profits always appears to the capitalist to be because demand is too low and costs are too high.

In studying the crisis in both its production and market dimensions it is necessary to look at two kinds of real phenomena – factors that counteract the tendency of the rate of profit to fall, and the problems of realising surplus value, which means introducing the sphere of circulation, competition and credit into the analysis. Many of the specific simplifying assumptions made for the purposes of value analysis, specifically Say's Law and the assumptions that commodities sell at their values, have now to be relaxed for analysis to proceed further.

In the process of accumulation social productivity is raised by reducing the number of production workers in relative terms and increasing the constant capital (both in terms of its size and its value) that they work with. Other things being equal this will cause the rate of profit to fall. But this tendency is usually checked by various counteracting influences which enable capital for long periods to enjoy crisis-free growth. Four have been of practical importance in the historical development of capitalism.

First, the rate of exploitation (s/v) has increased. This is not surprising since, as has been pointed out above, raising it is the object and purpose of increased investment in constant capital. It has been increased by reducing the number of productive workers, introducing machines that raise output, and reorganising work methods with the aid of such techniques of 'scientific management' as time-and-motion study.[14] By itself, however, these moves are rarely enough to wholly offset the tendency of the rate of profit to fall, since capitalists are not free agents. Competition from other capitalists forces them to concentrate production, adopt the latest techniques and machinery and so increase their outlay on constant capital. The increase in the rate of exploitation that these bring is not always sufficient to prevent the rate of profit on total capital from falling.

Secondly, technological advance may well have a capital-saving bias. If the elements of constant capital are continually being cheapened by the discovery of, say, more efficient ways of extracting raw materials or by the invention of machines of much greater productive capacity, then the value of constant capital will not rise so fast as its mass is increasing. This is, of course, the normal pattern of development. The quantity of machines and raw materials used up in production has grown prodigiously in the last hundred years. But the portion of total value which these represent has obviously increased nowhere near as fast, and in some periods it is probable that it did not increase at all. In the long run, however, the capital-saving bias of technological innovation is unlikely to be sustained. It is only capital-saving, in any case, as regards the sector producing consumer goods. For the capital-goods sector, its ability to cheapen some of the inputs of the rest of the economy depends on its own innovations being labour-saving. As these spread to the rest of the economy (as appears to be the case at the moment)[15] so the organic composition of capital may rise sharply.

The third main counteracting force is the constant pressure towards extending the scale and scope of capital accumulation. This means sucking into the orbit of capital whole new populations both inside national frontiers and without. The stimulus to such expansion is that with new populations the rate of exploitation is generally higher, the organic composition of capital generally less. Hence both the rate of profit and the mass of profit are higher than for those sectors where accumulation is already at an advanced stage. This explains the ruthless penetration of capital into less-developed areas of the world. Other modes of production are systematically destroyed. The over-all effect of this is the construction of the world market, the dragging of all peoples and economies into trading with one another, a world division of labour. For a long time, therefore, accumulation in new areas of the world market can offset for the capitalist the tendency for the rate of profit to fall. In the long run though the world market has obvious limits. Indefinite expansion is ruled out. Even capital eventually runs out of populations it can exploit profitably, and the cost of maintaining its domination of the world market becomes burdensome, as even the United States has found.

Finally, another factor that counters the tendency of the rate of profit to fall is the rising absolute mass of surplus value – the increasing of surplus at the disposal of the capitalist. Baran and Sweezy's tendency for surplus to rise is not an alternative to the tendency of the rate of profit to fall. It is only another aspect of the same phenomenon. As capital is accumulated on an ever-greater scale, as each increment in surplus value is fed back into the production process, employing more workers, more machines, more raw materials, so the mass of surplus value must rise whatever happens to the rate of profit. The latter is calculated on the total capital that is advanced. So it can decline relatively to total capital whilst still growing in absolute terms. Surplus value is not the same as surplus, and the share that capitalists have of the national income does not depend on the share or the rate of profit as it is normally understood. For as Sismondi wrote on this question : 'Of those who share the national income among themselves, the one side (the workers) acquire every year a fresh right to their share by fresh work; the others (the capitalists) have already acquired, by work done originally, a permanent right to their share.'[16]

At the end of a production cycle the capitalists have changed M for M'. This increased amount of exchange-value, even if it is only won by a fall in the rate of profit, is still sufficient to compensate the capitalist for that fall. When they have not only successfully produced but realised an increased surplus value, the capitalists must then divide it. A part must be consumed as revenue and spent on the goods and services they need. The rest they must transform back into capital and throw into production to accumulate. From the standpoint of capital all private consumption by the capitalist is robbery perpetrated against accumulation. So there develops, in Marx's words, a 'Faustian conflict' in the breast of each capitalist between accumulation and consumption. All surplus value that is consumed as revenue is lost forever. Only capital constantly increases.

Yet the tendency for the organic composition of capital to rise and the rate of profit to fall means that capitalist crises risk becoming ever more severe. So to offset these dangers and keep accumulation profitable, a growing proportion of the increasing mass of surplus is diverted from accumulation to consumption. Like all such consumption it is unproductive in relation to capital. Only consumption and labour that increases surplus value can be considered productive in the capitalist sense. Yet the growth in capitalists' consumption is not directed at increasing their private consumption of actual goods and services, though this may increase. From the standpoint of the system as a whole, it is directed far more at creating conditions under which surplus value can still be produced and realised. The two most important categories of such expenditure, as noted by Baran and Sweezy, are the sales effort and government spending. But this kind of expenditure is a *deduction* from surplus value, not an additional means of 'disposing of surplus'. They can only properly be understood as expressions of the tendency for the organic composition of capital to rise and the rate of profit to fall. They are not planned, they are necessary; and their necessity derives not from political considerations or the inadequacy of markets but from the nature of capital accumulation itself.

It is in this sense that the organic composition of capital must be understood. Seeking to measure it directly by attempting to convert values into prices mistakes the real problems and the level of analysis. What can be directly measured is not the organic composition of capital itself but its effects – in particular, the narrowing base of capital accumulation, the growth of state and unproductive expenditures, the concentration of capital, and the creation of a world market. These are all consequences of the basic nature of capital accumulation which the concept of organic composition of capital was formulated to express. Capital constantly develops towards its furthest limits. It overcomes the barriers to its further development by breaking through them. From one aspect, state expenditure has the effect of preventing a drastic rise in the organic composition of capital by taking away from individual capitalists most of the cost of infrastructure, research and development, and the training and maintaining of an efficient labour force. From another aspect, it maintains a high level of effective demand, so enabling surplus value to be realised, by ensuring that goods produced are sold. Yet the very means of breaking through barriers to accumulation eventually raises still greater barriers. In the case of the state, public expenditure intensifies the 'Faustian conflict' between accumulation and consumption. It undermines the reserve army of labour and it unleashes permanent inflation in its bid to secure full employment and prosperity.

The basic cause of crisis in capitalism is thus the barriers inherent in the very process of capital accumulation which rear up whenever accumulation falters. But the form of every crisis is always a crisis of markets, of realising surplus value. In the production cycle there are two phases M (Money) $\rightarrow C$ (Capital) constant and variable and $C \rightarrow Cm$ (Commodities) $\rightarrow M'$. No matter how much surplus value can be produced in the first phase, it will be of no consequence to capital unless it can be realised through the sale of the finished goods. At the beginning and end of the production cycle, exchange-value intervenes. It is the hoop through which all production must pass, if values existing at the beginning of production are to be preserved and expanded. Without realisation of surplus value the social basis of capitalism crumbles. Every real crisis of accumulation, therefore, is simultaneously a crisis of realisation. It appears as a conflict between production and consumption. There is too little effective demand in relation to productive capacity. At the same time, the fact that this is only the appearance and not the cause of the crisis is shown by the apparently contradictory fact that, in a crisis, costs and particularly wages are always singled out for being too high. They must be lowered to make investment profitable once more. Yet the most obvious feature of the crisis is that consumers do not have the money to buy all the output of industry. Over-production and excess capacity are everywhere. Goods pile up in warehouses, new cars in disused airfields and bricks in builders' stacks. Purchase and sale are broken apart. Rather then change money back into capital and throw it back into production, the capitalist hoards it. The crisis can be mitigated by the government stepping in to increase effective demand through its spending and deficit financing. But for accumulation to resume on an extended scale once more, the barriers to accumulation have first to be overcome. These barriers are always political and economic in nature and grow out of the process of accumulation itself. In the early stages of capitalism crises were normally sharp, but did not last long. Recovery was swift. A fall in real wages brought about by a rise in the industrial reserve army of unemployed often sufficed. The paradox, however, is that as the accumulation of capital has progressed, so the barriers have grown larger. Booms and slumps are magnified. The scale of the productive forces makes booms times of unparalleled prosperity and economic progress. By contrast, the slumps threaten to be graver, deeper and longer lasting than ever before. The forces that nourish the boom do so by preventing the organic composition of capital from rising and the rate of profit from falling. When they are exhausted, as at present, capital meets its limits. Further development of the productive forces, even maintenance of their existing level, cries out for the abolition of the social basis of capitalist production.

VALUE AND PROFIT : THE PRESENT CONTROVERSY

There has always been a current of thought within Marxism which has tried to amend Marx's approach to capitalism, usually on the grounds that it was no longer applicable. A major issue is the vexed question of whether the falling rate of profit, usually regarded as central to Marx's crisis theory, is essential for explaining the depth and nature of the present crisis.

The questions of how crucial this tendency is, what are the causes of a particular fall, or indeed is there a fall at all, have long been preoccupations of serious Marxist scholarship. The positions taken in such a controversy, both political and technical, are difficult for even the most committed to comprehend. Yet some mention must be made of them for even orthodox journals now see fit to publish articles tackling such problems. One of the leading organs of U.K. finance capital, *Lloyds Bank Review*, published an article in 1973 by two aptly named gentlemen, Panic and Close, which set out to tackle the problem empirically. Entitled 'Profitability of British Manufacturing Industry', the article tried to reassure readers that predictions of 'the imminent collapse of the economic system' as a result of the United Kingdom's long-term decline of profitability were unnecessarily panicky. Their results, however, cannot have given much cheer. For they concluded that 'there has been a decline in the rate of

profit in the manufacturing sector over the last two decades'. They
attributed this to increased competition, and the inability of firms
to pass on all their costs in higher prices. Yet they still argued that
the term 'crisis in profitability' was inapplicable because the 'U.K.
experience was not all that different from what happened in
West Germany',[17] and, anyway, most of the decline occurred
during the 1950s.

On their calculations for the rate of profit, measured as the
rate of return on capital employed in the United Kingdom and
West Germany, they obtained the following results. In the United
Kingdom post-tax returns fell from 9·5 per cent in 1961 to 7·8
per cent in 1969. Whilst in West Germany they remained much
steadier, being 5·2 per cent in 1961 and 5·4 per cent in 1969.
They believe that these figures indicate that there is a profits
problem, but not a profits crisis. The comparison with West Germany is meant to indicate that a falling rate of profit does no
serious harm to the economy.

Are the present signs, therefore, of a widespread profits crisis
throughout the O.E.C.D. area, coupled with inflation, and rising
unemployment and short-time working, illusory? Recent empirical evidence seems solid enough – yet it is not merely a factual
question. For facts are processed, produced and handled within
theories and analytic frameworks. The national income figures
for the United Kingdom do not show rates of profit, only the
absolute share of profits in the national income. Even at the level
of technical calculations there is hot dispute. This is because
these questions are never really technical but theoretical and
political.

One recent study by M. A. King, 'The U.K. profits crisis :
myth or reality?',[18] argues that many of the assumptions in studies
of profitability have been loose scientifically. However, his own
rather more careful analysis still confirms that there is a profits
squeeze. King calculates the share of gross trading profits (before
and after tax, with and without deductions for capital consumption and stock appreciation) generated by manufacture. His
principal conclusions are that, from 1950 to 1973, there has been
a downward trend in the share of profits before tax, that tax
concessions seem to prevent a post-tax fall, that if one deducts
stock appreciation (high in periods of inflation) from profits,
then even the post-tax profit shares declined after 1966, with a

particularly sharp fall in 1969–71. The *National Institute Economic Review*[19] for January 1975 also shows a fall of profits in the share of G.D.P., net of stock appreciation, from 14·8 per cent in 1963 to 11·6 per cent in 1969 and 9·6 per cent in 1973. Another important study by G. J. Burgess and A. J. Webb, which reviews various measures of profitability, including those of Glyn and Sutcliffe, concluded : 'All the profit-share or rate-of-return series which we have considered indicate similar trends when allowance is made for cyclical factors. Before tax, both profit shares and rates of return have been in decline since the early 1950s. After tax, there is evidence that profit shares have been in decline at least since the mid-1960s, whilst rates of return have been falling from the early 1960s.'[20]

These important empirical studies conducted by establishment economists, have been discussed by socialist economists attempting to relate trends within capitalism to Marx's value analysis and his predictions of an eventual decline in the rate of profit. The first socialists to raise the issue before a large readership were Andrew Glyn and Bob Sutcliffe in their important work, *British Capitalism, Workers and the Profits Squeeze* published in 1972. They convincingly put the evidence for a fall in the rate and share of profits. Unfortunately they tend to have a rather Ricardian model of the relationship between capital and labour, which treats workers' gains as capital's losses and vice versa. This 'zero-sum' conception of capitalist society implies that a gain by one class is a loss for the other. However, this is oversimplified. In periods of expansion and rapid growth, rising real incomes (in percentage and absolute terms) can be coupled with an increase in the absolute amount of profit as well as in the rate of profit. Despite such criticisms, the book was of major importance in stimulating Marxist political economy. Indeed Glyn and Sutcliffe are in the vanguard of serious attempts to develop empirical measures of Marx's concepts.

Glyn's important recent article in the *Bulletin of the Conference of Socialist Economists*[21] reviews the evidence on profits since the original book appeared. Some of the attempts to measure the rate of profit aim at the real rate, but fail to take out stock appreciation from profits or to revalue capital, in which case, 'neither the monetary or real rate is measured'. He cogently argues that the figures used by Panic and Close are completely useless because of this. In general, he is able to show that the various studies that have appeared recently, either confirm the original Glyn and Sutcliffe thesis about the trend of the rate and share of profit, or else use different measures and assumptions which are inadequate. He demonstrates this particularly in discussing how a price index should be constructed to deflate the rising money value of capital. Taking the consumer price index as King suggests in his article falsely implies that the driving force for capital accumulation is capitalists' own consumption. Since the real driving force is the accumulation of exchange-value the monetary profit rate should be deflated by the over-all price index for production as a whole. This would give the real profit rate. Glyn agrees that the figures show that both wages and profits have declined after tax. The big expansion has been in the proportion of national income taken by government. The squeeze on profits was maintained after 1970 and became critical in 1974.

Empirical evidence, therefore, points to a marked and continuing squeeze on profits. This is the traditional indicator of crisis in a capitalist economy. But given that such a squeeze exists, how is it to be explained? Is Marx's value analysis really relevant?

THE FALLING RATE OF PROFIT : THE LONG DEBATE

Ever since the publication of Marx's *Capital*, there has been incessant debate between Marxist economists over which propositions are central and which are relatively incidental to Marx's theory of capital accumulation and crisis. In Volumes I and III of *Capital*, applying the labour theory of value, Marx demonstrates that there is an inherent tendency for the capitalist system of production to stagnate and fall into crisis as a result of the falling rate of profit. This prediction, which is stated as a tendency rather than some iron law, may be countered by forces which can prevent its occurrence during particular historical periods. The uncovering of this long-term tendency was regarded by Marx as one of his major achievements. Many Marxists have commented on the difficulties of operationalising the concepts in a way that allows them to be empirically tested. One obvious objection to such tests is that the tendency is a very long-term relationship, whilst most empirical work is done with relatively short-term statistical series. The importance of Glyn and Sutcliffe's work mentioned above is that it seeks to find econometric measures which are consistent with Marx's assumptions. Despite such endeavours, the empirical questions remain at the centre of political and theoretical controversy. The complexity and importance of the debate can best be seen by examining briefly the arguments of two recent contributions, both of which are articulated with considerable scientific skill.

Geoff Hodgson has discussed the question in an article in *New Left Review*[22] in which he attempts to refute the 'theory of the falling rate of profit' on the grounds that there is no justification, either theoretical or empirical, for assuming that the organic composition of capital rises in the course of capitalist development. Marx's view was that the general rate of profit is given by the rate of profit in value terms, its surplus value, divided by value of capital invested. Marx initially treats the whole economy as a single Capital and equates the general with the average rate of profit. Hodgson believes that this is unjustified. On theoretical grounds he tries to show that 'if the physical and value aspects of accumulation are separated, then there is no reason to suppose that technical change will have any particular bias in the long run'. The actual bias of technical progress cannot be predicted from any model of capital accumulation. In saying this he chooses, as David Yaffe points out, to reject Marx's method of analysis in *Capital*, claiming it is Hegelian and idealistic. The question is, what does he have to put in its place?

Hodgson also reviews the empirical evidence for an increase in organic composition, ignoring the fact that, since organic composition is a value concept, it cannot be measured directly; only its effects are observable. The only major studies that have been carried out are by Gillman and Mage which have been widely criticised on the grounds that they do not measure value relationships, that is the ratios between amounts of socially necessary labour-time. (See J. M. Gillman, *The Falling Rate of Profit* (London, 1957) and S. H. Mage, 'The Law of the Falling Tendency of the Rate of Profit', Columbia University, Ph.D. thesis.) In some respects, Mage comes nearest to an operational division. Moreover, the data that he collected does show a small upward trend in the figures. Hodgson interprets these figures differently, arguing that one must discount the high figure in the years of depression. The rise was caused by the depression, not vice versa. Hodgson argues from this and other evidence, particularly Kuznet's figures on capital–output ratios, that the law of the tendency of the rate of profit to fall should be rejected. The question why the rate of profit is falling becomes 'an investigation into the causes of concrete socio-economic convulsions'. Glyn and Sutcliffe adopt a similar position. They also believe that the profits squeeze is not due to rising organic composition of capital. It is falling because of increased international competition and worker militancy. The weakness of such positions is that they cannot explain why international competition and worker militancy should themselves increase. As in Keynesian and marginalist analysis, these factors have to be imported into the analysis from outside, as self-sufficient principles to provide explanations. That is because only the market phenomena of capitalism are analysed, however much they may be fitted into a 'value' framework.

David Yaffe makes value analysis central to Marxism in several important recent articles.[23] He argues that abandoning the organic composition of capital argument is to reject Marx's whole value analysis, which leaves Marxism reduced to Ricardian economics plus crude factual empiricism. As Yaffe indicates, a scientific analysis of capitalism can only explain the phenomenon of the market, and in particular competition, if it is based upon notions of value, and capital in general. So long as one class has to sell its labour-power to live, and another owns the means of production, then capitalist production will be subject to specific laws of motion. Marx's analysis of value in terms of labour-time reveals that labour is treated as a commodity for capitalists – labour-power. The development of the social productivity of labour under capitalism finds expression in a rising organic composition of capital because constant capital grows faster than variable capital. If the rate of exploitation does not increase sufficiently then the rise in the organic composition will cause a fall in the rate of profit. He quotes Marx :

The tendency of the rate of profit to fall is bound up with a tendency of the rate of surplus value to rise, hence with a

tendency for the rate of labour exploitation to rise. . . . Both
the rise in the rate of surplus value and the fall in the rate
of profit are but specific forms through which growing productivity of labour is expressed under capitalism.

Yaffe also stresses that, despite impressions to the contrary,
Marx did not treat value and price as the same thing. The transformation problem is based on a misunderstanding, on a futile
quest to find a way of making values proportional to prices. Yet
that does not mean value can be dispensed with. As Marx states,
'if the limits of value and surplus value are given it is easy to
grasp how competition of capitals transforms value into prices
of production and further into mercantile prices, and surplus
value into average profit'. If value is not the starting point, how
is it possible to understand how and why things get produced?
Without social labour-time as a standard, price has no meaning,
nor have changes in the general rate of profit any explanation.

Yaffe underlines the fact that Marx develops a theory of
money which has been generally ignored. Yet without a theory
of money, it is not possible to talk about the relationship between
value and price. Few Marxists have ever understood Marx on
money. Money acts both as a measure of value and as a standard
of price. Marx attacked those, like Proudhon and other 'labour-
time chitters' who wanted to overthrow capitalism by overthrowing money.

> The first basic illusion of the time chitters consists in this,
> that by annulling the nominal difference between real value
> and market value, between exchange and price – that is by
> expressing value in units of labour-time itself instead of in a
> given objectification of labour-time, say gold or silver – that in
> doing so they remove the real difference and contradiction
> between price and value.[24]

Yaffe's position is the most authoritative reading of Marx at
present available. He justifies Marx's method of analysis by
showing the inadequacy of other approaches. It alone can show
how money and fiscal crises are and must be related to a crisis of
production. To abandon value theory is to pursue an empty and
anchorless empiricism. Marx's method must first be understood
before empirical tests of his concepts are attempted. Any measure

of the rise in the organic composition of capital has to take into account the massive size of the state sector. For the state now provides much social capital; it socialises the costs of capital accumulation and is the most visible expression of the unproductive sector of the economy. It does not produce surplus value for capital directly in most of its operations, yet these operations are necessary for any capital accumulation to exist at all. The long debate is not over; it has taken a new turn. Only value analysis provides a framework in which the present crisis and its confusing manifestations, such as inflation, can be adequately discussed. The role of the state is central, but is only possible to understand the role that it plays by relating it to accumulation. The science of crisis reflects the politics, as yet still unresolved.

5

The End of the Boom

The right remedy for the trade cycle is not to be found in abolishing booms and thus keeping us permanently in a semi-slump; but in abolishing slumps and thus keeping us permanently in a quasi-boom.

Lord Keynes, *The General Theory of Employment, Interest and Money* (London : Macmillan, 1973) p. 322.

THE GREAT DEPRESSION

In many ways the 1930s marked a watershed. Far from being some accidental interruption to the smooth path of capitalist development, the depression exposed the tendencies inherent in capital accumulation. It clearly revealed the changing structure of capitalist markets and the need for the state to play a much greater role in the capitalist economy. By the 1930s production had become increasingly concentrated to take advantage of economies of scale and because relentless competition between capitals allowed the successful companies to grow at the expense of the rest. This tendency towards monopoly was further strengthened by the centralisation of capital – the amalgamation of different firms into much larger units under co-ordinated financial control. By the 1930s the economies of the most advanced capitalist states had already assumed their familiar modern look; a division between corporate capital, the sector of giant financial and industrial companies which dominated their own markets and industries, and small capital, the sector of numerous but small firms, of declining importance in the economy.

Corporate capital was clearly the main agent of the accumulation of capital by the 1930s. Not only was its rate of growth higher and its profits bigger, it was also the instrument by which 'private' labour and 'private' production were increasingly becoming social, collective and interdependent. It was the main agency by which technological innovation was integrated into the production process, and it also accounted for the bulk of foreign investment and foreign trade. How such corporate monsters could have emerged out of the placid marginalist world of perfect competition remains a real mystery for many economists. But it was the outcome predicted by Marx's model of capital accumulation.

The second feature of the Great Depression that needs to be noted is that it was the period when the central importance of the state in modern capitalism was widely recognised. State sectors and public expenditure had been growing, but little attention had been paid to these phenomena. When the crisis broke, however, all the new radical political solutions for overcoming it stressed the role of the state. This was as true for those plans that were not adopted, like Oswald Mosley's and Keynes's in the United Kingdom, as for those that were, like the New Deal in the United States, or the National Socialist policy in Germany. During the 1930s it became apparent that the powers of the state had to be employed if high levels of output and employment, let alone growth, were to be assured. The orthodox still preached the conventional wisdom of the nineteenth century – a balanced budget, monetary restraint, cuts in real wages. That had ended most previous slumps. Many economists argued, and still do, that the 1930s slump was only a rather more severe example of the traditional downswing in the trade cycle, and could be cured by the same medicine. The realists pointed to the changed nature of the economy. Prices were no longer highly flexible, so the political consequences of standing aside and allowing millions of unemployed to solve the accumulation problems of monopoly capitalism were frightening. A much easier weapon lay to hand. By expanding domestic money supply through government spending, effective demand, output and profits could all be raised together.

This was the policy pursued in Germany, Sweden and the United States and advocated in the United Kingdom. In the United States between 1929 and 1931 industrial production declined 28 per cent, wholesale prices dropped by one-third and wages fell 39 per cent. Yet despite these massive price falls, unemployment in 1931 rose to 14 million or 23 per cent of the working population, and 50 per cent of total productive capacity stayed unused. So long as prices were falling business would not invest; only if wages were to fall even further would profit expectations improve. The degree of flexibility in prices that was required was too great. The New Deal, by contrast, inaugurated by Roosevelt in 1933, aimed at relieving distress and aiding recovery by raising both prices and incomes. The gold standard was suspended which gave the federal authorities the necessary control over the economy. Budget deficits, loans to industry, new public-work schemes, payments to the unemployed, all were attempted in order to damp down social unrest and get the economy moving again.[1]

THE LONG BOOM

Despite the greater appreciation of the role the modern state could play in restoring the conditions for profitable accumulation, the international barriers to growth made further prosperous development under capitalism remote in the 1930s. The New Deal did not rescue the United States from depression. The economy slumped again in 1938. Output fell 30 per cent and unemployment increased sharply. In 1939 it was still 17 per cent. The only way out seemed to be that course of action employed by Germany, which found that forcibly holding down wages by means of political terror and providing huge arms orders for industry allowed highly profitable production and hence a burst of accumulation. Politically, such a path led directly to war in an effort to secure the extra markets and raw materials German industry so badly needed and could not, at that time, secure by other means.

Other major barriers included the fragmentation of the international monetary system and world market and the absence of major new industries that could generate a high level of primary and secondary investment. Capitalism increasingly seemed stuck in a mire of stagnation and excess capacity. Wages and costs were too high; there was overproduction and markets proved inadequate. The basic cause was insufficient profits to finance accumulation on an expanded scale again.

The Great Depression, the greatest and longest period of crisis and stagnation the capitalist economy had known, ended in the Second World War. All those who believed that the fundamental cause of the depression was inadequate markets also believed that the economy would lapse back into permanent stagnation once the short post-war boom was over. Yet the short post-war boom turned into the longest and fastest period of expansion capitalism has yet known. If our analysis is correct, then it should be possible, in describing the factors that made the long boom possible, to describe also the present barriers to further accumulation and the present phenomena of capitalist crisis. For both are rooted in the way capital is accumulated. In this sense there are three main factors that sustained the boom and are now barriers in the path of further accumulation: the international monetary system, the rate of profit, and the state.

THE INTERNATIONAL MONETARY SYSTEM

One of the consequences of the accumulation of capital is the creation of the world market. Capital constantly pushes beyond the bounds of the nation state and the existing economy searching for the highest rates of return and new sources of profit. In this way all other nations and populations outside the capitalist economy are gradually pulled into its orbit. Universal exploitation, constant increase in surplus labour, is the result.

The creation of the world market extends the sway of capital and maintains profitable accumulation. At the same time it creates new problems for capital. These problems lie in the nature of money and the nation state. As argued earlier, the capitalist economy has to be analysed as a system of production and as a system of markets. These do not exist independently of one another. In the real world they always exist together, so that the tendencies of production find expression only through the workings of the market. The production cycle is ruled by exchange-value which appears on the market in the form of money. Money therefore has a contradictory role in a market economy – it is both a medium of exchange and a standard of value. It must circulate in the market all the commodities that are produced, but it must also represent the value of these commodities. It is their common standard, the universal equivalent. If it is to perform this task adequately, it must measure the only aspect of commodities that is common to all of them – the labour-time required to produce them – and it must itself remain reasonably stable in value. That is why gold and the other precious metals became the adequate form of money in a market economy. Gold is a commodity and must be produced like any other. It embodies a part of total social labour-time. Since its production requires expenditure of labour-power its supply cannot be increased indefinitely. Provided the metal is not itself debased it follows that it is a stable standard of exchange and value. It is a universal equivalent in which everyone has confidence. Gold itself need not circulate. A paper currency may replace it, provided it is backed by gold and can be converted into it. The central monetary authority that issues the notes guarantees their value.

At the international level, however, problems arise. Once accumulation of capital and trade push beyond national boundaries, the need arises for an international money. Once again a commodity that is both an efficient means of exchange and a stable standard of value must be discovered. Yet, in a world of separate nation states, there can be no international monetary authority to enforce and police the use of one form of money in exchange. How can different countries each with different levels of output and productivity exchange their commodites except by barter? What is needed is some measure of international labour-time to ensure that goods are exchanged fairly. No such measure exists, or is on the agenda for the future. The exchange-value of commodities appears on the market not as labour-time, but as price. How can the prices of different commodities produced in different countries under different conditions and expressed in different currencies be established, in a way that each nation feels is fair and just, so that trade may be promoted?

The answer once seemed straightforward. If labour-time is the objective form of exchange-value, then gold is the objective form of money. Gold alone, because it is a commodity and has a labour-time value like any other commodity, can command international confidence and be used to settle debts. Governments can control currencies they themselves print. They cannot control gold. It is beyond their grasp. That makes gold internationally acceptable, and makes it inevitable that gold should normally be the favourite foundation for the international monetary system.

There is no special mysticism about gold, at least no more than there is for any other commodity. What gives gold *value* is not something inherent in it but its capacity to represent exchange-value – the different quantity of labour-time embodied in each commodity. The international monetary system that developed in the nineteenth century was based upon gold – known as the gold standard. All national currencies were given a fixed price in terms either of gold or of sterling, which was itself pegged to gold. Trading deficits had to be settled ultimately by the countries exporting gold to their creditors. Moreover, their domestic money supply was tied to gold, because all notes and coins in circulation were convertible into it. So if gold had to be exported, causing the reserves to fall, action would have to be taken to reduce the domestic money supply, thus freezing credit and raising unemployment. In full operation the gold standard meant real internationalism – national governments lost control over their domestic money supply. Adjustments were automatic, and seemed to be part of the natural order. Within this framework free trade was expected to promote maximum efficiency and economic progress, creating a world division of labour by encouraging countries to specialise at what they could produce most cheaply.

The beauties of the gold standard prevented recognition of certain realities. It was initially established and only worked because of the industrial and commercial supremacy of one nation state – the United Kingdom. This meant that, alongside gold, sterling was acceptable as an international currency. Holding sterling gave access to the U.K. market and the products of U.K. industry. This enabled the United Kingdom to export huge funds overseas and to extract maximum benefit from free trade which, for a time, allowed her industries to exploit their competitive advantage in the world market.

The gold standard crumbled, however, when the imperial power of the United Kingdom and the *laissez-faire* phase of capitalism declined. Free trade was increasingly rejected by the United Kingdom's major new rivals, like Germany and the United States, who preferred to build up their industries behind tariff walls. As the competition between nation states and their rival capitals grew more intense, so imperialism expanded, and almost the entire world was divided up between the major powers

by the end of the nineteenth century. There appeared a growing
contradiction between the international nature of world production and the territorial division for appropriation of profits and
control of markets among nation states. This intensified the political, cultural and strategic conflicts of nations which ultimately
erupted in the First World War.

In the inter-war years, the United Kingdom made a vain
attempt to rebuild the gold standard and with it its own power,
but her industrial strength was now below that of her rivals, particularly the United States. Sterling was, as a result, no longer
such an acceptable international currency. Adhering to the gold
standard had increasingly disastrous consequences in the age of
advancing monopoly capitalism. It meant for the United
Kingdom, after her return to the gold standard at the pre-war
parity in 1925, the need to cut wage rates. This open revelation
of the class structure of society led to the great General Strike of
1926. Its defeat was followed by several years of stagnation. The
rest of the world economy was booming during the late 1920s.
Still more important it meant that, faced by the slump of
1929–32 and the Great Depression, governments remaining on
the gold standard had no means of using domestic monetary
expansion to prevent unemployment. The gold standard was
unwieldy and tended to be inflexible. Mere governments had no
choice. At the height of the slump in the United States, the
Federal Reserve, far from trying to increase the money supply
and expand credit, raised interest rates so as to stem the outflow
of the reserves. Country after country was eventually forced off
the gold standard, because the internal costs of settling international debts in gold and shackling the domestic money supply to
the gold reserves were too great. The United Kingdom abandoned gold in 1931 after the fall of the Labour Government,
which split over measures to balance the budget and so safe-
guarded sterling by cutting the dole of the unemployed. The world
market rapidly fragmented into a number of currency blocs –
based on the pound, the dollar, the mark, and gold. There was
no generally acceptable international currency any more – currencies were now mostly inconvertible, so trade had to be
arranged in bilateral deals. Trade naturally recovered very little.
By 1939 world trade was only what it had been at the beginning
of the 1920s.

After 1945, however, the international monetary system was reorganised and reunified under U.S. leadership. The United States emerged from the war as by far the strongest and most advanced industrialised nation in the world. Furthermore, its industrial capacity was still intact, whilst that of all its rivals was either in ruins or severely depleted. The United States imposed, as the United Kingdom had done, a new economic and political order on to the world economy and sought to promote free movement of goods and capital through the world market once more. In one respect, however, U.S. control was less than that dominance once achieved by the United Kingdom. The Soviet Union, and subsequently China, were shut out from the world market and refused to take part in the new arrangements. So almost one-third of the world was denied, at the outset, to U.S. penetration, and became organised as a separate power bloc within the world economy. The Soviet and Chinese currencies stayed inconvertible, and trade between them and the rest of the world was arranged only on a bilateral basis.

The new monetary arrangements that established dollar hegemony over the rest of the world were set up at Bretton Woods in 1944. It was called a gold exchange standard, because, like the modified gold standard of the 1920s, world money included not just gold but acceptable international currencies as well. Currencies were no longer freely convertible into gold within each national economy, but remained convertible, in principle, internationally. The dollar was given a fixed price in terms of gold, $35 an ounce, and all other currencies were then fixed in terms of the dollar. In the early years other currencies were not freely convertible into one another or into dollars because of the immense dollar shortage that existed. The United Kingdom's early attempt, at the insistence of the United States, to make sterling convertible in 1947 led to a devastating run on sterling, and had to be abandoned. But by the end of the 1950s the world economy had revived sufficiently for all the major currencies to be freely convertible.

The dollar assumed a contradictory role in the new international monetary system. On the one hand, it was not convertible into gold domestically, so there was no external control over domestic money supply. U.S. governments could expand and contract it according to their view of the needs of the domestic economy. On the other hand, the dollar was convertible into gold internationally. That meant it was acceptable as an international currency, and because there was a dollar shortage due to the desire of the rest of the world to buy U.S. goods, the dollar appeared for a long time to be 'as good as gold'. In the early post-war years, when the rest of the world had a desperate need for industrial goods of all kinds but no industrial capacity to produce them, or to produce exports to pay for them, the United States extended loans, credit and aid – the most famous being Marshall Aid – to provide the dollars that were needed. In return the hegemony of the dollar was assured.

The international currency status of the dollar reflected the higher productivity of the U.S. economy compared to any other, just as the strength of sterling had reflected the United Kingdom's industrial superiority in the nineteenth century. But there was a crucial difference between the gold standard and the gold exchange standard. Under the first, paper currency could be exchanged into gold both domestically and internationally, and this meant there was an automatic constraint on expansion of the domestic money supply and on the building up of trade deficits. This applied to the United Kingdom no less than to the other countries that adhered to it. Under the gold exchange standard there was no such check on an indefinite expansion of the domestic money supply. This meant also that there was no automatic constraint on the country holding the major reserve currency to prevent it running balance-of-payments deficits and financing them by making other countries hold more of their international reserves in dollars.

This is exactly what the United States did. After running enormous trading surpluses in the first few years after 1945, the U.S. balance of payments began to deteriorate. This was because there was an increasing outflow of funds abroad. The two main kinds of expenditure were foreign investment and overseas military spending. Dollar hegemony allowed U.S. capital to roam the world market seeking out the most profitable investments, and overseas military spending by the U.S. government became necessary to make and keep the world free for U.S. capital and goods. U.S. imperialism was closely connected with the international currency status of the dollar.

After 1952 the deficit on the U.S. balance of payments became marked. U.S. liabilities caught up and passed her reserves. The dollar gap was replaced by a dollar surplus. By the end of 1968, liabilities were two times as great as her holdings of gold, foreign currency, and reserves in the International Monetary Fund. In the meantime the boom had occurred, which the new international monetary arrangements had assisted. Japan and West Germany had recovered their industrial strength, and experienced rapid, export-led growth. If the United States were to continue to run deficits, she needed to persuade her main industrial rivals to pay for them by increasing their reserve holdings of dollars. For a time Europe was prepared to do this. The dollar was still 'good as gold'. Dollars in European banks became the foundation for the Eurodollar market that grew so enormously during the 1960s. There was, however, a growing conflict between the interests of the United States and of Europe. The deficits run up by the United States were paid for in dollars which increasingly ended up in the European banks. The countries which held most dollars were precisely those whose industrial strength had recovered and so no longer had any need of dollars to buy industrial goods in the U.S. market. Dollars were increasingly worthless to them. Unlike gold they were not an objective form of money, not a reliable standard of value, and as the supply of dollars was continually expanded, so their attractiveness declined further. The countries that were short of dollars – the poor nations of the Third World – lacked the means to acquire them. There developed a growing contrast between the short-term financial strength of Europe and the short-term indebtedness of the United States. In the long term of course the U.S. economy was still ahead of its rivals, both in level of output and productivity. Its overseas assets if liquidated were more than enough to pay off all the debts it had accumulated, and its ability to earn surpluses on its export trade was undiminished. But its short-term liquidity problem grew. In order to solve it the United States needed to cut back drastically on its military spending and on its foreign investment. It was naturally willing to do neither. These were the fruits of dollar hegemony, and the substance of U.S. power. Without the overseas markets they helped protect, it was widely feared the U.S. economy could not maintain full employment at home.

By the 1960s all the conditions for renewed international

monetary crisis were present. What accelerated the process of disintegration were the 'new economics' of the Kennedy administration and the Vietnam War. The first meant a concerted effort by the U.S. government to use Keynesian techniques and government control of domestic money supply to the full, in order to reduce the relatively high unemployment and excess capacity of the U.S. economy of the 1950s, and to achieve faster growth. It was very successful. The United States entered the longest period of expansion in its history. The growth rate rose to 4 per cent fuelled by a large budget deficit. This monetary expansion was continued after the commitment of U.S. forces to Vietnam in 1965. Its immediate result was to raise the burden of overseas military spending enormously. By 1968 the United States was spending $4 billion on troops abroad, $4·3 billion on 'aid'. The trade surplus was only $4·4 billion. Both the U.S. deficit and the U.S. money supply rose rapidly. The former led to increased holdings of dollars abroad, the second to inflation as costs began outstripping productivity. Given the importance of the U.S. economy, inflation there was quickly transmitted to other countries in the shape of rising costs and rising interest rates. Speculative pressure in the international money markets intensified. This exacerbated the problems of fixed exchange rates. They now had to cope with countries inflating at different speeds, with much larger trading surpluses and deficits.

The Vietnam War helped precipitate the exchange crises of the late 1960s and 1970s. Sterling was the first to go. Established after the Second World War as a second reserve currency by the United States, sterling was no longer backed by U.K. industrial superiority. After 1945 sterling liabilities were four times as great as foreign exchange reserves. Maintaining sterling as the junior international currency became one of the accepted priorities of U.K. government policy, in a vain bid to cling to the United Kingdom's old power and role in the world market. It helped accelerate the decline of the U.K. economy relative to its main rivals. Because of the deficits on its balance of payments, the United Kingdom constantly encountered exchange problems. It had the industrial strength neither to increase its exports sufficiently nor to finance the volume of overseas military spending and renewed foreign investment that the international status of sterling encouraged it to undertake. The City prospered whilst

F

the rest of the economy stagnated. Given the inadequacy of the reserves, every balance-of-payments crisis caused a run on sterling and produced measures to deflate demand and cut credit and investment. The 'stop–go' cycle that this produced meant that the larger U.K. firms aided by the financial expertise of the City increasingly diverted their funds overseas into more profitable outlets. Industrial capacity declined still further, as did international competitiveness. The growing severity of sterling crises finally caused the second post-war devaluation in 1967.[2] This put the dollar in the front line.

The dollar crises that followed reflected the underlying weakness of the dollar in the post-war economy. There was a contradiction between its two roles : it could only be 'as good as gold', a stable standard of value, if its supply was fixed. The U.S. government was not prepared to renounce control of the U.S. economy to provide such international harmony. For that would mean re-establishing the gold standard, and so preventing the United States from running a permanent deficit to maintain and extend its power throughout the world. The United Kingdom had financed its military spending and foreign investment in the nineteenth century from the surplus on its export trade. The costs of imperialism have today become too great for that.

Maintaining the policies which dollar hegemony made possible ultimately destroyed this hegemony and helped produce a raging world inflation. Despite strenuous efforts to avoid it, the dollar had finally to be devalued in 1971 and subsequently made inconvertible. Other currencies were first revalued in terms of the dollar – the Smithsonian Agreement (hailed by ex-President Nixon as the most significant monetary agreement in the history of the world). A few months later hopes for this also crumbled as all major currencies were floated. The regime of floating rates spelled the end of the firmer agreement of the Bretton Woods system. It meant too that there was little further check on the rate of world inflation. Under the regime of fixed exchange rates, all countries, except the United States, were obliged to correct deficits when they arose, and could not afford to inflate their domestic money supply too fast for fear of pricing their exports out of world markets. Under rules of the International Monetary Fund devaluation was only a last resort. Only if the United States had rapid inflation would prices increase generally throughout the world economy. Under floating exchange rates, however, all countries gain the freedom of the United States and the world money supply rises effectively as fast as every country expands its domestic supply. The consequences for competitiveness can be partly offset by allowing the currency to depreciate on the foreign exchange markets. The only constraint left is the impact on import prices.

From being a support and a cause of expansion, the post-war international monetary system has therefore turned into a barrier. Its difficulties have been made worse by the problem of recycling the vast and growing oil revenues which now have to be paid to the oil-producing countries, but which, for the most part, they have nothing to spend on. As a result these revenues have to be held in increasingly worthless paper currencies attracting a negative rate of interest.[3]

The dramatic difficulties which oil revenues present, however, can lead to the more basic problem being overlooked. If inflation is to be mastered, if the capitalist economy is to expand again, if trade is again to start increasing for more than short periods, then a new stable monetary system is indispensable. Continuation of the present chaos risks a steady slide into protectionism, currency blocs, even trade wars — of the kind that characterised the 1930s. Yet how can agreement be found? Re-establishing the gold standard means the United States renouncing its rights to run deficits, and all countries renouncing their right to use monetary expansion — easier credit and budget deficits — to smooth out the trade cycle and counter unemployment. It would force them instead to rely on wage cuts. If they are not sufficient it could mean depression on a greater scale than occurred in the 1930s. Maintaining floating exchange rates means accelerating world inflation unless all national currencies are replaced by some fictitious international currency like Keynes's *bancor*, whose supply is controlled by a world monetary authority, an international central bank. That requires the presently utopian detail of a world government. The alternative under floating exchange rates is that all countries should rigorously control their domestic money supply. That is something no government has managed to do unaided — because of the domestic political risks.

The third alternative is some new form of gold exchange standard. Many ingenious technical solutions have been put forward. But all require political agreement. As a result of the long boom, no one nation in the capitalist economy can impose its conditions on the rest. Any solution has to be agreed. Yet the dollar remains the only possible international currency, because of the still marked industrial superiority of the United States. To re-establish it means concessions by the latter – the elimination of the deficit that brought the fall originally. To eliminate the deficit would mean reducing U.S. power abroad substantially. The consequences are already discernible. The world market is beginning to shrink as U.S. domination crumbles. The world will no longer be so free for U.S. capital following the major defeat of U.S. power in South-East Asia by the Vietnamese and Cambodians. The socialist world is expanding again, and cracks in the U.S. shield are appearing everywhere, even in Europe. If nations and nation states could be wished away, then a unified world economy could be built. But it is one of capitalism's contradictions that capital constantly expands beyond the nation state to the further limits of the world market, yet all the time it still needs the nation state to guarantee the dominant framework under which it operates and appropriates surplus value.[4]

PROFITABILITY

The second main factor that promoted and sustained the boom was that investment and accumulation became profitable once more. Many of the reasons concern the reconstruction of the international monetary system on the one hand and the intervention of the state on the other. There are other factors that deserve to be mentioned here. They divide into two main categories. First, there was the appearance of new fields for investment that raised productivity and yielded high returns, and secondly, many inputs were cheapened. Both acted to raise the rate of exploitation and so speeded accumulation.

Among investment outlets construction and cars were probably most important. The enormous physical destruction of the war created a building boom throughout the O.E.C.D. area which lasted right through the 1950s. Cars too experienced a great leap forward and encouraged all kinds of subsidiary investment. The car industry became the dynamic growth leader in every economy. Another industry that was important and highly profitable was armaments particularly in the United States.

As regards cheap inputs the ex-fascist countries, West Germany and Japan, benefited particularly. Since their trade unions had been suppressed in the 1930s firms were able after the Second World War to start production with very low wage costs and, therefore, a very high rate of exploitation. The devastation of these economies was particularly great. German output in 1946 was back to the level of the early 1920s, and West Germany had for a time to resist U.S. attempts to destroy all its industry and turn the whole country over to grazing land. When recovery did start, it meant that not only was the rate of exploitation very high, but the opportunities for investment were enormous.

Another major boost to the boom was the supply of cheap raw materials and primary products. From the 1950s, the terms of trade moved in favour of the industrialised countries and against the less-developed nations of the Third World. Most important of all, a cheap supply of energy became available. The oil industry not only grew into the largest and most profitable industry in the capitalist economy – it also supplied for Western Europe and Japan the energy that was needed to hasten growth at a very low rate. In the period 1950–70, world energy consumption grew at 5 per cent a year and oil consumption at 7·6 per cent. (Information from P. R. Odell, *Oil and World Power*, Harmondsworth, Penguin, 1974.)

In the 1950s, therefore, a number of factors combined to make accumulation highly profitable and more rapid than it had ever been before. The pace of economic advance quickened, the interdependence of nations increased and a continual flow of new techniques entered the production process. Yet the favourable conditions could not last. Some were obviously limited. The building boom, for instance, fed by the needs of reconstruction, had eventually to diminish. More important, the very recovery of the various nations of the capitalist economy meant a sharpening of competition both for markets and for scarce raw materials. Accumulation was so rapid that soon all the tendencies of the accumulation process began to show themselves. There was another great leap in concentration of production. The gap between the monopolistic corporate sector and the small business sector widened further in all the advanced capitalist countries. This was paralleled by an increasing centralisation and internationalisation of capital. The second half of the 1960s saw a great merger and takeover boom in many countries, and the phenomenon of the so-called multinational companies, mostly, in fact, originating in the United States, began to be noticed and publicly discussed.

Competition for raw materials also grew. The very rapidity of expansion meant an accelerating demand for raw materials to feed industry. Since both the scale and extent of industrialisation were now much greater than ever before, so the demand on the world's resources was much greater. It was obvious to many that low prices of raw materials could not last for ever. The market situation of their owners was constantly improving as industrial demand grew. The contradiction between accumulation of capital and the division of the world market into nation states had eventually to assert itself. The uneven distribution of resources and raw materials around the world had eventually to create a politics of scarcity in which the bargaining power of the poorer primary producers would tend to improve, at least at certain times. Oil has been the most dramatic example of this reversal, but the same may happen with other raw materials. As more countries industrialise, the situation from the point of view of the industrialised nations that must import their raw materials can only grow worse.

The most important consequence of the long boom, however, has been the trend of technological innovation. A combination of increasing international competition and rising labour costs has produced a growing switch to labour-saving techniques. This has recently been discussed by Michael Barratt Brown.[5] For the first time since the early industrial revolution, technological innovation once again has a pronounced labour-saving bias. The switch from handicraft to industrial manufacturing caused a massive displacement of labour from the productive process and the creation of an industrial reserve army, and led Marx to formulate both his theory of the tendency of the organic composition of capital to rise and his theory of the trade cycle. Since that time capital-saving innovation has been the general rule. Along with increasing state intervention to socialise costs, the creation of the world market, and the enormous increase in productivity, it has helped prevent the organic composition of capital from rising directly, so the rate of profit has not fallen dramatically. In the 1970s, however, the result of the greatest boom and most rapid accumulation capitalism has ever experienced has been to stimulate a new wave of labour-saving innovation, based on electronics and computers. Increasingly large numbers of workers are displaced from the productive process and have to find jobs in the burgeoning service sector. As Marx foresaw in *Grundrisse*, the historic tendency of capital accumulation is to reduce necessary labour to the minimum so as to increase surplus labour to the maximum. The rate of exploitation is raised by employing ever fewer workers, ever more machines and thus increasing productivity to its furthest extent. Capital accumulation drives towards the automation of production. As Professor Meade has noticed, this would eventually have remarkable consequences :

> There would be a limited number of exceedingly wealthy property owners; the proportion of the working population required to man the extremely profitable automated industries would be small; wage rates would thus be depressed; there would have to be a large expansion of the production of the labour-intensive goods and services which were in high demand by the few-multi-multi-multi-millionaires; we would be back in a super world of an immiserized proletariat and of butlers, footmen, kitchen maids and other hangers on. Let us call this the Brave New Capitalists' Paradise.[6]

Yet such a 'paradise' is unlikely to arrive. The nearer it approaches, the stronger will be the tendency for the rate of profit to fall and the weaker will be counteracting factors. At present, this is showing itself in productive capacity outrunning demand. In all capitalist countries unemployment has been rising for the last few years, overproduction and falling demand have begun appearing once more, because opportunities for profitable accumulation have been declining. All the sales effort, all the public spending, all the private credit are no longer enough to compensate capital for this. They merely exacerbate inflation. Profit rates in manufacturing have fallen significantly before tax in the United Kingdom, the United States and West Germany. The absolute mass of profits has risen enormously, but it has become more and more difficult to maintain the rate of profit. Indeed, the inflation rate has often outstripped the profit rate altogether.

It is very difficult for any firm to raise its rate of profit sufficiently to justify investment; its cash income is being devalued at approximately 20 per cent per annum, and the rate of interest paid on local government bonds is well above the expected return on new manufacturing investment and carries no risk.

Corporate liquidity has severely declined. Because the trade cycle has been mild, and the price level has not fallen since 1945, debts have simply accumulated. In the United States the liquidity ratio of non-financial companies declined from 73·4 per cent in 1946 to 19·3 per cent in 1969. Debt has swelled. A few major bankruptcies now put enormous pressure on the banks. In the United Kingdom the total increase in bank advances accelerated in the 1970s to well over £1000 million a year. Total bank credit increased more than five times between 1967 and 1973.[7]

THE STATE

The role of the state has become so overwhelming in modern capitalism that some have argued it constitutes a new stage in capitalist development.[8] Certainly the development of the modern state poses special theoretical problems for all economists. The nineteenth-century liberal view of the state that treats it as just another economic household with special responsibilities is moribund. At that time the main functions of the state were upholding the legal basis of capitalist social relations, maintaining a stable currency, and managing defence and external relations. The services supplied by the state were financed by taxes that fell almost exclusively on the propertied classes. The requirement of sound finance, that the state should always aim to balance the budget and restrain public expenditure, was therefore the prime aim of public policy.

Such a view of the state, cemented in the ideology of *laissez-faire*, which prescribed as little state interference as possible, was undermined by the progress of capital accumulation. As production became more concentrated, so the age of the trusts and monopolies began; so too the costs of accumulation increased. These costs were both economic and social and led to growing political pressure from both capital and labour for measures of state intervention. In this way state spending and state involvement in the economy began to increase. By the 1930s the size of the state sector was already so large in all the advanced economies that a new relationship between the state and the economy became necessary; one that was often conscious and planned. The devotees of sound finance still preached the virtues of balanced budgets which meant refusing to use the obvious powers of the state to counter slump when accumulation faltered. The economic 'radicals' like Keynes saw that the modern organisation of industry was such that unless the state intervened in the economy and discarded its old nightwatchman role, permanent stagnation could settle on it.

The contribution of the state to promoting and sustaining the capitalist economy may be briefly summarised. The state plays three crucial roles in the modern capitalist economy. It manages demand, it socialises costs and it seeks to maintain social peace and political stability. All were essential for the long boom. The contradictions that were involved, however, in the state performing them have slowly ripened, until now it is the organisation of the state itself that appears as a major barrier to further accumulation.

A. *Economic management*

Whether adopting Keynesian ideas or not, governments throughout the western economy all became closely involved after 1945 in regulating demand, smoothing out the trade cycle and formulating general economic goals. The ability of national governments to control economic conditions rested on control of the national currency. Money supply, and hence private credit and government spending, could be varied as an instrument of domestic policy. The emphasis differed from country to country. Some like West Germany, Japan and France built up a very close and successful partnership between government and 'big' capital.[9] In the United States the main contribution of the federal government to the level of effective demand in the economy and the profits of industry was the arms budget, and the free rein given to the growth of credit. Several governments, notably those in the United Kingdom and the United States, committed themselves to maintain full employment. An elaborate array of counter-cyclical and stabilisation devices were built up to cut short downswings in the cycle and accelerate recovery. A typical example was the U.S. recession of 1957–8. Industrial production fell in nine months by 13 per cent; unemployment rose to five million, 7·5 per cent of the work force; production of consumer durables and capital goods fell by 27 per cent and that of cars and steel by 40 per cent. The government responded not by balancing its own budget but by unbalancing it. Government spending was increased, particularly military spending. A public-works programme was launched and the budget deficit soared. Interest rates were brought down and private credit expanded. Recovery began in the spring of 1958. In the past the slump and stagnation phase of the cycle had usually lasted at least three years.

The result of counter-cyclical policies and the very strong forces sustaining the boom was that the old trade cycle was greatly moderated. As one economist observed : 'Had the idea of the business cycle not existed, it would hardly have been invented to describe the post-war fluctuations in Europe.'[10] In the United States between 1918 and 1939 the economy was in recession and declining for 42 per cent of the period. Between 1945 and 1965 the figure was only 18 per cent. Crises in the nineteenth century were marked by bank failures (62 out of 63 banks in New York had to suspend payments in 1857), falling prices, financial panics, bankruptcies in hundreds of thousands, strikes and lockouts. Wages were regularly reduced by 20 or 30 per cent as unemployment soared, often as high as 25 per cent of the working population. The period of recession allowed restructuring and reorganisation of capital; it deflated the debt structure, reduced costs, and made those companies that remained highly liquid and potentially profitable again.[11]

After 1945 there was no generalised cycle throughout the O.E.C.D. area. The United States suffered recessions in 1948–9 and 1957–8. But the United Kingdom was immune from the first and West Germany and France from the second. For the fast-growth countries, particularly West Germany and Japan, it appeared for a time that they had abolished the cycle altogether. Their growth was uninterrupted; the most they ever suffered was a slackening in the rate of growth, never an actual fall in output. The United States too, in the early 1960s, had appeared to learn the lesson. After a slight recession in 1960–1, the new economic programme of the Kennedy administration which produced a budget deficit of $4000 million, a cheap credit policy and wage–

price guidelines, propelled the U.S. economy into the longest period of continuous expansion in its history. The annual growth rate rose to 4·7 per cent. Only the United Kingdom was unable to join the magic roundabout of uninterrupted growth.

In 1966–7 there occurred the first generalised fall in output and demand throughout the O.E.C.D. area in the post-war period. The West German economy was particularly affected. It recorded its first downturn since the Second World War. This was also the period in which sterling finally collapsed, and the defences of the dollar breached. The response of the United States, embroiled in Vietnam, was to attempt to spend its way out of the crisis. The behaviour of the world economy grew steadily more erratic, sharp booms alternating with steadily longer periods of stagnation. Inflation began accelerating as governments kept expanding their spending and stimulating private credit to maintain prosperity. The boom of 1973 saw the fastest rate of growth ever recorded by the O.E.C.D. area. Even the United Kingdom grew at a rate of 5 per cent. It was followed in 1974 by the start of the most serious recession the O.E.C.D. area had faced since 1945. With raging inflation and rising unemployment existing side-by-side with each other the counter-cyclical policies of the post-war years seemed no longer very effective.

B. *Socialisation of costs*

The second major function of the modern state has been to socialise costs. The state intervenes to take the burden of many costs from private capital. It finances, in a sense, the overhead costs of the whole process of capital accumulation. By doing this, as we have shown, it prevents the organic composition of capital rising. Without the huge volume of state spending, capital would make no profits at all.

During the 1930s public expenditure in the United Kingdom represented less than 25 per cent of G.D.P. It rose enormously during the Second World War and was maintained at a high level by the post-war Labour Government. After falling in the early 1950s after the Conservatives came to power, it began to rise steeply again after 1958. By 1964 when the Conservatives left office it was back to the level, around 41 per cent, that it had been in 1951. Since then it has continued to climb. By 1973 it was

TABLE 5

Size of state sector

	1965	1966	1967	1968	1969	1970	1971	1972	1973
Total public expenditure	14,143	15,314	17,528	19,119	19,795	21,874	24,365	27,372	31,979
G.D.P. at factor cost	31,153	33,042	34,854	37,333	39,180	43,012	48,432	54,390	62,176
Percentage	45·4	46·3	50·3	51·2	50·5	50·8	50·3	50·3	51·4

Source: *National Income and Expenditure, 1963–73*, tables 1, 50.

more than 50 per cent. Mixed capitalism had truly arrived. The private sector, at least in terms of expenditure, was in retreat.

James O'Connor's important book *The Fiscal Crisis of the State* reveals that this change is true of the trend for all capitalist countries and is in no way confined to the United Kingdom alone. O'Connor shows that around 45 per cent of the West German G.N.P. is public expenditure. In the United States spending by the U.S. federal government rose from 12·8 per cent of G.N.P. from 1945 to 1950, to 22·4 per cent from 1966 to 1970. Local public expenditure also rose from 5·9 per cent of G.N.P. from 1946 to 1950 to 11·5 per cent from 1966 to 1970.[12]

O'Connor divides up state spending on what he calls 'social capital' into social investment and social consumption.[13] The former raises productivity, the latter lowers labour costs. By doing so, both raise profits. Examples include all the various ways in which the state produces inputs for the economy – spending on infrastructure, like roads and ports, spending on research and development, spending on education, retraining and health. In many countries the nationalised sector of the economy grew enormously after 1945. In the United Kingdom the industries that were taken over were mostly either declining industries, like railways and mining, or the suppliers of essential services, like gas and electricity. The nationalised industries were run at huge losses in the 1950s and again in the early 1970s in order to provide direct subsidies to private industry. Other industries, like aircraft and shipbuilding, have become completely dependent on government orders, particularly, as in the United States, for arms. State holding companies, like the Italian I.R.I., and the very close co-operation achieved between the state and industry in West Germany, Japan and France has received much attention. Not only must the state socialise the costs of accumulation, but it must do it on an ever-increasing scale. Whatever measures one takes of the size of the state sector – expenditure, employment, fixed-capital formation – all show a large and continuing increase in the involvement of the state in the economy. Two further examples from the United Kingdom may be cited. In 1973 the public sector employed 6,541,000 people which was more than 25 per cent of the total employed labour force. By that year, too, over 50 per cent of the costs of all scientific research and development were met by the government.[14]

C. Consensus and stability

Besides economic management and the socialisation of costs the
state has also to try to ensure political stability and social peace.
It has to legitimate the structure of class inequality with the force
of law and mobilise the politics of consent rather than coercion.
These different functions can often be contradictory. Maintaining political stability may involve a growing burden of 'social
expenses', expenditure that is necessary, but at the same time
burdensome. The problem is how the state is to be financed.
There are two ultimate sources of income in a capitalist society –
wages and surplus value. State expenditure is always a deduction
from surplus value in the short run, however much it may help
increase surplus value in the long run. From the standpoint of
capital it is unproductive expenditure. It does not directly increase
value. This does not mean that the state is financed purely from
taxes on capital, as it largely was in the nineteenth century. On
the contrary, the state now collects a large part of surplus value
directly by taxing wages. Income taxes, national insurance contributions, and indirect taxes, as well as corporation taxes, supply
the revenue the state needs.

The 'fiscal crisis of the state', however, has grown. Spending
shows a constant tendency to outrun revenue. Legitimacy and
political stability have been maintained in the major capitalist
countries since 1945 through political markets. These produce a
great throng of pressure groups and political parties through which
demands and grievances are filtered. Group bargaining around
the annual increment in output and national income generates
enormous pressure for the maintenance and expansion of government spending. The relative strength of different lobbies and
pressure groups varies from country to country. In the United
States the military–industrial complex is dominant and military
spending is the largest component of the U.S. budget. In the
United Kingdom, spending on social services has had a higher
priority, although this has not prevented the erosion of many
features of the Welfare State.

The massive expansion of public spending since the Second
World War has been a marked feature of all capitalist countries.
Public spending both underpinned the boom and permitted the
construction of a welfare consensus which created a political

context for instrumental bargaining and the integration of the
working class into the political system. For a long time, therefore,
the creation of the mixed economy aided rather than hindered
capitalism. The expansion of public spending was 'unproductive'
but it did not conflict with accumulation. On the contrary it
meant accumulation was smoother and more prolonged than it
had ever been.

Sociologists actually discussed the thesis that 'tellys make
Tories', the affluent worker being considered a candidate for assi-
milation into the middle class. The 1950s and 1960s witnessed the
media triumph of capitalist ideology – class was meant to be a
thing of the past. The same observers who were busy writing off
Marxism as redundant, argued that workers were not revolutionary because they were instrumental. Underpinning the apparent
reduction of class conflict was the commitment to full employment
and the steady growth of incomes. Both have been undermined
since 1968. The so-called 'embourgeoisefied', 'privatised' or
'normatively converging' workers were bound to capitalism only
so long as it delivered the goods. The theorists of 'erosion' and
'institutionalisation' of class conflict failed to grasp that class
inequality is more acceptable in a period of expansion than of
recession. The labour movement has shifted to the left in the
United Kingdom, driven by the same instrumentalism which
previously encouraged compromise. The cash nexus at the centre
of the unequal exchange between capital and labour remained
unaltered throughout the 1950s and 1960s. In the 1970s the
smoke screen of affluence has disappeared.

The contradictory role of the state has become clear in the
last few years. It is expressed in the dilemma facing governments
during the present crisis. Whatever their response, whether they
contrive a contraction or expansion of state activity, it will
increase their political difficulties. One of the main pressures on
governments from the political market is to maintain full employment. If public expenditure and credit are contracted, then unemployment rises, and governments must either reflate or face defeat
at the polls. If they maintain or increase expenditure, they help
refuel inflation. The actual course of the mixed economy has produced a public sector which threatens to dwarf the private sector.
State expansion which helped provide a bedrock for post-war
capital accumulation now threatens the continuation of accumu-

lation itself. The contradictory nature of the state sector and its functions themselves prove a barrier to capital.

INFLATION

It is in the context of the concrete circumstances of the political economy of modern capitalism that inflation must be understood. Inflation is a monetary phenomenon that appears in the market as the most obvious and pressing economic problem. But inflation cannot be *explained* in monetary terms. It has to be understood as an expression of deeper problems concerning production and accumulation. The real problem is not inflation but slump and depression. Inflation is a means of postponing or avoiding them, delaying the arrival of actual crisis. In doing so it makes the crisis potentially more severe.

Sustained inflation can only occur if the money supply is expanded faster than output. The question is always why and how is the money supply so expanded. When the money supply consisted largely of precious metals, the main means open to government, anxious to increase their income and spending without raising taxes, was to steadily debase the coinage. Obvious physical limits existed to this process. It was the introduction of purely token money, paper currency and credit, that made unlimited inflations impossible. The only barrier is the speed with which money can be manufactured. In the German inflation of 1923, the government employed 133 extra printing firms using 1783 extra machines to produce sufficient notes. All the rapid inflations of prices have been on a paper rather than a metallic base.

Paper currency and credit developed enormously, of course, once a capitalist market economy was established. Yet the dangers inherent in its use were countered in the nineteenth century by the adoption of the gold standard, which effectively took control of money supply away from governments. Only during wars did the need for high government spending cause the abandonment of the principles of sound finance. The result was that, although prices fluctuated during the nineteenth century, rising and falling with the trade cycle, the over-all trend was slightly down. In the United Kingdom in 1914 prices were slightly below what they had been in 1816.

Historically, the progress of accumulation and the tendency of the rate of profit to fall led on the one hand to the growth of corporate capital, controlled markets, administered prices and, on the other, to growing intervention by the state in the economy. Governments increasingly became responsible not merely for maintaining a stable currency but maintaining the conditions for profitable accumulation. The two aims which once had been so much in harmony were by the 1930s increasingly in conflict. Sound finance in the circumstances of the modern capitalist economy meant stagnation and depression. One of the chief consequences of the Great Depression was that, after 1945, sound finance was generally sacrificed. Governments became interventionist, determined to maintain markets, output, employment and profits.

The consequence has been that the post-war mixed economy has contained an inherent tendency to permanent inflation. Private credit and government spending have both grown enormously, and have been consciously used as counter-cyclical demand. A high and stable level of effective demand to maintain full employment has been one of the first priorities throughout the O.E.C.D. area.

Permanent inflation at an 'equilibrium' level, around 3 per cent per annum could have been tolerated. It remained at this level in most countries during the 1950s and 1960s. What caused it to accelerate were the developments discussed earlier. This disintegration of the international monetary system was marked by a great surge in prices caused by insistence of the United States upon paying her debts in her own currency. This was followed by floating exchange rates, the sudden reversal of the terms of trade for the industrialised countries, and the consequent steep rise in primary commodity prices – they trebled between 1971 and 1974. Finally, the increasing costs of maintaining profitable accumulation were reflected in rising money wages, increasing international competition, and falling profits, and more particularly by the growing burden on accumulation of the unproductive sector, represented by the state.

The post-war role of the state in the capitalist economy was of major importance in assisting accumulation to get under way again. After a time, however, the implications of its new role brought an increasing conflict between prosperity and accumulation. The costs of maintaining the latter began to loom too large. Inflation was the direct result. Governments kept pumping their own spending into the economy and aiding the expansion of private debt and credit to maintain demand. This meant that the money supply kept outrunning output. To raise output meant raising profits and increasing productivity. This obliged governments to begin intervening much more directly in the economy – helping to restructure capital into larger units, redistributing income to companies through the tax system, and confronting trade-union claims for more pay and better conditions directly. The struggle for incomes policies or some means of restraining wage increases became the central focus of the strategy of many governments. To keep accumulation going, higher returns had to be guaranteed to investment. Under the old trade cycle the tendency for real wages to rise during the boom because labour became scarce relative to the needs of accumulation brought the crisis; a time when output fell and unemployment rose. The growth in the reserve army of industrial workers caused wage rates to fall. The very success, however, of post-war governments in maintaining full employment and moderating the cycle meant that yet another automatic regulator of capitalism was dispensed with. As Marx remarked in *Capital* :

> As soon as . . . adverse circumstances prevent the creation of an industrial reserve army and, with it, the absolute dependence of the working class upon the capitalist class, capital . . . rebels against the 'sacred' law of supply and demand, and tries to check its inconvenient action by forcible means and state interference.[15]

To maintain the mixed economy has required increasing resort to 'forcible means' and 'state interference', even by force of arms. Yet this conflicts with the third aspect of the role of the state – maintaining social peace and political stability. They are maintained partly through welfare spending, and partly through the political market which integrates the bulk of the population into the political system by giving access to government to a multitude of parties and pressure groups. In so far as social peace and class rule are maintained in this way it becomes difficult to pursue single-mindedly the policies necessary to restore health to the accumulation of private capital. To cut public spending on welfare or to make workers the scapegoats for inflation are difficult policies to sustain faced by the short-run pressures of the political market. That is why in the mid-1970s we hear mutterings about the incompatibility of political democracy with economic realities. The modern state sector is largely unproductive for private capital – it produces no surplus value directly. It has to be financed from revenue, whether gathered at source in the form of deductions from workers' pay packets or in taxes. But without it no surplus value would be produced at all. The state is indispensable in the three ways we have mentioned for maintaining accumulation and ensuring it is profitable. Without it the organic composition of capital would long ago have risen so much and the rate of profit fallen so low that accumulation of capital would have ceased. Yet even the state has been unable to keep expansion going forever. Once accumulation falters the state's concern to revive it and maintain prosperity comes into conflict with it. In the eyes of many it is the size of the state itself that places the burdens on capital and prevents it expanding. It is state spending and state control of the money supply that are unleashing inflation. To overcome the increasing severity of inflation, which the role of the state in the economy permits and promotes, the state must be extended still further or rolled back. Both courses have their advocates – both endanger the continued rule of capital.

Inflation, therefore, cannot be blamed solely on trade unions or on multinational companies, although their market behaviour and organisation provides the perfect transmission mechanism for inflationary pressure to be translated into rising profits. Yet neither can it be blamed in any simple-minded way on governments increasing their money supplies. They are not free agents in the matter. The pressures on them to do so come from the very structure of the balance of forces shaping the mixed economy. It is the legitimacy and organisation of the mixed economy that made growth and prosperity possible. With accumulation faltering, the world market tottering, and commodity prices soaring, the only course open to governments is to permit inflation to accelerate by increasing the money supply. Only in this way may the slide into recession and slump be postponed. Industrial militancy, increasing international competition, rising supply of money and accelerating inflation are only the market expressions of a deeper disorder – the crisis in the process of accumulation itself. That is why technical solutions and all manner of fine-tuning are no longer enough. The crisis is not confined to immediate problems. It is a crisis of the whole post-war mixed economy, a crisis of the welfare consensus, an impasse that only fundamental political changes can overcome.

6

Political Prospects

> He who supposes that an Englishman of the present day can
> find his way either to intellectual certainty or political consis-
> tency, without doubts, hesitation and errors, shows little
> appreciation of the gravity or the complexity of the situation.
>
> John Strachey, *The Coming Struggle for Power*
> (London : Gollancz, 1932) p. 7.

THE APPROACH TO DOOMSDAY

Amidst the gloom and dire warnings of disaster that surround us,
two particular scenarios for catastrophe stand out. One concerns
the ecological crisis, the other the prospects for hyperinflation and
slump. Robert Heilbroner has noted 'the pervasive unease of our
contemporary mood'; it is an unease that, at times, approaches
panic and proclamation of the apocalypse. Reality as it unfolds
will undoubtedly be more mundane.

The ecological argument that catastrophe is awaiting industrial
man has swelled in noise and volume during the last few years.
Every new development, whether it be the oil crisis or the latest
figures on world population, is seized on as confirming it. A series
of scientific reports, such as *Limits to Growth* and *Blueprint for
Survival*[1] have attempted to substantiate the claim that 'the
principal defect of the industrial way of life with its ethos of
expansion is that it is not sustainable' (quotation from the
second-named work, p. 15). The ecologists see three main dangers
that are held to threaten the world not merely with an end to
economic development but with actual extinction. They are the
physical exhaustion of resources of raw materials; the pollution
caused by industrial society and economic growth; and finally,

the threat of global famine due to population growth outrunning food supplies. Ecologists argue that the combination of the three makes industrial society and growth impossible to sustain for longer than one hundred years. Some estimates make it much less. All agree that the industrial way of life is doomed, and that if humanity is to survive at all, we must revert to patterns of living, of production and of consumption, that are in closer harmony with the natural environment.

The ecologists attack not just capitalism, but industrial society as such. Its exploitation of nature, its enormously wasteful consumption, its mutilation of the environment and disruption of the balance of natural processes makes the pursuit of economic growth a voyage to disaster in every way. Economists' concern about relative prices and the allocation of resources within an expanding economy appears hopelessly shortsighted. According to E. F. Schumacher, in a newspaper interview, 'they're spending their time re-arranging, with enormous ingenuity, the deckchairs on the *Titanic*'.

Other evidence, however, reveals that the general claims of the ecologists are exaggerated, however true many of their individual warnings may be. For example, one of their most familiar arguments is the idea that, at present rates of consumption, known reserves of the most important raw materials will be exhausted within one hundred years. If demand grows as fast as in the last thirty years, the process will be accelerated. Mercury, for instance, would run out in 13 years, tin in 15 years, lead and copper in 21 years, aluminium in 32 years and iron in 93 years.[2] The situation with the fossil fuels is as serious and, in the case of oil, critical. The essence of the ecologist's case is that 'indefinite growth of whatever type cannot be sustained by finite resources'.[3]

Such an approach has rightly been called 'Malthusian'. It shows dramatically the consequences of present consumption of non-renewable resources, but it does so only by assuming that the type and level of resources is fixed. The counter argument is that the level of resources is never fixed in this way. What determines the availability and exploitation of resources is, first technology, and secondly price. Scarcity of one resource can cause a shift to substitutes or a change in the pattern of consumption. The problem of actual exhaustion of resources is not a problem that will be faced by the industrial economies for a very long time, if ever.

The real problem is not a sudden cut-off in supplies that brings
growth to a stop, but whether economies can be adjusted successfully to the new conditions of relative scarcity in resources.
Recycling of minerals, development of new forms of energy, and
new technologies can offset the depletion of resources. The question is whether the capitalist industrial economies can accommodate the changes that will be needed. Certainly, the price
mechanism will not be sufficient. This is the real issue, not
exhaustion of supplies as such. Connelly and Perlman's major
study of non-renewable resources concludes that all metal ores are
still very abundant, though not all concentrated in rich deposits,
and that the main threat is a rise in the cost of extraction unless
new technologies are introduced to counter the decline in ore
grades. As far as oil is concerned, only an actual cut in supplies
will have serious effects.

The ability of industrial economies to adjust to new and
changing situations makes the crisis of raw material resources
unreal for them. But the ecologists are right to point out that the
reckless consumption of fossil fuels and other raw materials partly
results from treating them as 'income' rather than 'capital'. The
market economy prevents any long-term view being taken of the
world's resources. Consumption and production are both controlled by the desire for immediate and maximum profit. The
profit orientation of the market, enforced through competition,
means that no individual firm can afford to take the long view.
Immediate gratification guides consumption with profit maximisation governing production, so the ruling political and economic
pressures operating against any policy of conservation are enormous. As Schumacher points out, the dangers inherent in modern
technology and unplanned exploitation of nature steadily
increase : 'Economic growth, which viewed from the point of
view of economics, physics, chemistry and technology has no discernible limit, must necessarily run into decisive bottlenecks when
viewed from the point of view of the environmental sciences.'[4]
Economic growth threatens man's survival most through the pollution it causes, the long-term effect on the atmosphere and the
soil from the kinds of poisonous waste and new compounds that
are being injected into them in ever greater quantities. Such
dangers are hard to assess, but they are certainly increased by a
production process in which it pays to ignore them. The confi-

dent predictions that the oil crisis can be overcome by a massive switch of resources into nuclear power are a typical example. For a temporary solving of the energy problems of the industrialised economies it is proposed to create huge amounts of radio-active waste which will need to be sealed off for 25,000 years. The lunacy of the short-run view over the long run was never more vividly demonstrated.

The food crisis is another matter. This is always presented as though it were solely about too rapid an increase in population. The real problem, however, is not the availability of food supplies, nor the capacity to supply enough food. It is a problem of distribution. It is clear that famine and hunger can be eliminated. They have been eliminated in China. What prevents their elimination elsewhere is not the growth of population as such, but the systematic distortion and plundering of the economies of the Third World through their incorporation into the world market. As Geoffrey Barraclough points out,[5] it is only two years ago that the U.S. government stopped paying $3 billion a year to its farmers *not* to grow food. Most food production in the Third World is controlled by international 'agribusiness' and local landowners, who use the bulk of the land to grow export crops to supply markets in the advanced industrial countries. Ability to pay has always been the only right recognised in the capitalist market. It takes between four and seven pounds of cattle feed to produce one pound of meat, and it is estimated that 'the livestock population of the United States alone . . . consumes enough food material to feed 1·3 billion people'.

Only redistribution of the land and reorganisation of production can end famine and underdevelopment, and raise incomes to a level at which birth control will become practicable. The view of one expert, Professor Jay Forrester of the Massachusetts Institute of Technology, that population will always outrun food production and that, therefore, some populations had better be left to starve, simply ignores the experience and success of socialist reconstruction in China. Social revolution will solve the problems of the Third World, nothing else.

For the industrial economies the issues raised by the ecologists are more difficult. Marx's view of socialism was a society which, utilising the production forces that capitalism had established, organised production for use rather than for profit. But it was still an industrial society. It was still based on the subjection of nature, with the aim of liberating humanity from endless toil. The essential precondition of freedom for Marx was to achieve a society in which all people would have free time. The division between mental and manual labour, rich and poor, would be gradually abolished. The realm of necessity – labour that had to be undertaken to provide basic subsistence – could be reduced to an absolute minimum by the social application of science and technology to production. What remained would be the realm of freedom. The historical justification of capitalism was that it had so raised productivity and surplus labour that it made such a society possible once the social basis of capitalism had been discarded.

Marx shared the view of nineteenth-century science that mastery of nature and unlimited progress were within man's grasp. With the knowledge we have in 1976 it is easy to see that he was too optimistic about the conquest of nature by industrial techniques. Modern technology itself often involves a domination of nature that destroys and damages it. The productive forces cannot simply be taken over and developed under socialism. They must to some extent be remodelled. Solutions urged by the ecologists involving recycling, the ending of much wasteful consumption, the development of small-scale technology – all these become essential for socialism in an already industrialised economy. In many areas large-scale production and technology may have to be reversed and a society of more or less stable growth established. Not merely social relationships but the technical organisation of industry itself will have to be changed if industrial society is to be preserved. Yet in its central aspect Marx's vision remains accurate. In the long run, the modern industrial productive forces can only become the basis for increasing real freedom if they are organised for use not profit. Marx saw clearly, which many ecologists do not, that the relationship of the human species with nature is necessarily exploitative. Humanity must dominate nature if we are to wrest more than subsistence from it. That is why, even under socialism, the realm of necessity would still exist. It is an inescapable aspect of existence. The question for Marx was under what circumstances did real freedom, based on freedom from forced and specialised labour, become possible, not merely for one class, but for all classes. The issue raised by the ecologists is how large any future realm of freedom can actually be. The dream of abundance and everlasting material progress is being rejected by some Marxists. Hans-Magnus Enzenburger has written :

> The wealth of the overdeveloped consumer societies of the West, insofar as it is not a mere mirage for the bulk of the population, is the result of a wave of plunder and pillage unparalleled in history; its victims are, on the one hand, the peoples of the Third World and, on the other, the men and women of the future. It is therefore a kind of wealth which produces unimaginable want. . . . The productive forces which bourgeois society has unleashed have been caught up with and overtaken by the destructive powers released at the same time. . . . Socialism, which was once a promise of liberation, has become a question of survival.[6]

As long as the mode of production is capitalist, humanity is threatened with disaster, because capitalism *must* expand. The basic orientation of production to profit which lies at the heart of capital finds its expression in competition and the impersonal laws of the market. In this way the laws of capitalist production are felt by each individual capitalist as external coercive laws : 'It compels him to keep extending his capital in order to preserve it, but extend it he cannot, except by means of progressive accumulation.'[7] That is why any steady-state or zero-growth capitalism is impossible for long. While capital rules production its drive must always be to increase exploitation and increase consumption. The outcomes of the capitalist market economy are unplanned and uncontrollable. Only a different mode of production could make a choice between more growth or no growth workable. No growth is not an option of capitalism. It is a manifestation of crisis.

SLUMP AND HYPERINFLATION

The ecologists see the doom of capitalism and all industrial societies to be all-embracing and inescapable, yet still some way distant. The more recent prophets of gloom make its collapse much more immediate. Capitalism, according to them, runs no risk of exhausting the world's resources and ruining the natural

environment, because it will not grow any more. It faces slump
and depression on a massive scale – output and consumption will
fall, not rise. In this case the ultimate constraint of resources on
economic growth recedes. The problems of capitalism are more
pressing.

Three chief contributors to doom have received most attention.
To some extent, all are related. They are oil, the financial
system and inflation. Acting alone or together they are thought
sufficient by a growing army of pundits to bring growth to a
complete halt for the foreseeable future and by some to plunge
the world economy into a slump more severe and more prolonged than that which occurred in the Great Depression of the
1930s.

There are still a few optimists about. Samuel Brittan, for
example, has queried : 'Is there an imminent world economic
catastrophe on the scale of the 1930s? I am rather sceptical. . . .
Ever since I have been in economic journalism, hardly a year has
passed without solemn predictions of a depression like that of the
1930s.'[8] Yet even he acknowledges the intractable nature of the
problems facing the world economy.

In this situation it is important to avoid rhetoric and too
simplistic comparisons with economic events in the past, and we
should analyse carefully the concrete prospects for the world
economy. This is difficult with phrases like the 'crash', 'world
slump', 'hyperinflation', proclaimed on all sides, with even
journals like *The Economist* joining in the cry.

First, oil. The reason why the quadrupling of the oil price after
the Arab–Israeli War in 1973 presents a threat is by now fairly
widely known. The real problem is not so much the actual
increase, but absorbing the revenues that it creates. Spending on
oil and energy represent only a tiny proportion of G.N.P. in the
O.E.C.D. countries, that is around 1·5 per cent. Yet access to
abundant and preferably cheap energy is essential for economic
growth. The difficulty arises because the increased oil revenues
are paid to countries that cannot possibly spend it all. In 1974,
the oil producers were paid around $110,000 million for their oil.
It has been estimated that by 1980 unspent oil revenues could
total $250,000 million in constant prices (from F. Cairncross
and H. McRae, *The Second Great Crash*). Another estimate
reckons that the four OPEC countries with the smallest popu-

lations – Saudi Arabia, Libya, Kuwait and Abu Dhabi – will be running an annual surplus of $60,000 million by 1982 (from P. Connelly and R. Perlman, *The Politics of Scarcity*).

The size of the oil bill, coupled with the big rises in other primary commodities, has pushed the O.E.C.D. area, for the first time, into massive deficit on its trade with the rest of the world. Yet the deficit cannot be met simply by increasing exports to the oil-producing countries, because they do not have a large enough need for all the goods that would have to be supplied. The oil-producing states face a dilemma. Either they must use their money within the existing market or they must stop production. They can use their revenues by investing in the industrial economies, by buying goods and services, by lending the money back to the countries that buy the oil, or by stockpiling raw materials. All have drawbacks. Buying goods and services is inadequate, stockpiling other raw materials would cause a massive increase in their price which could not be sustained for ever; eventually the market would crack. Buying up industrial companies on a massive scale would risk retaliation and possible nationalisation or exclusion.

The practical choice for the Arab sheiks is between lending their revenues back to the oil importers so that they can finance their trade deficits and go on importing oil, or cutting supply and letting their oil appreciate in the ground. It is clear that most of the members of OPEC ask nothing better than to be admitted as permanent shareholders in the western economy, drawing the rentier incomes that will support the luxury and privilege of their ruling élites, altering the semi-feudal social structures in their countries as little as possible. For this reason, unless, and this is always possible, another Arab–Israeli conflict breaks out, the 'oil weapon' is unlikely to be used. On the other hand, the Arabs can hardly be happy at depositing their vast revenues in banks in London and New York and receiving a rate of interest which is often negative when compared to inflation rates. It may seem ideal, from the point of view of the O.E.C.D. economy, that the oil problem should be dealt with by paying the Arabs in depreciating paper currency. In fact, at present, the western countries have a positive interest in seeing some degree of inflation continue and accelerate. If prices were stable, the debt owed the Arabs would seem much more of a burden. This may explain the strange equanimity with which the oil problem is discussed, and the complacency with which deficits, once unimaginable, are now contemplated. By destroying money as a stable standard of value, inflation makes debts unreal. If sufficient time is won they will disappear. The Arabs, however, are hardly likely to be deceived, and this is what poses the real threat – that they will seek to maintain the real value of their revenues, whether by more price rises or selective cuts and reductions in supplies. They also have the financial strength to sabotage many of the O.E.C.D. economies simply by withdrawing their funds from it. The United Kingdom is now heavily dependent upon Arab money to finance the deficits on the balance of payments which reached £3828 million in 1974. Any sudden withdrawal of Arab money would force the freezing of sterling balances and suspension of the pound's convertibility into other currencies. If the Arabs retaliated by cutting supply, the United Kingdom would be plunged into a siege economy, similar in certain respects to wartime.

Such dramatic developments are improbable, even if possible. Although little progress has been made in developing recycling schemes, that is getting the Arabs to return (invest) their revenues to the countries that have paid them, the interest of the Arabs in the short to medium term seems overwhelmingly to lie in maintaining stability. Yet the oil crisis does highlight a more general problem. As the world economy moves into an era of relative resource scarcity in many fields, control of raw materials and access to them is bound to loom larger in the political and economic strategy of each nation state. This will increase international tensions and breed international rivalries, which raise the risk of wars. This fear has been voiced a lot as regards oil, especially the possibility of military intervention by the western powers to secure their supplies, but it applies generally.

The state of the financial system causes anxiety, because of the memory of the Wall Street Crash of 1929. The history of past crises in the history of capitalism is, in part, the history of financial panics. These usually preceded the downturn in output and employment, as in 1929. The increasing use of hire purchase and other forms of private credit meant that during booms the hope of short-term gains led to intense speculative activity and the multiplication of claims and debts. The pyramid of credit would grow progressively, sustaining and feeding on the boom and the rapid rise in prices. Once there was a check, however, and expectations altered, the whole edifice would come crashing down. At every stage of the financial structure loans would be called in to meet claims for repayment, prices would tumble, and bankruptcies soar.

Those who today fear another great financial crisis point to the massive increase and huge volume of credit and private debt that has accumulated during the longest boom in the history of the world economy. In the United States private debt rose 150 per cent as a percentage of G.N.P. between 1946 and 1974. In current prices it increased from $153·4 billion to $1335 billion.[9] The capitalist economy has never been more dependent on expanding credit to maintain its high level of activity. If it should cease to grow, if accumulation should falter for long, and a real slump occur, then there could well be an unprecedented financial collapse, and huge numbers of companies dependent on bank loans would have to be declared bankrupt. Only it will occur this time after the downturn, rather than before. At present, several fringe banks and finance companies in a number of countries have collapsed – Herstatt in West Germany, the Franklin Bank in the United States; in the United Kingdom, several finance companies have failed. Banks themselves have started to go bankrupt. Despite this, the financial system has stayed firm. Prices on the Stock Exchange fell in 1974 even further than they did in 1929, but now a recovery is under way. The expected crash is long overdue.

The fact that it has not come reflects the much greater involvement of the state in the economy. To allow major banks to go bankrupt and the financial system to collapse would have incalculable consequences. They have to be shored up at all costs. Yet this leads to huge problems. Even the giants are not safe. The structure of claims and debts is international and a collapse of one part could bring the whole lot down. The Eurodollar market is one example. Eurodollars are not issued by any government – it is stateless money. A huge structure of loans has been built up upon the deposits. If banks suddenly had to repay the holders of deposits it would cause them serious difficulties. There is no lender of last resort to turn to. In such circumstances a run on the bank is made more rather than less likely. The size, the security and financial strength of the banks have never been greater. But their liabilities have never been so huge. The problem of handling, in addition, the huge oil revenues puts the system under severe strain. So long as the economy does not crack, the financial system is unlikely to break. But that means capitalist governments are highly restricted in their policies. To prevent everything collapsing around them, they must reflate the economy, stimulate private credit still further, pump in more government spending and expand the money supply. In other words, they must preserve inflation at all costs. This explains the turn to reflationary policies in the United States and West Germany in 1975. The slump is to be postponed a little longer.

Inflation is the third reason for gloom. For it is argued that if inflation cannot be checked because of the depression that would ensue, then it will go on accelerating in stages until it becomes hyperinflation. At this point, the monetary system will finally collapse, and the long postponed slump will finally arrive, with added ferocity. Hyperinflation as such, however, is unlikely. It is nearly always in the power of governments to avert a hyperinflation. Hyperinflations have only occurred historically either as a deliberate act of government policy or because no real government existed. Continuing 'strato-inflation' of the Latin American type is, however, much more probable. Many economic observers predict a recovery in the world economy for 1976 followed by still higher inflation and deeper recession in 1977–9.[10] Inflation will continue so long as governments try to maintain the post-war mixed economy. Permitting inflation becomes their only option. In the meantime, social, political and economic tensions all increase, and class struggle becomes more open.

To understand why governments find it easier to maintain inflation rather than suppress it is not difficult. Throughout the history of monetary economies, governments have found the temptation to allow money to depreciate too strong. During an inflation, those who lose are creditors, savers, rentiers of all kinds, as well as all those on fixed incomes. Small businessmen and wage earners suffer also – the first because increased uncertainty about costs and returns makes calculation and planning much more hazardous; the second because, despite media mythology, wage earners are almost always left behind in an inflationary upsurge, and only catch up, if at all, after a timelag. When wages (real take-home pay) do appear to be rising faster than prices,

it is usually because in the period before prices rose much faster
than wages. A perfect example of this occurred in the United
Kingdom in 1970. A real increase of around 6 per cent followed
a long period of pay restraint, 1966–9, when other costs rose
much faster.[11]

Those who gain from inflation are debtors of all kinds, since
in real terms their debt is constantly decreasing. Companies and
banks in the corporate sector gain too, because they take the
decisions to raise and fix prices, and they have the flexibility to
move funds around the world to extract maximum gain from
whatever opportunities arise. Techniques perfected by multinational companies, in particular for switching prices and rigging
their internal price structure, manage not only to exploit the
profit opportunities inflation creates, but often to sabotage the
power of national governments to pursue effective monetary
policies.

The greatest gain from inflation still accrues to government. It
makes financing of a large state sector and budget deficits very
much easier. It is in this sense that inflation is the greatest tax
gatherer of all. Increased government spending financed by
printing more money permits government to appropriate a
larger share of resources by making the incomes of all other
groups depreciate. Moreover, the real burden of interest
payments on the existing national debt is continually reduced,
and this allows it to be expanded faster than would otherwise be
the case. Inflation also means higher tax receipts (the process of
fiscal drag) as wage earners move into higher tax brackets and
as a higher proportion of their income comes to be paid in tax.

Looking back it is not surprising that in the 1950s a mild
inflation was regarded so tolerantly. It helped lubricate the mixed
economy, and stimulated economic growth. Now, however, it is
seen as the major economic problem, threatening an end to
growth if it is not checked. The danger inflation presents to
the mixed economy is the impact it is believed to have on profits.
'U.K. industry is bleeding to death', cry the headlines. The profits
squeeze has apparently become so intense that whole sectors are
threatened with bankruptcy, and the cause is 'inflation'. But on
the face of it this is rather puzzling. It is, after all, the big companies that have the power to raise their prices and keep ahead
of the falling value of money. In Latin America, where double-

figure inflation is the rule, multinational companies have found no difficulty in adjusting to it. Why should it endanger profits in the O.E.C.D.?

Various answers are given. The best researched book on the profits squeeze in the United Kingdom appeared in 1972, written by two Marxist economists – Andrew Glyn and Bob Sutcliffe. Despite some challenges and some abuse[12] their conclusions about a fall in the rate of profit both before and after tax for U.K. companies from 1950 to 1970 appear to be substantially correct. Their belief that this is partly caused by worker militancy also happens to be that favoured by the Confederation of British Industry and many orthodox economists. Glyn and Sutcliffe argue that the structure of the modern economy now consists of monopolistic institutions – trade unions and companies. But whereas trade-union bargaining power became unfettered after the Second World War because of the government commitment to maintain full employment, companies were still subject to international competition. The result was that, as a class, labour possessed greater bargaining power. As international competition intensified in the 1960s, companies found themselves obliged to accede to wage demands, sometimes unable to pass the full increase on in higher prices. The result was a steadily growing squeeze on profits which reached critical proportions in 1970.

In his article on the profits squeeze in the *Bulletin of the Conference of Socialist Economists*[13] Andrew Glyn shows, on one estimate, that if we deduct indirect taxation from post-tax share of profits in G.D.P. at factor cost, there is a sharp fall between 1962 and 1970 from 16·8 to 10·7 per cent. For Marxist analysis, however, the crucial factor is the rate of profit. Glyn demonstrates that the rate of profit fell even faster than the share of profits over this period and has not recovered since 1970. This fall in profitability cannot, as Glyn sometimes suggests, simply be put down to the strength, militancy and affluence of the working class. Glyn's own figures (Table 6) show that, during this period, there is a sharp fall in the post-tax share of incomes going to wages and salaries.

There is a 5·5 per cent fall in post-tax wages and salaries. Glyn argues that this in no way demonstrates that increases in money as against real wages were *not* a pressure on profitability.

G

TABLE 6[14]

Percentage of net domestic product at factor cost

	1955	1964	1970
Wages and salaries before tax	73·3	74·5	78·8
After direct taxes	64·5	63·0	61·5
After direct and indirect taxes	55·6	53·6	50·2

For if money as well as real wages had been held back, then there would have been no need to redistribute to private firms by increasing the tax burden on the workers. It is true that the government has increasingly taken on one role of money by restoring profitability through taxation. But it is unclear that this is a result of working-class militancy. Rather it expresses the contradictory role of the state in the later stages of capitalism. For both the share going to wages and salaries and that to profits has fallen. What has risen is the share taken by the state. Now Glyn chooses to argue that some public expenditure must be regarded as payment to the working class. But in value terms, since all income comes from wages or surplus value, state expenditure itself must represent costs for capital, not income for the working class, so long as capital rules production. Using Glyn's argument, we would have to believe that the state has functioned *primarily* for the welfare of the workers.

The collapse of profits is seen as threatening the continued existence of a private-enterprise economy. In the short term it means a steep fall in investment. Accelerating inflation to prop up prosperity only brings further losses, because of the havoc it wreaks with the book value of companies. An increasing proportion of declared profit becomes no more than paper profit, reflecting the rising price of stocks. In extreme cases, real profits become negative so that companies are, in effect, consuming their capital. Stopping inflation thus becomes identified with restoring profitability. Since inflation is itself falsely identified with wage-push, restoring the health of the mixed economy means permanently reducing the bargaining power of trade unions.

Yet, as we have argued throughout, it is not, in fact, the unions that are responsible for inflation, or the crisis, nor is it primarily wage demands that have squeezed profits. Certainly unions play an important part in the process, and stand at the centre of the political debate. But the crisis cannot be understood simply in terms of the struggle between labour and capital, between unions and employers. This see-saw model will not explain how, in a crisis, the incomes of both workers and capitalists can suffer. The class struggle has to be related to the overall development of the capitalist economy, the way in which the post-war opportunities for accumulation of capital have now turned into barriers. The crisis of the mixed economy appears once more in contradictory form – wages are too high and demand is too low. Its causes lie deeper. As Glyn and Sutcliffe note, the rate of profit has fallen but company income, in general, has not. Governments have redistributed income to companies through the taxation system. Real take-home pay of workers has not risen. But this has only alleviated the profits squeeze. It has not removed it, because its causes lie in accumulation. Companies will not invest sufficiently to keep the economy fully employed and expanding because profit expectations are too low. The investment required to raise the rate of exploitation is too great. This is the real impasse of the mixed economy. If accumulation revived, high wages and a large state sector would be no problem. They would be necessary to provide an adequate level of effective demand. With accumulation faltering, however, both appear as an increasing burden and constraint on capital. That is why wages and public spending are the main targets of attack. Maintaining them, in present circumstances, means accelerating inflation. This makes the impasse of the mixed economy political as well economic. A shift in political power has become essential to resolve its problems. For if capitalism is to be maintained, the state has to expand and contract at one and the same time.

THE END OF CONSENSUS

Whenever the present crisis is discussed, comparisons with the 1930s are made so readily that many are listening apprehensively for the sound of jackboots. But since the form of the present crisis is quite unlike that of 1929–32, its political outcomes are liable to be very different. The actual outcomes are rarely what the orthodox expect. Writing on the Great Depression in the 1930s,

Lord Robbins saw four essential conditions for recovery – business confidence had to be restored by stabilising currencies and foreign exchanges; all barriers to international trade had to be removed; all 'inflexible' elements in the economy, particularly wage rates which did not fall far enough, had to be eliminated; and to make recovery complete, governments should refrain from all interference in the economy. In fact, recovery took a quite different form; not a restoration of what had existed, but a development of the economic structure, in particular a great extension in the role of the state.

The state's role was extended in different countries by very different political parties and political means. In every case, however, its extension was the key to recovery, although several countries, including the United Kingdom, had to wait for the Second World War and its aftermath to discover that. Economic orthodoxy could neither explain the slump nor how to bring recovery. That was because, then as is the case in the 1970s, it had little grasp of how economies actually worked and missed the political dimension of the problem. Economists merely lamented the shattering of their beautiful toy. Keynes had much more insight, but a naive belief in the power of ideas. He felt confident that only vested interests, ignorance and stupidity stood in the way of applying ideas which everyone could rationally accept. For Keynes, the problem was a technical one.

Yet, in 1931 in the United Kingdom, the problem was anything but technical. The ideas for overcoming the depression and speeding recovery were present. Keynes, Lloyd George and other groups, including Oswald Mosley's New Party were advancing policies which, if adopted, would have at least alleviated the situation. But none of them were adopted, because all meant an extension of the state, and a shift in the balance of class power. Retrenchment was the favoured policy because a balanced budget was the best way of preserving the dominant interests of the ruling class and keeping its capital intact. So the dole of the unemployed was cut and unemployment itself was allowed to rise to three million. No practicable political alternative for the ruling class existed. The political market was divided between Conservative, Liberal and Labour. No party had a majority in the 1929 Parliament – it was apparent that the only possible majority was for a policy that upheld the ruling consensus. The Labour movement had no forward policy, never mind a reformist policy. When the Cabinet split over the proposed cuts in the dole, a National Government became the inevitable political instrument for forcing through retrenchment and riding out the depression. The National Government helped divide the Labour movement and rallied the rest of the electorate behind it.

The United Kingdom, however, was exceptional. Elsewhere, policies of retrenchment were not enough. In the United States conservative forces strongly urged retrenchment, cuts in income tax on those with high incomes, and the ending of federal intervention in industry. But the impact of the depression was much greater than in the United Kingdom. Alternative strategies were put forward. Roosevelt's New Deal was one. In the opinion of one historian, Roosevelt 'sensed the danger of revolution unless the demand for change was satisfied within the limits of the existing order'.[15] The New Deal was incoherent and unplanned. But it fulfilled the need for policies that staved off major social unrest and pushed aside the spectre of revolution. As President Truman later declared : 'In 1932 the private enterprise system was close to collapse. There was real danger that the American people might turn to some other system. If we are to win the struggle between freedom and communism, we must be sure that we never let such a depression happen again.'[16]

Such sentiments explain much about the post-war welfare consensus and the present impasse of the mixed economy. The triumph of orthodoxy and retrenchment in the United Kingdom during the 1930s was only temporary. It contributed to the election of the first majority Labour Government in 1945. The Second World War showed that modern governments could secure full employment and produced in the United Kingdom a major shift of opinion and power in favour of organised labour. The welfare consensus established after the war was based on adherence to the Atlantic Alliance, the Cold War, and the continued preservation of sterling as an international currency. But it also involved the maintenance of full employment, a much enlarged state sector, and greatly increased government spending on welfare. The political concessions of the welfare consensus were the costs accepted by both governing parties for preserving and strengthening private capital. In government both parties were concerned to administer the existing state, not transform it into socialism or roll it back.

For a time the mixed economy, the reunified international monetary system, and the new opportunities for profitable investment, meant that capitalism flourished as never before. For a period even class conflict dwindled, the working class had never seemed more integrated into the political system, socialism never more irrelevant. 'The class war is over and we have won it', Macmillan announced after the 1959 General Election. But it was a premature boast.

As the mixed economy developed, so too did its underlying contradictions. Once accumulation began to falter, the burden of high wages and state spending became too great. Inflation was one result. Yet relatively high wages and state spending were not features of the mixed economy that could be easily removed. They were the heart of the welfare consensus, the political settlement with organised labour. One response in the United Kingdom during the 1960s was to attempt to overcome the problems of the mixed economy by extending the state still further. This involved increased spending to modernise and rationalise industry, to develop new infrastructure, improve education and training; experiments in planning to co-ordinate the corporate sector and make nationalised industries more efficient; and aids of all kinds to industry to promote growth, mergers and technological advance. All these and more were tried. If the United Kingdom grew faster, it was reasoned, then the cost of increasing real wages and welfare spending would be paid for out of increased output. In return, the trade unions might voluntarily accept an incomes policy which would stop wages rising faster than productivity. So inflation would be checked, U.K. exports would remain competitive, and U.K. industry profitable.

The ruins of this policy are strewn all through the 1960s. Stagnation and accelerating inflation were its only obvious fruits. The policy was hamstrung by the priority of defending sterling in the interests of the City, and increasingly by the appearance of new obstacles to further expansion of the world economy. So the final release from sterling in 1967 was not the herald of a new era as it might have been earlier. Indeed, it is since 1967 that the welfare consensus has slowly started to crumble and disintegrate.

In order to prop up the mixed economy governments came to

lay the blame for inflation more and more upon the trade unions, and attempts at compulsory restraint of wages and attacks on trade-union bargaining power began to be made. Governments began to intervene directly in the workings of the labour market. Government policy swung between attempts to obtain voluntary restraint and, alternatively, compulsion. Selwyn Lloyd's 'pay pause' of 1961 was followed by the National Incomes Commission, Labour's Declaration of Intent, and the Prices and Incomes Board in 1964. In 1966 Labour declared a new wage freeze and in 1968 produced, in the form of a White Paper, legislative proposals – *In Place of Strife* – to curb union power. In every case it was trade-union power that was made the scapegoat for the failings of the economy. The trade unions were expected to bear the burden. Underlying the administration of the welfare consensus and the mixed economy was the profound belief, shared by both governing parties, that maintaining the profitability of the private sector must be given priority. If there were no investment and no growth, then none of the other reforms and improvements that were urged would be possible. If profits are squeezed, so are all other things. Social democracy depends on a healthy private sector. With Labour 'garden-party' logic it follows that the interests of the working class are not served but betrayed by militancy. If militancy means lower profits, lower profits for capitalism means higher unemployment and slower growth. All governments undertook to act in the 'real' interests of the workers, attempting to blow away their 'false consciousness' by cajoling and compelling unions to restrain wage demands.

The policy met limited success. Yet governments had more powerful weapons. Inflation and taxation could be used to deprive wage earners of most of their gains and preserve the share of profits in national income. But even this did not stop profitability falling. By 1970, inflation was accelerating, strikes and industrial militancy were swelling and profits still declining. The greater intervention of the 1960s had achieved very little; it had not rescued the welfare consensus; it had only exposed how fragile it was. In the 1970s there was a turn to new policies. With the growing impasse of the mixed economy and the evident economic decline of the U.K. economy, the disintegration of the welfare consensus began.

THE CONSERVATIVE PREDICAMENT

In 1931 the Conservatives dominated the political market in the United Kingdom and were the normal party of government. In the inter-war years they were only out of power in three of the twenty years, and then they faced weak minority governments. The absorption of much of the Liberal support had made the Conservative Party the spokesman and instrument of all sections of property, to which was added widespread electoral support amongst the middle and working classes. Its ability to identify defence of the Constitution with the maintenance of existing property relations and the Empire, through policies of sound finance and retrenchment, made it the ideal governing instrument for the ruling class. Yet, since the establishment of the welfare consensus, the position of the Conservative Party has been steadily eroded. For a time it seemed they had been successful in adapting, but during the last fifteen years their real weakness has begun to show. The problem in administering the welfare consensus has been reconciling the interests of organised labour with the interests of corporate capital. The Conservative Party, no less than the Labour Party, has been very responsive to the interests of the latter. But the mass base of the party is rooted in the declining and neglected small-business sector. The electoral ideologies reflect this, stressing the principles of free competition, self-help and individual initiative. Electoral ideologies, however, are no guide to how the parties have governed. Instead of rolling back the state, the Conservative Party extended it. Instead of reducing public spending, it increased it. In power it had to recognise the realities of the welfare consensus and mediate between the dominant interests in the state – the big industrial companies and banks, and the trade unions. A growing split emerged between the Conservative leadership and its supporters. This did not matter very much in prosperous times. In the mid-1970s the scenario is very different. Growing economic difficulties and the increasing failure of central policies of the welfare consensus have produced a considerable reorientation of the Conservative Party away from government and the realities of power towards the interest and ideological concerns of the rank-and-file.[17]

The first sign of this shift occurred during the second half of

the 1960s when the party was in opposition. By 1970 when
it returned to government it was committed to a programme
that seemingly overturned many of the priorities of the
welfare consensus. State intervention in industry was to cease,
taxation was to be reduced, bankrupt companies were not to be
propped up, the bargaining power of the trade unions was to be
curbed through legal means, selectivity was to replace universal
benefits in welfare. Above all, the party declared itself firmly
against incomes policy. Heath's new course presented a substantial ideological victory for Enoch Powell and the bulk of the rank-
and-file of the party against the leadership. But the realities of
power were soon busy re-educating the new ministers. Despite
the new emphasis in policy, no substantial attempt was made to
dismantle the state sector and reduce government expenditure.
Whilst taxation was reduced, spending was not, and the budget
deficit soared. The Industrial Relations Act brought direct confrontation with the trade unions. Inflation and wage demands did
not abate even though unemployment was rising. The Conservative Government pursued an indirect incomes policy by attempting to hold down wages in the public sector. Following major
defeats inflicted by the struggle of the miners and railwaymen in
1972, the new course was abandoned. Instead, it introduced the
most comprehensive statutory control of prices and incomes the
United Kingdom has ever seen in time of peace.

This conversion to the Keynesian strategy for controlling inflation and preserving the mixed economy reversed all the Conservative Party's pledges to its supporters. This might not have
mattered if it had been successful. But it was not. It eventually
brought major industrial confrontation, again with the miners,
followed by the fall of the government. In 1974 the Conservatives called an election on the issue, 'Who Governs Britain?', and
they lost. Plainly, it was no longer the Conservatives. In the two
elections of 1974 the Conservatives suffered a serious electoral
haemorrhage. Much of their support in Scotland moved to the
Scottish Nationalists; the Ulster Unionists severed their connec-
tion; in Wales and the North of England the Conservative vote
declined substantially; in the South many votes were lost to the
Liberals. The task of rebuilding the national strength of the Conservative Party and formulating a credible policy for government
have become immense. The replacement of Edward Heath by

G*

Margaret Thatcher as leader represents a further decisive swing in the orientation of the leadership – away from the problems of government towards the gratification of the interests and ideologies of the party rank-and-file. It had never been in greater danger of becoming a middle-class protest party.

The Conservative way out of the impasse of the mixed economy is a more extreme version of their 1970 programme. They propose to roll back the state and create a 'social market' economy. There will be a big reduction in taxation and public spending, an end to all state intervention in industry and the labour market and new legislation against the 'monopoly power' of the trade unions. The aim is to secure greater choice, greater competition, faster growth and higher profits. Inflation will be halted by adopting the programme of the monetarists – rigorous control of the money supply. Mass unemployment would result.

It is hardly surprising if the programme has a 'desert island' look. It is no longer the Labour Party whose proposals are irrelevant and impracticable. The ideology of the social market flourished in West Germany in the 1950s at the time of the German economic miracle. Such times are no longer with us. The programme ignores entirely the division of the economy into corporate capital and small business; it ignores how deeply involved the state has become in maintaining the mixed economy at all levels; it ignores the way markets are organised and controlled; it ignores the power of the trade unions; it ignores practicable politics.

According to Sir Keith Joseph in a recent speech, U.K. industry is in danger 'of bleeding to death from loss of profits' (*Financial Times*, 9 August 1974). He blames it on inflation and the interventionist policies of successive governments. The solution is to end these interventionist policies. Sound finance, balanced budgets, rigorous control of money supply – this is what the Conservatives now demand. To achieve them requires a major confrontation with organised labour – a reversal of the gains and concessions embodied in the welfare consensus. In particular the government must abandon its commitment to full employment. Here would be the real difficulty faced by any Conservative Government committed to monetarist measures. It would mean permitting unemployment to go way beyond 1·5 million. Unemployment in the low millions for the rest of the decade is Mr

Peter Jay's forecast in *The Times* for overcoming inflation by monetarist means. In effect the monetarist prescription is for governments to cease propping up the mixed economy by policies that are inflationary and instead allow an old-fashioned crash. The crash is intended to restore sanity, labour discipline and profits to the capitalist economy. Yet unemployment in the low millions is a displeasing prospect. It is hardly compatible with regular elections, and it promises the kind of social upheavals that many countries faced in the 1930s. Hence it could only be maintained in practice if the political market were closed down, an authoritarian regime established, and trade unions effectively suppressed.

LEFT TURN

A drift into some kind of authoritarian system cannot be ruled out. It is certainly one scenario for the future, earnestly canvassed and discussed by those who talk darkly about the threat which inflation poses to democracy and about the circumstances under which the armed forces might gradually come to play a larger and larger role in government. Thankfully, it is not the most probable course of development. The drift is much stronger in the other direction. This is so even within the conventional bounds of the political market. It is apparent that the Conservatives suffer from a growing isolation, whilst Labour commands a greater degree of authority and a greater degree of acceptance in the political establishment than at any previous time even if its support in the country is declining. After the first election of 1974 the Labour Cabinet was suddenly discovered by the press to have much more 'weight', experience and talent than its counterparts. This was not a matter of personalities. It was because it was widely recognised that, at that moment at least, the Labour Party was the only possible instrument of consensus government. Its ministers, therefore, naturally appeared more competent. The Labour Party was regarded quite simply as the last chance of holding the welfare consensus and the mixed economy together.

Never have the pressures and the difficulties been so great. After its election the Labour Government tried once more for voluntary wage restraint, through the 'Social Contract'. The contract was a formal agreement between unions and government

for wage restraint in exchange for government guarantees on
employment, welfare spending, redistribution of income, renego-
tiation of the Treaty of Rome, trade-union rights, public ownership and price controls. The hope was that by increasing union
political power and influence, stronger foundations for the survival of the private sector would be laid.

Labour leaders, no doubt, conceived the Social Contract as a
holding operation, but it soon became clear that its sieve-like construction did not allow it to hold very much. The squeeze on
profits continued, inflation reached record levels, public spending
still grew. The situation is not sustainable. All previous governments have eventually been compelled to try to control wages
directly. Yet matters are confused in the United Kingdom. The
impasse of the mixed economy is such that mere patching is no
longer enough. On the left, as well as on the right, solutions for
breaking out of the impasse have emerged. Within the Labour
Party the most noted spokesman is Tony Benn.

Benn is very rare indeed among Labour Party politicians. He
takes a longer view, and tries to relate his policies to a wider
historical and political analysis of U.K. society. It is for this
reason that his ideas are thought dangerous, and he receives such
merciless denigration in the press. It is also why, in the present
situation, his ideas are so influential. Everyone else is preoccupied
with short-term survival.

Benn's arguments are very simple. He bases them on the economic structure that has developed in the United Kingdom –
production dominated by fewer and fewer giant companies, many
of them multinationals. Benn argues that for U.K. industry to
revive this power structure must be changed. The post-war mixed
economy has failed in the United Kingdom. Successive governments have presided over a twenty-five-year decline of the U.K.
economy, and the country is now fighting for its industrial survival. The basic cause is low investment, and this is matched by
the neglect of social investment, producing all the problems of
poverty, poor housing, low pay and high regional unemployment.
Benn argues that the solution is not to put the blame on scapegoats, whether industrial militants or speculators, but to tackle the
real causes. That means making the state provide the investment
the private sector no longer can. Benn thus calls for a big extension of public ownership in the profitable corporate sector of the

economy. At the same time he does not advocate the establishment of extra Whitehall bureaucracies. In his view, nationalisation plus Lord Robens does not add up to socialism.[18] Extending public ownership will only be effective if it enlists active support and pressure from workers. Benn sees the problem no
longer in technical terms, as he did when Minister of Technology
in the 1960s, but in political terms. He plans to use workers' participation in industry to harness the enormous defensive power of
trade unions as a positive power. The aim, he has declared, is
to bring about 'a fundamental and irreversible shift in the
balance of power and wealth in favour of working people and
their families'.[19] Benn's language is populist. He talks about the
loss of confidence in the U.K. establishment. Working people, he
claims, have not lost confidence. The industrial problem is a
political problem – gaining consent. To gain consent means
achieving greater equality and enabling working people to shape
their own lives.

Benn's way out of the impasse of the mixed economy is, therefore, a shift towards a planned economy, that is public control
of investment and workers' participation in management,
achieved through such instruments as the National Enterprise
Board and the Industry Bill. He does not believe such changes
will come about through parliamentary action alone, but through
trade-union pressure. He therefore argues consistently for
measures, like forcing companies to disclose information to their
workers, that will increase trade-union bargaining power and
influence.

Populist rhetoric is one thing – class power is another. It is
much harder to achieve real shifts in the balance of political
power than most radical social democrats believe. Benn's supporters are a minority even within the Labour Party, even more
so within Parliament. In Parliament itself the most obvious
majority is for a national government, united over the European
Economic Community, the need for wage restraint and preserving capitalism. Yet a national government is unlikely, if only
because its position would be so precarious; it would be faced by
a militant left-wing party and the possibility of prolonged confrontation with the unions. The long-term interests of capital seem
to require that the Labour Party stays intact, if it is at all possible. Capitalism needs the present Labour Government; socialism

does not. Circumstances are not at all favourable for a new experiment in national governments, which would entail splitting the Labour Party. It still remains, however, as Edward Heath realised, the best chance for the Conservatives to return to government.

CONCLUSION

Despite all the prophecies of doom, the world economy is unlikely to suffer a catastrophic slump, at least for the next few years. It is still within the power of governments to prevent that. Yet the costs of so doing are likely to become ever more burdensome in the next ten years: alternating bursts of inflation and rapid expansion, mounting unemployment, shrinking markets, fiercer competition, low profits and low investment. The risks of a crash will grow, and so will political unrest, class struggle and attempts to find political solutions to the impasse. The nature of capitalism and the accumulation of capital is such that it is not possible to overcome the barriers to further expansion by retro-gression – trying to re-create the capitalism of 1920 or 1900. The development of capitalism is cumulative; it imposes its own logic and conditions for the solution of crises. The great historical achievement of capitalism is the creation of social labour and social production. It has made the productive forces so vast and each branch of production so interdependent that it has created the material basis for a new kind of society, that is a socialist society. In the process it has radically undermined the relevance of all free-market ideologies, resting as they do on the independent sovereign individual producers. There are very few left, and there can only be very few in the circumstances of modern production. This means that capitalism itself has made the right to work a social right, no longer an individual obligation, because the means of production are now so clearly social, not individual in character. Even individual ownership has declined markedly.

The impasse of the mixed economy is international. Solutions to it can only be effective if they take account of its basic causes and the structure of the modern capitalist economy and world market. The creation of a social market may be ideologically attractive to some; it shows little realism. The actual choice is between attempting to ride out the storm, and between creating a new order by extending further the role of the state. The first choice is, of course, the instinct of most politicians, committed as they are to the short-run view. Government is conceived as a series of temporary expedients to keep the system afloat until something turns up to rescue it, whether this be a new expansion of the world economy, electric cars or oil from the North Sea. To be viable tighter controls on wages would be necessary, but not so tight that it provoked confrontation. This balancing act will require experiments with indexation, import controls, and all manner of devices, perhaps including rationing.[20]

Steering such a middle course amidst the present economic and political turbulence requires great skill; at any moment the balance may collapse – either from external or internal developments. So long as such a policy persists, however, no really drastic changes can be expected, and no recovery from capitalism's long-term decline. The most probable scenario is that the stalemate will continue. This is because any overcoming of the problems of the mixed economy requires its transformation into something else. It requires above all either an assault on the trade unions or an accommodation with them. This is crucial for understanding the different forms which the political extension of the state would take. The monetarist programme would be mere camouflage for policies that shackled the trade unions. The state would not be rolled back. It would be extended as it was in Germany in the 1930s. An authoritarian regime would need to suppress unions and free elections but at the same time, to ensure its own stability, it would need to maintain relatively full employment. Wages would be controlled and profits raised, but private capital would also need the state to shoulder still more of the costs of accumulation. Merely curbing trade unions does not solve all the accumulation problems of capital. The armed forces are no substitute for increasing the rate of exploitation.

The alternative in the United Kingdom is for a persistent drift towards some kind of radical social democracy propelled by the demands and struggles of the mass of working people. The logic of events points in that direction, even if most Labour Party actions and rhetoric do not. It would have to involve a shift in the balance of political power towards the working class, much more than that contemplated in the 'Social Contract'. Whether more public ownership and worker participation would become the basis for a new invigorated and more profitable capitalism, or whether it would prove explosive, creating the conditions for more far-reaching change, for the transition to socialism, is not possible to predict.

What seems clear is that any attempt to extend the state to overcome the problems of the mixed economy must involve permanent wage and price controls (indexation is one form). This appears to be the direction in which all capitalist countries are moving. It is clear that such controls in a capitalist society cannot ever be just to both labour and capital. The existing distribution of income arising from production is not equal or 'fair' in any sense on which the two classes could for long agree. It follows that eventually either labour or capital would launch an all-out attack upon them. Under the Conservatives' Counter-Inflation policy, it was eventually the labour movement that fought and won. The policy was intended to favour private capital and boost profits. To win the confrontation against labour permanently would require the adoption of authoritarian measures, bringing in the armed forces more and more to keep order and maintain essential supplies, and eventually suppression or emasculation of the unions.

If, on balance, policy favoured the working class, then capital would eventually be forced to fight out in the open. Its most obvious weapons would be an investment strike and a large-scale flight of capital. This would cause any social democratic government to back down, or force it to take counter measures. A recent pamphlet by the Cambridge Political Economy Group[21] has examined the kind of strategy a radically left government could take. The Group estimates that the major problems facing such a government would be the stranglehold of the City and multinational companies over the U.K. economy. It therefore proposes temporary freezing of all capital movements and suspension of the Stock Exchange, followed by an extensive rundown of the City's operations and the nationalisation with full compensation of foreign multinational assets in the United Kingdom. The compensation would be paid to avoid retaliation and would be financed by requisitioning and selling U.K. assets overseas, which are valued at around £12,000 million. Loss of City earnings would not be disastrous as it accounts for only 10 per cent of all invisible exports and less than 4 per cent of total exports. In the meantime, such a government could take over the top 200 firms which would bring the bulk of all industrial production under its control, but small-scale enterprise would be left alone. The pamphlet estimates that, over a period, resources worth 16·9 per cent of G.N.P. could be freed for other uses, after such items as upper-class consumption and military expenditure were drastically reduced.

Such plans appear utopian and far from present political realities. Yet the underlying situation in both the economy and the political system is highly unstable. The weaker national economies in the world market are vulnerable. The United Kingdom's long economic and political decline, stretching back now over one hundred years, has finally reached its decisive stage. During times of crisis, political parties and movements on both Left and Right can in their quest for mass support and political power, adopt one of three perspectives – catastrophe, accomodation or intervention. Parties of catastrophe expect and hope for some kind of economic or political breakdown which will provide the opportunity for revolution or *coup d'état*. Parties of accommodation defer to the established consensus, which reflects the existing balance of power between classes and interests in the state. They pursue the policies that are politically practicable within these confines. Parties of intervention propose to reshape existing institutions and change the balance of power between classes, using the power of the state to overcome opposition, in order to remedy the causes of the crisis and restore stability and progress.

In the United Kingdom at every moment of crisis in this century, parties in power have followed the path of accommodation to the dominant interests in the state. The basic policy consensus and institutional structure established on the basis of U.K. capital's nineteenth-century dominance of the world market has been modified but never fundamentally changed. Even the construction of the welfare state and the consequent incorporation of the Labour Party into the political system did not shake its central pillars. Interventionist programmes to arrest the long national decline, and interventionist politicians, like Chamberlain, Lloyd George and Mosley to carry them out, have surfaced at various times. None have gained the power to act. The stalemate consensus among the various élites that make up the governing class – politicians, civil servants, bankers, industrialists, trade-union leaders, journalists and broadcasters – has always blocked any radical action. Colonies, overseas investments and earnings, victory in two World Wars, have helped to prevent the upheavals seen elsewhere. The result has been continuing, inexorable decline.

Catastrophe rarely overtakes a political order except in time of war. The German communists waited in vain for German capitalism to fall apart in the 1930s. The Nazis, with the backing of the army and industry, sucessfully intervened. Intervention from Right or Left is likely in the United Kingdom too before catastrophe strikes. So paralysed and inept has the U.K. governing class become, however, that it is for the most part unable to think about intervention at all. In the last ten years the only two major politicians that have had any fresh thoughts and begun to discuss intervention – though in very different political directions – are Enoch Powell and Tony Benn. Powell would intervene on behalf of 'capital', Benn on behalf of 'labour'. Both have been mercilessly pilloried in a sustained effort to discredit and isolate them. Yet all they have done is suggest that reversing the United Kingdom's decline is impossible within the framework of the mixed economy and the existing consensus : both have attracted considerable popular support. Meanwhile our brave coalition of moderates, bereft of any constructive or forward policy, drained of ideas, united only in their common bankruptcy, have scuttled to the flag of the Common Market, in the evident hope that the E.E.C. will somehow achieve what they now shrink from – the reshaping of the U.K. economy and the U.K. state.

Staying in the Common Market, however, will do nothing to arrest the decline. It only ensures that the decline will go on. The decisive victory of the pro-Marketeers in the Referendum of June 1975 is certainly a significant triumph for consensus politics and particularly for the leadership of the Labour Party. Harold Wilson immediately compared the result with the landslide for the National Government in 1931. The comparison was more apt than he knew. The 1931 Coalition was a great political triumph for the established consensus. It brought political immobility for a decade, because it ruled out the adoption of an interventionist strategy for coping with mass unemployment. The result of the Referendum also condemns the country to a further period of immobility and another dose of the familiar 'consensus' remedies – wage restraint, higher unemployment and cuts in government spending. Such a programme will lower living standards and raise profits by reducing costs but, in the absence of a major revival of world trade, profits will not rise high enough to bring economic revival on a scale that can make the mixed economy viable again. The consensus remedy will merely prepare the way for further decline. The free play of market forces ordained by the Common Market will further encourage the steady exodus of capital and labour from the United Kingdom.

So long as the present political leadership remains in control of the levers of state power there will be no attempt to develop the kind of interventionist policies to plan production, trade and incomes that alone can cut short the decline. The pattern is familiar in U.K. history. Only twice in the last one hundred years has state power been used to break the stranglehold of the world market and the dominant interests of U.K. capital over the economy; both were during times of war. The result of the Referendum will not encourage a new attempt. Despite the endless chatter of the media about how the trade unions now dictate policy, the speedy removal of Tony Benn from the Department of Industry immediately after the Referendum is a useful reminder of where the balance of power lies in the state, and whose influence is decisive. Nevertheless, the defensive power of the trade unions and the radical 'left' is still formidable. That is why political immobility will continue for a while yet.

So long as capitalism (in the form of the mixed economy) survives, inflation and unemployment will continue and grow worse. The demand by the unions for higher wages to keep pace with the cost of living, and the demand of capital for higher profits to justify investment have become irreconcilable. Short bursts of prosperity will be followed by still more severe declines. The cost in terms of living standards and political freedoms of restoring the mixed economy to health is very high. Socialist planning is no longer a matter of ideology, but increasingly the only practicable policy for overcoming our economic difficulties. Only by planning production for use instead of planning production for the market and profit can new institutions and social relationships be developed that make economic security and development possible, and which hold some hope for the future survival of some kind of industrial society.

As the U.K. decline continues during the next few years, so the chances of an interventionist strategy succeeding will grow. All governments since 1945 have failed in their economic policies. Despite the Referendum vote, the hold of the major parties over the electorate and even over their own rank-and-file is much weaker than it was. Secession from the Union of both Ulster and Scotland has become a possibility.

The apparent calm and immobility of U.K. politics may be deceptive. At present most of the discussion of ways to solve the crisis centres around how best to do it at the workers' expense. Yet as Geoffrey Barraclough has noted : 'There is, after all, a basic contradiction when an economic system which claims to have discovered the secret of rising living standards for all can only find a way out, when the crisis develops, by reducing living standards.'[22] It is a contradiction which the structure of the mixed economy, the nature of accumulation, and the crumbling of U.S. power in the world market, make increasingly difficult to overcome. The political prospects are uncertain but contain some hope.

Notes and References

CHAPTER 1

1. 'Can Social Democracy Survive', *The Times*, editorial (18 Oct 1974).
2. *The Times* (16 Aug 1974).
3. 'The Growth of Output 1960–1980' (Paris : O.E.C.D., 1970) p. 220.
4. Cf. John Westergaard and Henrietta Resler, *Class in Contemporary Britain* (London : Heinemann, 1975).
5. D. Jackson, H. A. Turner and F. Wilkinson, *Do Trade Unions Cause Inflation?* (Cambridge University Press, 1972).
6. Ibid.
7. A. R. Prest and D. J. Coppock (eds), *The U.K. Economy* (London : Weidenfeld & Nicolson 1972) p. 264.
8. A. Glyn and B. Sutcliffe, *British Capitalism, Workers and the Profits Squeeze* (Harmondsworth : Penguin, 1972).
9. Robin Blackburn, 'The Heath Government : A New Course for British Capitalism', *New Left Review*, no. 70 (Nov–Dec 1971).
10. *The British Economy: Key Statistics, 1900–1970*, London and Cambridge Economic Service (Times Newspapers Ltd) table 17.
11. Frances Cairncross and Hamish McRae, *The Second Great Crash* (London : Methuen, 1975).
12. W. Beckerman, in *Crisis '75 . . . ?* (London : Institute of Economic Affairs, 1975) p. 59.
13. *The Second Great Crash*, p. 36.
14. See *Crisis '75 . . . ?*, p. 22.
15. J. M. Keynes, *Economic Consequences of the Peace* (London : Macmillan, 1919) p. 220.
16. 'Inflation and the Retail Price Index', *Labour Research*, vol. 64, no. 3 (Mar 1975) pp. 59–60.
17. *Financial Times*, editorial (20 Feb 1975).
18. *N.I.E.R.* (Feb 1971) p. 39.
19. These are extracted from *Economic Trends* (Sep 1974) and Prest and Coppock (eds), *The U.K. Economy*, pp. 280–82.
20. O.E.C.D., *Economic Outlook* (July 1974).

21. Westergaard and Resler, *Class in Contemporary Britain*, and cf. L. Taylor, P. Walton and J. Young (eds), *Critical Criminology* (London : Routledge & Kegan Paul, 1975) for an account of differential prosecution in propertied societies.

22. *Facts in Focus*, Central Statistical Office (Harmondsworth : Penguin, 1974) table 155, p. 189.

23. Tony Cliff, *The Crisis: Social Contract or Socialism* (London : Pluto Press, 1975).

24. L. A. Dicks-Mireaux, 'Inflation in Post-War Britain', in *Inflation*, ed. R. J. Ball and Peter Doyle (Harmondsworth : Penguin, 1969).

25. Ibid. p. 320.

26. Extracted from *National Income and Expenditure* (1966) tables 1, 2, 18; (1963/73) tables 1, 2, 20; (1970) table 18. These figures do not add up to 100 per cent because of direct public benefits. Also see Westergaard and Resler, *Class in Contemporary Britain*, for detailed analysis.

27. L. R. Klein and R. J. Ball in *Inflation*, p. 338.

28. Ibid. p. 297.

29. Ibid. p. 135.

30. M. Parkin, 'The U.K. Evidence on the Causes of Inflation', in *Inflation and the Unions* (London : Institute of Economic Affairs, 1972) p. 76.

31. Jackson, Turner and Wilkinson, *Do Trade Unions Cause Inflation?*

32. Alec Nove, *The Times* (30 Oct and 31 Oct 1974).

33. E. Mandel in *Inprecor* (16 Jan 1975) p. 15.

34. Jackson, Turner and Wilkinson, *Do Trade Unions Cause Inflation?*, pp. 5, 8, 9.

35. Ibid. p. 61.

36. Ibid. p. 117.

37. Anthony Robinson, 'Return from the Verge of Disaster', *Financial Times* (28 Feb 1975).

38. Alan Walters, *Crisis '75 . . ?*, p. 98.

39. Cf. M. Barratt Brown, *What Economics is About* (London : Weidenfeld & Nicolson, 1970).

40. *Financial Times* (20 Feb 1975).

CHAPTER 2

1. Cf. M. Dobb, *Theories of Value and Distribution Since Adam Smith* (Cambridge University Press, 1973). Within the marginalist paradigm there were important differences of

emphasis. The 'Austrians' rejected general equilibrium analysis and the quantity theory. Marshall favoured a partial equilibrium approach.

2. L. Robbins, *The Nature and Significance of Economic Science* (London : Macmillan, 1935) p. 16.

3. G. S. Shackle, *The Years of High Theory* (Cambridge University Press, 1967) pp. 4–5.

4. J. Strachey, *The Nature of Capitalist Crisis* (London : Gollancz, 1934) p. 15.

5. Ibid. p. 161.

6. See J. M. Keynes, *General Theory of Interest, Employment and Money* (London : Macmillan, 1936). Useful commentaries on Keynes's thoughts are L. Klein, *The Keynesian Revolution* (New York : Macmillan, 1949); M. Stewart, *Keynes and After* (Harmondsworth : Penguin, 1972); D. Winch, *Economics and Policy* (London : Hodder, 1969); and A. Leijonhufved, *On Keynesian Economics and the Economics of Keynes* (Oxford University Press, 1968).

7. Two typical collections of the time were S. E. Harris (ed.), *Saving American Capitalism* (New York 1948) and K. Kurihara (ed.), *Post-Keynesian Economics* (London : Allen & Unwin, 1955).

8. Cf. H. G. Johnson, 'The Keynesian Revolution and the Monetary Counter-Revolution', *American Economic Review*, vol. 61, no. 2 (May 1971) pp. 1–14.

9. See G. Harcourt, *Some Cambridge Controversies in the Theory of Capital* (Cambridge University Press, 1972).

10. Cf. D. Patinkin, *Money, Interest and Prices* (New York : Harper & Row, 1965).

11. Some of the most important work was done by the Polish economist, Michael Kalecki, who in fact developed the analysis of the 'General Theory' independently in the 1930s. See his *Theory of Economic Dynamics* (London : Allen & Unwin, (1965).

12. See the discussion by F. Machlup, 'Cost Push and Demand Pull', in *Inflation*.

13. A. W. Phillips, 'The relationship between unemployment and rate of change of money wage rates in the U.K., 1861–1957', *Economica*, vol. 25, no. 100 (1958) pp. 283–99.

14. See F. W. Paish, *Studies in an Inflationary Economy* (London : Macmillan, 1962).

15. Ibid. p. 311.

16. Cf. Machlup in *Inflation*.

17. F. A. Hayek, *A Tiger by the Tail* (London : Institute of

Economic Affairs, 1974) and G. Haberler, 'Incomes, Policies, and Inflation', in *Inflation and the Unions* (London : Institute of Economic Affairs, 1972).

18. Cf. J. K. Galbraith, *The New Industrial State* (Harmondsworth : Penguin, 1969).

19. Cf. R. Miliband, *The State in Capitalist Society* (London : Weidenfeld & Nicolson, 1969) ch. 6.

20. Cf. Haberler in *Inflation and the Unions.*

21. Cf. C. Levinson, *Capital, Inflation and the Multinationals* (London : Allen & Unwin, 1971).

22. Kalecki, *Theory of Economic Dynamics.*

23. J. R. Hicks, 'Economic Foundations of Wages Policy', *Economic Journal*, vol. 65 (1955) pp. 389–404.

24. H. G. Johnson, 'The Keynesian Revolution and the Monetarist Counter-Revolution'. See also M. Friedman, *The Counter Revolution in Monetary Theory*, I.E.A. Occasional Paper, 33 (1970).

25. M. Friedman and A. Schwartz, *A Monetary History of the United States* (Princeton University Press, 1963). See also A. Walters, *Money in Boom and Slump* (London : Institute of Economic Affairs, 1969).

26. Hayek, *A Tiger by the Tail.*

27. F. A. Hayek, *Studies in Philosophy, Politics and Economics* (London : Routledge & Kegan Paul, 1968) p. 298.

28. For discussion see W. Rees Mogg, *The Reigning Error* (London : Hamish Hamilton, 1974) and R. Hinshaw (ed.), *Inflation as a Global Problem* (Baltimore : Johns Hopkins, 1972) especially the contributions from Mundell and Machlup.

29. Hinshaw, 'Introduction', in *Inflation as a Global Problem.*

30. E. Mandel, *Decline of the Dollar* (New York : Monad Press, 1972) and R. Segal, *The Decline and Fall of the American Dollar* (New York : Bantam Books, 1974).

31. Hayek, *A Tiger by the Tail*, p, 298.

32. Ibid. p. 294.

33. See *Inflation and the Unions* (London : Institute of Economic Affairs, 1972).

34. M. Friedman, *Monetary Correction* (London : Institute of Economic Affairs, 1974).

35. M. Bronfenbrenner, in *Post-Keynesian Economics*, p. 48.

36. Cf. J. K. Galbraith, *The New Industrial State* and A. Jones, *The New Inflation* (Harmondsworth : Penguin, 1972).

37. Cited in Hinshaw, *Inflation as a Global Problem*, p. 99.

38. M. Friedman, *The Counter Revolution in Monetary Theory.*

39. Cited in Hinshaw, *Inflation as a Global Problem*).

CHAPTER 3

1. A. Shonfield, *Modern Capitalism* (Oxford University Press, 1969) p. 3.
2. Cf. C. Kerr *et al.*, *Industrialism and Industrial Man* (Harvard University Press, 1960).
3. M. Barratt Brown, *From Labourism to Socialism* (Nottingham : Spokesman Books, 1972) table 4.8, p. 111.
4. Karl Marx and Friedrich Engels, *The Communist Manifesto*, in Selected Works (Moscow : Foreign Languages Publishing House, 1962).
5. Karl Marx, *Preface to A Contribution to the Critique of Political Economy*, in Selected Works (Moscow : Foreign Languages Publishing House 1962).
6. Their main works are P. Sweezy, *Theory of Capitalist Development* (New York : Monthly Review Press, 1942); *The Present as History* (New York : Monthly Review Press, 1953); *Modern Capitalism and other Essays* (New York : Monthly Review Press, 1972); P. Sweezy and H. Maydoff, *Dynamics of U.S. Capitalism* (New York : Monthly Review Press, 1972); P. Sweezy and P. Baran, *Monopoly Capital* (Harmondsworth : Penguin, 1965); P. Baran, *The Political Economy of Growth* (Harmondsworth : Penguin, 1965).
7. Sweezy, *Theory of Capitalist Development*, p. 143.
8. But see Chapter 4.
9. Sweezy, *Theory of Capitalist Development*, p. 180.
10. Baran, *The Political Economy of Growth*, p. 133.
11. Adam Smith, *Wealth of Nations* (London : Methuen, 1961) p. 353.
12. Baran, *The Political Economy of Growth*, p. 215.
13. *Monopoly Capital*, p. 215.
14. Ibid. p. 63.
15. Cf. Sweezy, *Modern Capitalism and Other Essays*.
16. N. Kaldor, *Essays on Economic Stability and Growth* (London : Duckworth, 1960).
17. A. Glyn and B. Sutcliffe, *Workers, British Capitalism and the Profits Squeeze*.
18. Cf. R. Lekachman, *The Age of Keynes* (London : Allen Lane, 1967).
19. K. Marx, *Grundrisse* (Harmondsworth : Penguin, 1973).
20. *Monopoly Capital*, p. 138; F. M. Fisher, Z. Grilliches, C. Kaysen, 'The Costs of Automobile Model Changes since 1949', *Journal of Political Economy* (Oct 1962).

21. *Monopoly Capital*, p. 150.
22. Ibid. pp. 239–43.
23. Sweezy, in R. Lekachman, *Keynes' General Theory* (New York : St Martin's Press, 1964).
24. *Monopoly Capital*, p. 177.
25. One study of the arms economy and its importance to modern capitalism is M. Kidron, *Western Capitalism Since the War* (Harmondsworth : Penguin, 1968). See also his *Capitalism and Theory* (London : Pluto Press, 1974).
26. *Monopoly Capital*, p. 150.
27. Ibid. p. 24.
28. J. Gillman, *The Falling Rate of Profit* (London : Dobson, 1956) p. viii.
29. J. Steindl, *Maturity and Stagnation in American Capitalism* (Oxford : Blackwell, 1952).
30. M. Nicolaus, 'The Unknown Marx', *New Left Review*, 48, (Mar–Apr 1968).
31. E. Mandel, 'The Labour Theory of Value and Monopoly Capitalism', *International Socialist Review*, 28 (July–Aug 1967).

CHAPTER 4

1. See the interesting article by M. Itoh, 'The Formation of Marx's Theory of Crisis', *Bulletin of the Conference of Socialist Economists* (Feb 1975) which also discusses the work of Professor Uno of Tokyo University on crisis theory.
2. There has been a flourishing school in Germany, of whom Roman Rosdolsky and Elmer Altvater have been prominent members. Also the work of Ernest Mandel, especially *Marxist Economic Theory* (London : Merlin, 1968).
3. Perhaps the single most important work on Marx's value analysis to have appeared since 1945 is Paul Mattick's *Marx and Keynes* (London : Merlin, 1969).
4. Recent works by Marx scholars have achieved a new and much higher level of scholarship in Marx studies in the English-speaking world. See particularly David McLellan, *Karl Marx: His Life and Thought* (London : Macmillan, 1973).
5. See our *From Alienation to Surplus Value* (London : Sheed & Ward, 1972) ch. 6, to be published by Macmillan in paperback in 1976.
6. Marx and Engels, *Selected Correspondence* (London : Lawrence & Wishart, 1934) p. 246.
7. Marx, *Capital*, vol. I, p. 72.

8. Ibid. p. 639.
9. Ibid. p. 634.
10. Ibid. p. 612.
11. Ibid. p. 219.
12. Marx, *Grundrisse* (Harmondsworth : Penguin, 1973) p. 706.
13. Marx, *Capital*, vol. III, p. 266.
14. An important recent study of the labour process is A. Sohn-Rethel, *Geistige und Körperliche Arbeit* (Frankfurt : Suhrkamp Verlag, 1972).
15. See Chapter 5.
16. *Capital*, vol. I, p. 585.
17. M. Panic and R. E. Close, 'Profitability of British Manufacturing Industry', *Lloyds Bank Review*, no. 109 (July 1973) p. 30.
18. M. A. King, 'The U.K. profits crisis : myth or reality?' *Economic Journal* (Mar 1975).
19. *N.I.E.R.* (Jan 1975).
20. G. J. Burgess and A. J. Webb, 'The Profits of British Industry', *Lloyds Bank Review*, no. 112 (Apr 1974) p. 18.
21. A. Glyn, 'Notes on the Profit Squeeze', *Bulletin of the Conference of Socialist Economists* (Feb 1975).
22. G. Hodgson, 'The Theory of the Falling Rate of Profit', *New Left Review*, 84 (Mar–Apr 1974).
23. D. Yaffe, 'The Marxian Theory of Crisis, Capital and the State', *Bulletin of the Conference of Socialist Economists* (Winter 1972); 'The Crisis of Profitability', *New Left Review*, 80 (July–Aug 1973); and 'Value and Price in Marx's Capital', *Revolutionary Communist*, no. 1 (Jan 1975).
24. Marx, *Grundrisse*, p. 138.

CHAPTER 5

1. On the Great Depression see G. Rees, *The Great Slump* (London : Weidenfeld & Nicolson, 1970); R. Skidelsky, *Politicians and the Slump* (London : Weidenfeld & Nicolson, 1967); D. Winch, *Economics and Policy* (London : Hodder, 1969). H. W. Arndt, *Economic Lessons of the 1930s* (Oxford University Press, 1944); C. P. Kindleberger, *The World Depression* (London : Allen Lane, The Penguin Press, 1973).
2. On sterling see S. Strange, *Sterling and British Policy* (London : Chatham House, 1972) and B. Johnson, *Politics of Money* (London : Murray, 1970).
3. For an analysis of the problem see F. Cairncross and H.

McRae, *The Second Great Crash* (London : Methuen, 1975); the journal *Politics and Money* (Jan–Mar 1974); and P. R. Odell, *Oil and Water Power* (Harmondsworth : Penguin, 1974).

4. For further discussion of the international monetary system and the world market see, M. Barratt Brown, *Economics of Imperialism* (Harmondsworth : Penguin, 1974); E. Mandel, *Decline of the Dollar* (New York : Monad Press, 1972), P. Sweezy and H. Maydoff, *Dynamics of U.S. Capitalism* (New York : Monad Press, 1972).

5. M. Barratt Brown, *From Labourism to Socialism* (Nottingham : Spokesman Books, 1972) ch. 1.

6. J. E. Meade, *Efficiency, Equality and the Ownership of Property*, (London : Allen & Unwin, 1964) p. 33. Cited in Barratt Brown, *From Labourism to Socialism*, p. 35.

7. P. Sweezy and H. Maydoff, *Dynamics of U.S. Capitalism*, and 'The long-run decline in liquidity'; see also *N.I.E.R.* (Jan 1975) table 12.

8. See, for example, the analysis in *Politics and Money* (Nov 1974–Feb 1975). This journal provides an invaluable, regular commentary on current developments. It is available on subscription from 14 South Hill Park Gardens, London NW3.

9. A Shonfield, *Modern Capitalism* (Oxford University Press, 1965).

10. Milton Gilbert, cited in *Modern Capitalism*, pp. 12–13.

11. M. Flamant and J. Singer Kerel, *Modern Economic Crises* (London : Barrie & Jenkins, 1968).

12. From *National Income and Expenditure*, 1963–73, tables 1, 50.

13. J. O'Connor, *The Fiscal Crisis of the State* (New York : St Martin's Press, 1973) ch. 4.

14. From *Annual Abstract* (1971) table 164.

15. Karl Marx, *Capital*, vol. i (Moscow : Foreign Languages Publishing House, 1961) p. 640.

CHAPTER 6

1. *The Limits of Growth*, Club of Rome (London, 1972); *Blueprint for Survival* (Harmondsworth : Penguin, 1972). See also E. F. Schumacher, *Small is Beautiful* (London : Abacus, 1974).

2. P. Connelly and R. Perlman, *The Politics of Scarcity* (Oxford University Press, 1975) table 2.3, p. 14.

3. *Blueprint for Survival*, p. 17.

4. *Small is Beautiful*, p. 23.

5. G. Barraclough, 'The World Crash', *New York Review of Books* (23 Jan 1975).
6. Hans-Magnus Enzenburger, 'A Citique of Political Ecology', *New Left Review*, no. 84 (Mar–Apr 1974) pp. 23, 31. For Marx's view on *nature* see A. Schmidt, *The Concept of Nature in Marx* (London : New Left Books, 1971) ch. 4.
7. Karl Marx, *Capital,* vol. i, p. 592.
8. Samuel Brittan in *Crisis . . '75?* p. 110.
9. P. Sweezey and H. Magdoff, *Dynamics of U.S. Capitalism* (New York : Monthly Review Press, 1972). See also R. Segal, *The Decline and Fall of the American Dollar*, ch. 6.
10. This has been predicted by leading economic correspondents on *The Economist, The Times* and the *Guardian.*
11. *Economic Policy Review*, no. 1 (Feb 1971) p. 13.
12. For the former see D. Yaffe, 'The Crisis of Profitability', *New Left Review*, no. 80 (July–Aug 1973). For the latter see the debate in the *New Statesman* during 1973.
13. A. Glyn, 'Notes on the Profits Squeeze', *Bulletin of the Conference of Socialist Economists* (Feb 1975). Glyn and Sutcliffe's original figures and conclusions on the profits squeeze were challenged by some, notably John Hughes, *Profit Trends and Price Controls* (Nottingham : Spokesman Books, 1974). More recent studies, however, particularly the studies by King and Burgess and Webb, cited by Glyn in the above article confirm their original analysis.
14. Ibid.
15. G. Rees, *The Great Slump,* p. 260.
16. Barraclough, 'The World Crash', p. 16.
17. This notion is examined in much greater detail in Andrew Gamble, *The Conservative Nation* (London : Routledge & Kegan Paul, 1974).
18. T. Benn, *Speeches* (Nottingham : Spokesman Books, 1974) p. 87.
19. Ibid. p. 77.
20. For proposals on indexation see M. Friedman, *Monetary Correction* (London : Institute of Economic Affairs, 1971). For import controls, see the *Economic Policy Review*, as cited in note 11.
21. *Britain's Economic Crisis* (Nottingham : Spokesman Books, 1974.
22. Barraclough, 'The World Crash'.

Index

accumulation, barriers to 122–5, 130–7, 169, 170
arms spending 80, 110
'Austrian School' 37, 71, 209

balance of payments 5, 6, 183
balanced budget 28
Baran, P. 88, 92, 94, 96, 97, 99, 100, 101, 103, 104–10
Barraclough, G. 178, 206
Barratt Brown, M. 84, 159, 211
Benn, T. 198, 199
breakdown, theory of 126, 130, 135–7
Bretton Woods 152
Brittan, S. 181

capital
  accumulation of 122–5
  concentration of 91, 109
capitalism
  laissez-faire 40
  monopoly 77–105
Cliff, T. 18
commodity fetishism 118–19
Conservative Party 194–7
credit 67

debt 182, 184
democracy 194, 197
dollar gap 154

ecological doom 175–9
energy 181–5
Enzenburger, H.-M. 180
Eurodollars 184
European Economic Community 119

floating exchange rates 157
food crisis 178
Friedman, M. 58, 61, 62

General Strike 151
Glyn, A. 139, 140, 187, 188, 189

gold standard 149, 150, 151, 152, 153
Great Depression 145, 146, 148

Haberler, G. 54
Hansen, A. 80
Hayek, F. A. 54
Heath, E. 195

incomes policy 193
Industrial Relations Act 195
inflation
  creeping 20, 21
  hyper 23
  strato 23, 24
  suppressed 22, 24
international monetary system 148, 149, 150, 151, 152, 157, 158

Jackson, D. 21, 22, 23
Joseph, K. 196

Kalecki, M. 48, 49
Keynes, J. M. 12, 42
Keynesianism 42–8, 48–50

Labour Party 191, 193
labour theory of value 112–19

Mandel, E. 22, 109
marginalist revolution 37–42
Marx, K. 79, 86, 102, 111, 112, 113, 118, 119, 131, 172
Mattick, P. 111
monetarism 58–74

National Government of 1931 190, 194
Nazi economic policy 146
New Deal 146

O'Connor, J. 167
oil 157, 160, 181, 182, 183

Paish, F. 52–3
Phillips curve 50–2

post-war boom   147–57
Powell, J. E.   195
profit   137–43

raw materials   176–7, 178
Robbins, L.   38, 190

Say's Law   126
Schumacher, E. F.   176, 177
Schumpeter, J. A. 80, 96–7
Shonfield, A.   81, 82
'Social Contract'   197–8
state   26, 162
Strachey, J.   40
strikes   7
surplus value   124
Sutcliffe, B.   139, 140, 187, 188, 189

Sweezy, P.   88, 92, 94, 96, 97,
     99–101, 104–10

taxation   14, 15
trade cycle   145, 163
Turner, H. A.   21, 22, 23

unemployment   3, 5, 31, 32, 164

Vietnam War   158

wage–price spiral   24, 25, 26
Wilkinson, F.   21, 22, 23
world market   6, 155

Yaffe, D.   142, 143, 144

THE

FIRST

THIRTY

DAYS

From the Ashes of Despair, a Melody of Hope Rises